SECRET SYMBOLISM
IN OCCULT ART

SECRET SYMBOLISM
IN OCCULT ART

by

FRED GETTINGS

HARMONY BOOKS/NEW YORK

Published by Harmony Books, a division of Crown Publishers, Inc., 225 Park Avenue South, New York, New York 10003

Originally published in Great Britain as *Visions of the Occult* by Century Hutchinson

HARMONY and colophon are trademarks of Crown Publishers, Inc.

Manufactured in Singapore

Library of Congress Cataloging-in-Publication Data

Gettings, Fred.
    Secret symbolism in occult art.

    1. Symbolism. 2. Occultism in art. 3. Symbolism in
    art. T. Title
    BF1623.S9G45   1987   133   87-3412

ISBN 0–517–56718–0

10 9 8 7 6 5 4 3 2 1

First American Edition

PICTURE SOURCES

196 Bibliothèque de l'Arsenal, Paris; 93 Bibliotheca Estense, Modena; 11, 42 Bodleian Library, Oxford; 47, 75, 104, 161, 189 British Library; 45, 48, 206 Bibliotheque National, Paris; 142 Moyse's Hall Museum, Bury St Edmunds; 51, 128, 129, 130 Monastery Sacra di San Michele, Val di Susa; 153 Museé Archeologique, Sousse, Tunisia; 77 Museé Conde, Chantilly; 136 Museo Civico, Vicenza; 76 Public Library, Lucca; 152 Romer Museum, Augst; 144, 148 Rhodes Museum; 191 Vadiana Kantonsmuseum, St Gall; 26 Victoria and Albert Museum

All other illustrations are drawn from the Charles Walker Collection, Images Colour Library, Leeds

Contents

Introduction: The Occult Veil   7

1 The Star Wisdom of the Occultists   23
2 The Astral World: The Invisible Sea   41
3 The World of Man   59
4 Earth Magic and Earth Spirits   74
5 Black Magic: The Use of Unseen Powers   90
6 Amulets and Charms: The Invisible Power of the Evil Eye   107
7 Demons: The Unseen Workers of Evil   122
8 Alchemy: The Secrets of Inner Rebirth   140

Index   158

Frontispiece *The occult world is said to be hidden from the ordinary senses by a thin veil. This illustration by Arthur Rackham shows Pandora opening the box from which demons fly – a mythological tale which expresses to perfection the idea that those who are not especially prepared for such undertakings may lift that thin veil only at their own peril. In the myth it is actually Pandora's box (which came with her as a present from the gods) which is opened by Pandora's husband Epimetheus. When all the evils escaped from the box into the world, Hope alone remained inside, still accessible to man. Occultism maintains that the veil is itself nothing more than the visible appearance of the world, behind which exists another reality, accessible only to those who develop a special insight or consciousness by the practice of occult initiation.*

Introduction: The Occult Veil

The word 'occult' comes from the Latin *occultus*, meaning 'hidden'. In modern times the word is used for those sciences and arts involved with looking into the secret world which is supposed to lie behind the world of our familiar experience. The poet Swinburne called the appearance of the familiar world 'that painted veil', and said that behind its coloured fabric was a rich spiritual world. The symbols which are called 'occult' are those used on this side of the material veil to point to meanings beyond it, in the spiritual realm. The occult symbols – the 'occult script' as such symbols are usually called – point to the existence of a hidden world to which very few men have access. It is our purpose in this book to examine some of the many different ways in which certain occultists have attempted to represent in symbols what they have perceived in that world hidden behind the veil.

If there is a veil, and if we are prevented from looking at what is hidden behind its flimsy fabric, how do we know about this occult world at all? How is it possible that something which is invisible has been described in visible symbols? The answer to this question is that some have been able to penetrate the veil and have returned to the familiar world with the urge to leave behind descriptions and symbols which will to some extent portray for ordinary people what this world is like. Those who have the ability to see beyond the veil are sometimes called 'initiates', 'clairvoyants' or 'occultists'. The greater part of the occult symbols which are known to us, and which are designed to point to the existence of a hidden and secret world, has been given to us by such people.

There are many occult sciences and arts, but the most widely known are those concerned with demonology, witchcraft, magic, alchemy, astrology and geomancy. Each of these sciences or arts is very ancient, and each one has developed its own specialized system of secret symbolism. It is only because each system uses secret meanings in a symbolism concerned with a hidden world beyond the senses that they are thought of as being occult at all. Generally speaking, there is no very clear connection between many of the occult sciences. One or two of them are described as dark sciences, because they are concerned with the lower levels of the hidden world – with such things as demons and with those realms in man which are nowadays termed the subconscious. The prime example of a dark science (if it may be described as a science at all) is witchcraft, but some of the practices in modern seance rooms are also linked with the darker side of occultism; this is especially true of those methods concerned with bringing the souls of the dead back to earth, in seances and so on. Other occult realms include astrology, which seeks to look into the higher levels of the hidden worlds – into the planets and stars, as well as into the soul life of human beings. There is very little connection between witchcraft and astrology, yet they are both called occult. They are occult mainly because they are both based on the assumption that there is a hidden world, and that the principles and truths of this hidden world may be represented in terms of symbols.

The practice of occult symbolism is so ancient that it has by now become part and parcel of everyday life. Very many of the symbols that we use in our ordinary lives are rooted in occultism, did we but know it. Even the alphabet we use was derived originally from magical symbols, sounds and numbers. Anyone who takes the trouble to look without prejudice into the occult roots of our language, and into our modern forms of writing, will be astonished to see what power there is in everyday words, letters and sounds. Most people use the alphabet without being aware that it is occult at all, without grasping the truth that it contains within its symbolism hidden ideas, energies and spiritual implications.

Indeed, it is not just our alphabet which is rooted in ancient magic. Very many of the symbols around us, which more often than not we take as so much decoration, and which we all too easily take for granted, are derived from the occult practice of symbolism and are really magic in origin. Most people are content to pass by such 'decorations', even when they suspect that they may have a hidden meaning; yet if they had the knowledge to look into the contents of such symbols, they would very quickly realize things which would change their lives. An understanding of the occult basis of symbolism is linked with the wish to pull back the painted veil and to gaze upon the real forms and lovely colours which lie behind it. The first steps in learning how to pull back this veil are involved with developing an eye which recognizes the hidden levels of meaning in the symbols that we encounter almost every day of our lives.

By means of symbols the occult realm penetrates into the familiar world of our ordinary experience on every side. It is simply that most of us have not developed the eyes to see their meanings. In fact, occult symbolism binds together a wide number of different things which the ordinary imagination might never connect together. An example of this may be seen if we study the 'secret' connections which may be drawn between things as different as two boats, a coffin, some graffiti and a gargoyle.

The picture in Figure 1 is instantly recognizable: it shows the prow of a gondola on the Grand Canal in Venice. The sailing boat in Figure 3 is moored in the harbour on the Greek island of Mykonos. The painting in Figure 6, from the end of an ancient Egyptian coffin, shows the body of a newly dead man bound to the back of a bull. The graffiti on the wooden shutters in Figure 8 were

2 *Five magical amulets. From left to right: the Seal of Solomon, zodiacal Gemini, the Egyptian ankh, a sacred eye and zodiacal Cancer (a stylized crayfish)*

1 *Magical figures on the prow of a gondola on the Grand Canal, Venice*

scrawled by would-be revolutionaries in the busy centre of Turin in Italy. The gargoyle in Figure 9 is from a church in the quiet village of Bottesford, on the border of Lincolnshire. What does this collection of pictures have in common, and what have they to do with occultism?

The surprising thing is that these five different pictures are linked together by a strain of magical belief. The prow of the gondola (Figure 1) is designed according to a tradition which was originally intended both to ward off demonic influences and to attract good fortune to all who ride in the boat. It does not take much imagination to trace in the three curvilinear patterns which jut out from the prow the symbol ♀. This is the Egyptian ankh, which may be seen among the magical amulets of Figure 2; it is one of the most powerful occult designs of ancient times – so powerful, indeed, that it was adopted into early Christian symbolism and is often said by occultists to be the origin for the modern symbol ♀, which represents Venus. The gondolier who plies his trade on the Grand Canal of Venice (a maritime city which rises from the sea) is protected by three symbols linked with the beautiful goddess Venus, who, according to ancient legend, also rose from the sea.

On either side of the prow of the Mykonos boat (Figure 3) is a six-rayed star. This symbol is also a powerful magical device, designed to ward off evil. A related symbol, sometimes called the Seal of Solomon, is also among the collection of modern magical amulets of Figure 2. In the tiny Greek museum across the waters of the Mykonos harbour is a Mycenean vase which is over 3000 years old. On it is painted exactly the same stellar

3 *Star symbols on a fishing boat in the harbour at Mykonos, Greece. This is by far the most popular of all amuletic devices among Greek fishermen*

4 *Rosicrucian diagram showing cosmic man and the planetary rulership over the spiritual organs of the body. From Georg Gichtel's* Eine Kurze Eroffnung . . . *(1799)*

pattern: it is there for precisely the same reasons – it was intended to bring good fortune to anyone who drank from the vessel. The magical basis for this protective symbol is said to be derived from the notion that an invisible trinity in the heavens, figured as ⅄, descends to meet and mingle with the image of the visible praying man on earth ⅄. It is a sun symbol ✳, because in ancient times it was widely believed that man prayed from his heart, which was the centre of his emotional life. This is why so many occult images of man portray the Sun, or a sun symbol, over the heart (Figure 4). Since the gods lived in the heavens, often symbolized by the Sun, the six-rayed star represented the link established between the human heart and the Sun.

In terms of this theory, the six-rayed star is symbol of a union between man and the gods, and its form is an outer sign of an inner perfection or stability which may not be easily disturbed by demons. In the picture of Venus from an astrological book (Figure 5) we see a six-rayed star over her private parts, between the images of the bull and the scales, which represent zodiacal Taurus and Libra. The scene to the right of this naked goddess shows the things over which she has rule – lovemaking, music and good food. The conditions which please Venus are those which are harmonious to the soul, and it is therefore no surprise that we should find a six-rayed star in this image, for it proclaims a peaceful relationship between earth and man, for the heavens have interpenetrated the earth. This is the reason why the six-rayed star is found so frequently as a protective symbol on boats and in magical amulets. As we shall see (chapter 6, p. 121), these

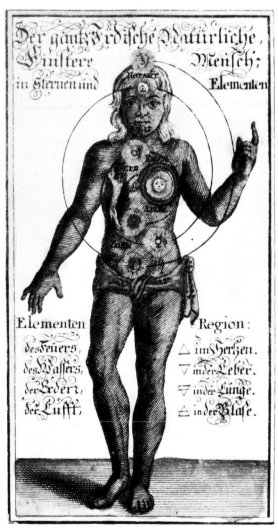

5 *Late medieval image of the planet Venus and the human occupations over which she is said to have rule. From a fifteenth-century French 'Shepherd's Calendar'*

6 *The dead Osiris on the back of a bull. Detail from an Egyptian coffin painting of the Middle Kingdom in the Museum of Egyptian Art, Turin*

six-rayed solar symbols have been incised on many of the chimneys on the houses of Mykonos (Figure 160), where they are expected to attract the protective goodness of the solar realm on those who dwell in the houses.

The body bound to the back of the bull in the Egyptian coffin picture (Figure 6) has a sun symbol at its feet. This is also a secret symbol – among the most sacred and secret of all Egyptian magical symbols. It is painted on the coffin to act as a protective talisman for the soul which was being carried into the underworld on the back of the bull. The solar disc was regarded as a powerful source of protective magic, and was as much a symbol of the spiritual realm as was the Trinity of the Christians. This is one reason why the Christian artists used halos to denote their saints, for the circles were symbolic of the fact that the individuals painted or drawn were linked with the spiritual realm or with the Sun. It is no accident that the Virgin and Child in Figure 7 both have halos and are surrounded by tongues of fire, for both halos and fire are symbols of the invisible spiritual world, the centre of which was the burning Sun. It is the Egyptian disc, marked with a central dot $\odot$ (itself a seed which might grow within the space around it), which was eventually adopted as the modern symbol for the Sun.

The symbol above the word *Toro* in the Turin graffiti of Figure 8 is also linked with the bull. The Italian *toro* actually means 'bull', and the name of the Italian city of Turin is from the Latin

10

tauronesis, which came from the word *taurus*, meaning 'bull'. The symbol itself, the interlinked \/, is the traditional Italian way of graphically representing the idea of fascism. Just as Nazism in Germany was linked with the swastika ⌗ (itself an ancient occult symbol), so was Italian fascism linked with an occult symbol. This \/ was derived from the Greek word *nike*, which means 'victory': we shall look into this symbol at a later point. To the right of the *Toro* graffito in Figure 8 is a symbol which closely resembles that used to denote one of the most important peace movements in Europe – CND. One might be tempted to see this symbol as the Trinity drawn inside a circle ⊕: however, the history of this form suggests an alchemical origin, itself just as deeply enmeshed in magic. It is, of course, very likely that the Italian revolutionary who scrawled this symbol did not know that he was drawing an ancient alchemical symbol filled with deep magical significance. He or she may have known that it was rather like the emblem of the Mercedes car company (Figure 155), but it is unlikely that he or she knew that in earlier times the form ⊗ was a symbol for phosphorus, which was one of the most secret and sacred of alchemical essences. We shall examine this alchemical symbolism more deeply in chapter 6, but here it is sufficient for us to note that even the most casual-seeming scrawl may be as deeply enmeshed in the occult tradition as a finely carved symbol on a boat or on a church wall.

What in fact has a gargoyle high on a church wall (Figure 9) to do with occultism? Surely one does not find occult symbols on or in a church? In fact, Christian art and occult symbolism are intimately interwoven, and in this case the gargoyle is not really a monster but a bellman – we can see the two bells he carries in his hands. He is the symbolic bellringer, as much a protection against evil as the solar symbols on the Mykonos boats and chimneys and on the Egyptian coffin. In medieval times, when this gargoyle was carved, it was believed that witches could not fly when bells were rung. For this reason it was commonplace for churchbells to be rung in all the villages at the time when the witches were supposed to fly to their Sabbats or witch gatherings. The magical basis for this notion goes back to the idea that beautiful sound – especially music – is a holy thing. The carved bellman was a projection in stone of this idea of the sound of bells – he is a symbol of perpetual sound, protecting the church from the demonic evils of witchcraft. It would seem that this church was in particular need of such protection, for (as we shall see in chapter 6) it was believed that witches were prevalent in this area during the seventeenth century.

It is interesting to compare the hidden symbols in these five pictures with Figure 10. Unless the significance of the prow symbols or of the sun symbols is pointed out, it is unlikely that a

7   *Sick people praying to a miraculous image of the Virgin at Alt-Oetting, Bavaria. The remains are wax models left by those who wish the corresponding organs to be cured. From* Das Buchlein zer Zuflucht zu Maria . . . *(1497)*

8   *Graffiti on a wall in a back street of Turin. Many of the modern political slogan symbols are unconsciously derived from occult sigils*

9 *Gargoyle, known as the Bellman, on the south face of the church of St Mary the Virgin, Bottesford*

non-specialist would realize their meaning. This is not so with the complex symbolism in Figure 10, which is the title page of Walter Raleigh's *History of the World*, published in 1614. Raleigh has made sure that the symbolism is evident even to the uninitiated, for he has written an explanatory word next to each of his symbols in order that there may be no mistake concerning their meaning. For example, as though the reader were not likely to realize it, the skeleton under the foot of the central figure is marked *Mors* (the Latin for 'death'), while the female who slouches against the skeleton is marked with the Latin for 'oblivion'. As the central figure holds aloft a map of the world – with South America actually touching the Antarctic – we may assume that this person represents that which overcomes both death and oblivion.

If we look closely at this plate we shall discover several symbols which we have already noted in the previous figures. For example, the central personage has a radiant halo around her head, while the angels of fame are both blowing trumpets (towards the eye, which is a symbol of all-seeing Providence), which have the same symbolic force as the gargoyle bells of Figure 9. Less obvious, perhaps, is that about a third of the way down the column to the left of the central figure (which is carved with strange emblems) is the Egyptian ankh symbol $\dagger$. Even less obvious is the fact that the lower three (Death, Oblivion and the central figure of the woman) may be seen as a triad reaching upwards $\curlyvee$, while the upper three (the two angels of fame, and the Eye of Providence), in the spiritual half of the picture, may be seen as triad reaching downwards $\curlywedge$, thus making a personified prayer symbol.

Now, for all that it is possible to see connections between Figure 10 and the preceding pictures, we must admit that the title page really belongs to a different tradition. The symbolic meaning in this plate is no doubt very clever, but there is really nothing hidden within it, in the sense that there are symbolic devices or magical powers hidden in the gondola, in the Egyptian coffin or in the gargoyle. These last are true examples of occult symbolism, for they are hidden and point to a secret power or meaning.

The occult world is the *hidden* world. But what is it hidden from? Well, the occultists themselves usually insist that the world with which they themselves are familiar is hidden from ordinary vision. Most occultists will say that, while it is quite possible for anyone to see this hidden realm, special preparation is usually needed. The majority of people are quite content to pass their lives immersed in the ordinary world of time and space, oblivious to the fact that it is a world interpenetrated by other worlds in which there is a different time and a different space.

The whole range of occult symbols which have come down to us from a remote past is concerned with giving us information about the nature of this different time and space which is hidden from ordinary sight. How is it possible for a hidden world, or an invisible realm, to be represented in ordinary pictures? Imagine, for example, something we have already mentioned, such as the flames which are used to denote the spiritual realm (we see these in Figures 7 and 10). When an

10   *Title page of Sir Walter Raleigh's* History of the World *(1614), which contains mainly occult and arcane graphic references*

ft reptile qddam quod gtecc dr salaman
ora. latine ü stilio. H oc simile est lacertule

ordinary person looks at a fire, he sees flames leaping upwards. He probably knows that the flames are fed by oxygen from the air, and that what he is seeing is incandescent gas. Now, when an occultist or an initiate looks with especially sensitized eyes towards the flames of a fire, he does not see only incandescent gases. He sees a sort of life force which is directly linked with the power of the Sun; he also sees that the fire is animated (like all earthly things) by a special soul-being. Such a soul-being is called by modern occultists a 'salamander'. Salamanders are famous in occult circles for of their volatility: they change their shape with extraordinary rapidity and love flames. Indeed, without flames they cannot live, just as humans cannot live without air. There are many occult drawings of salamanders luxuriating in the flames of fire (Figure 11).

When an artist wants to paint the flames of fire, he realizes that he cannot paint the movement. He has to adopt a convention and render the fire as though it were still, even though he knows full well that the important thing about a fire is that it is in constant movement and that it is hot. The two most important things about the fire – its movement and its heat – the artist cannot represent on paper. For this reason we accept the convention that the many tongues of flame, such as we see in Figures 7 and 11, represent fire. So it is when an occultist seeks to represent the nature of the salamander which he sees dwelling in the flames. He knows that the most important thing

13　*Detail of stars above the Virgin and Child on the eighth-century Pemmo Altar in the Cividale Cathedral Museum, Italy*

about the salamander is its life, its joy, its exuberant movement and its love of warmth. None of these things can he represent on paper, of course, and so he is reduced to representing this extraordinary creature as a newt, or tiny dragon, bathed in flames.

It was quite usual for the alchemists to symbolize fire with the simple drawing of a triangle △. This symbol indicates that the fire principle strives upwards, as though to the spiritual realm. The broad base of the triangle also indicates that the creative force of fire is well founded or stable, resting firmly and securely on the earth. In fact, this simple sigil for fire △ is the basis for the phosphorus symbol on the Mercedes car of Figure 155 (and, of course, for the CND symbol), for the form ⊕ is derived from a much older sigil for phosphorus, which showed an 'intense fire' – that is, a spiritual force which is somehow more than fire: △ . Anyone who has seen phosphorus burning will understand why this substance should be symbolized as being 'more than fire'.

If the artist experiences difficulties in representing exactly the nature of the familiar world of our experience, he faces greater difficulties when he is called upon to represent the nature of the hidden spiritual world with which only occultists are familiar. Almost all artists who seek to represent their vision of the higher world, which is occult to normal eyes, experience a sense of frustration. They find that they can only draw or paint the vitality and life of this higher world by means of

symbols in which the colours and purities of the higher world are imperfectly represented. Any artist who seeks to create such symbols soon discovers that he can best do this by means of a vast repertoire of symbolic forms which have been passed on from age to age, and which contain a rich series of meanings within their structures.

For example, the artist who carved the six-rayed star on the thirteenth-century façade of Amiens cathedral (Figure 12) obviously felt the wish to set out the idea contained within the prayer star ✳, and he therefore carved his star with six rays or arms. He also was seeking to show that the star was something more than a heavenly star – that it was a symbol of something even higher – and so he turned each of the rays into a sort of flame. We shall examine this star in relation to the men beneath it, who admire it with such fervour, in chapter 1 (p. 29), but for the moment we should note that, even in such a simple attempt to symbolize something which is essentially occult, the artist has made use of two strains of a well-established tradition of symbolizing. In this case he used both what we may call the 'numerology' of the star and the idea of flame to suggest spirituality. How different in feeling, and in symbolic importance, is the six-pointed star above the child in Figure 13. In this same image there is another star, though this time with only five rays. As we shall see, such is the subtlety of occult symbolism that a star with five rays has a

14 (left) *Zodiacal Scorpio on the north door of the western façade of Chartres Cathedral. Probably early fourteenth century*

15 (above) *Cancer (as crayfish) and Virgo – zodiacal details on the façade of Notre Dame, Paris. Probably early fourteenth century*

16 (right) *Medieval demon as a gargoyle overlooking Paris, from the parapet walk on the west front of Notre Dame, Paris*

very different significance from one with six rays.

It may be argued that the last two pictures we have examined do not seem to belong to an occult tradition at all – they are distinctly religious. It is certainly true that Figures 12 and 13 appear to deal with religious themes. For example, we may be tempted to take the star in Figure 12 as the star of the Magi, the one which guided the Wise Men to the cradle at Bethlehem; and since the carving in Figure 13 is from the back of a bishop's throne, it is obviously intended for religious purposes. However, the star of Figure 12 is not really the star of the Magi: occultists insist that it is in fact the star of initiation, an important symbol in alchemy, and the men gazing up at it are not the Wise Men of the Bible, but initiates, occultists with an inner vision. Without dealing in depth with this remarkable star symbol, we should at

least note that the symbolism of Christian art is permeated with what may only be described as occult symbols. Most notable among these are the vast number of astrological symbols which began to appear in churches and cathedrals after the twelfth century, when ancient Greek and Roman astrology (which had been preserved by the Arabs) was suddenly revealed to the Christian world. How else may we account for the presence of astrological symbolism on such important cathedrals as Chartres (Figure 14) and Notre Dame in Paris (Figure 15)?

It was not only astrological symbolism that was adopted into the art of the cathedrals and churches, however. At Notre Dame in Paris, and in a thousand other churches, we find hideous gargoyles (Figure 16) which belong more to the occult tradition of demonology than to Christian lore, as well as hundreds of decorative motives,

17 *Bi-tailed mermaid or siren, from the medieval westwork of San Michele, Pavia. Such half-fish, half-human images are generally linked with initiation cults, the symbolism indicating that the creature (which is in fact a symbol of an initiate) is at home in two elements, such as Earth and Water, which represent the material and spiritual realms*

such as mermaids (Figure 17) or basilisks (Figure 139), which are linked with the magical tradition of amulets, and hundreds of symbols which are alchemical in origin. The central façade of Notre Dame in Paris is perhaps the most famous of the 'alchemical books' in stone, for virtually all the images carved on this front are derived from ancient alchemical lore. A fairly obvious example may be seen in Figure 18, which shows (right) a woman holding a shield upon which a snake is seen curled around an upright staff. This is one of the most frequent of all alchemical images and appears in a number of guises, as, for example, in the alchemical diagram in Figure 19. This device is used to denote what alchemists call the Mercury principle: it is a healing force, the basic solvent, the most important liquid of the alchemical art, represented in a symbolic form which the great alchemist Fulcanelli says 'we meet with during the whole medieval period'. We shall see a development of this imagery in Figure 206, which is a picture of a dragon eating its own tail, a symbol of the healing power which the alchemists called the Azoth.

There is a sense in which occult symbolism cannot really be separated from either religious or ordinary symbolism, for both the Christian religion and the temporal world of art have always been refreshed by the depth of meaning to be

found in occult symbolism. It is really a question of on which level one is prepared to read the symbols involved.

We shall see this more closely if we examine the famous painting *Mars and Venus* by Botticelli (Figure 20). We can look at it on an ordinary level and assume that it is an allegorical painting of some kind, but that it is related to a classical theme in which the goddess Venus unaccountably looks after the sleeping Mars. If, however, we choose to look at this painting in the light of occult symbolism, we find a quite different meaning in the composition: we discover that the painting has nothing to do with Mars and Venus (which is in fact a modern title). As with all Botticelli's allegorical paintings, the symbolism is complex and difficult to reduce to a few simple statements. However, to approach this picture in the right way, we must recall that in the medieval occult system it was believed that the physical body of man was only part of the complete man – that he had several spiritual bodies.

In modern occultism the spiritual body most intimately connected with the physical is called the 'Etheric', but in the medieval period it had many names, including *Vegetabilis* and *Ens veneni*; in the later alchemical tradition it was called the 'Vital body'. As the last term suggests, it was the body of life, and not to be confused with the higher 'Astral body', which was the body of the passions. The medieval occultist imagined that the Etheric body, while invisible to ordinary sight, was a body of light, filled with undulating motion; it was of an opposite sexuality to the physical body.

If we bear this occult image of man in mind, we begin to see the *Mars and Venus* in a different way. Let us suppose that Botticelli was interested in portraying the relationship between the Etheric and the physical bodies. Let us suppose that he had learned about the Etheric from one of his friends (the circle in which he mixed was deeply learned in esoteric lore), and let us assume that he had heard the occult maxim that, when the physical body goes to sleep, the Etheric body is much freer and does not need to live so closely in the physical. Since the Etheric has the purpose of maintaining the physical body in a state of life, it does not go far away from the physical, but remains close, attentive to it, watchful and alert.

Here, then, Botticelli appears to have painted the sleeping physical body of a man guarded by his female Etheric body. The emphasis on the physical body as a sort of shell is expressed in the idea of the armour, which is nothing other than a protective metal shell placed around the body – in itself as lifeless as that body. The four young satyrs who play with the armour are each in their own way occult symbols. They each represent one of the four elements: one plays with the armour and represents Earth; one carries the lance

in a warlike way and represents Fire; another blows the shell and represents Air; while the fourth represents Water. This in itself is relevant, for the four elements (which play such an important part in astrology and alchemy) are said to be the basis of all physical and material form. The fifth element, the Quintessence, is that which links these four elements together (see chapter 1, pp. 28–9). It is often said in occult circles that the Etheric body is made from the Quintessence, which is thought of as an invisible, but powerful, surge of light and life.

If we look more closely at the diaphanous robe of the woman (whom we take to represent the man's Etheric body), we see that Botticelli has made every effort to suggest through the streaming draperies the ideas of movement and of life. There is a total contrast between the fluidity of movement of this female figure and the heavy stupor of the physical body of the man. Perhaps even more noticeably, he has attempted to illustrate in the attentive face of the woman the occult notion that the Etheric body is in love with the physical, that the physical is really nothing more than a heavy extrusion into space and time of the Vital body. The great occult poet William Blake expressed this idea most profoundly when he wrote: 'Eternity is in love with the productions of Time.' The occult tradition insists that the Etheric

19 *An alchemical rebus of a crucified snake, which is a secret symbol of the Philosophical Mercury which is achieved by practice of the arcane art of alchemy. Each of the constituents within the symbol is Christian, but they have been merged in such a way as to illustrate the alchemical notion that the inner serpent may be crucified yet still remain alive*

19

20 Venus and Mars
by Sandro Botticelli
(c. 1445–1510),
National Gallery,
London. In company
with many Renaissance
paintings, the arcane
significance of this
picture is not generally
recognized by art
historians

body really belongs to eternity, while the physical body is a 'production of Time'.

There is a sense in which the modern title for the picture is not so far wrong, for occultists would sometimes speak and write of the Etheric body as Venus. The physical body takes pleasure in the things of its own level – in good food, in music and in lovemaking. For this reason the Vital body, which guards man, ensures that these things do not harm him overmuch, and that he is able to take pleasure in the physical realm. We now see that the crude woodcut of Figure 5 is directly related to this magnificent painting by Botticelli, since the Venus of the woodcut is depicted as a spiritual being – for all she is naked, and for all she is admiring herself in a mirror, she stands symbolically in the spiritual world. This is why her feet rest on clouds, and why she has the signs of the zodiac over which she has rule at her feet. This is also why there is a six-pointed star above her head and another over her body, to show that she is a celestial being. All these are symbolic ways of showing that this Venus, though presented in the physical form of a woman, is a spiritual being. Botticelli uses a different technique for showing that his woman is a spiritual being, turning her flimsy dress into surface energy and making her face the face of a goddess.

This remarkable painting can be related even more closely to the occult tradition, but in a sense our examination of a possible deeper level of interpretation has served its purpose. We have seen that, once we are armed (however inadequately) with some knowledge of occult lore, we are able to see the world of art in a different way. For example, we will have realized that, to see Botticelli's art in the right way, we have to know a little about the medieval notion of the Etheric body and about Venus. Indeed, when we have some understanding of occult symbolism, we

shall be in a position to see many things – from the most profound artistic products made in the service of religion to the mercantile magic of advertising art – in a different way.

The reason for this is relatively simple. The moment one begins to see that genuine occult symbolism is concerned with an invisible world, in which the governing laws are different from those applicable to the physical world, then one allows a new dimension to enter into one's grasp of symbols. For example, it is quite true to say that the star of Figure 12 could be, on one level, the star of the Magi. However, if it were only the star of the Magi, then it could have any number of rays. There is nothing in the Bible or in tradition which insists that the star of the Magi had only six rays, no more than the Bible insists that there were three Wise Men! When an artist portrays a star with six rays, and also turns that star into a fire symbol, we are at once alerted to the fact that he is pointing to something above and beyond the symbolism of the Magi.

To begin to develop an awareness of occult symbolism one has to encourage a feeling for the finer points of symbolism, which works through such things as numerology (in this case, the symbolism of six) and esoteric traditions (in this case, the symbolism of fire). Occult symbolism is concerned with much more than the subjects of popular occultism, such as astrology, witchcraft, divination and so on – it is concerned with portraying accurately the inner nature of the invisible world.

We have so far approached the hidden world of the occultists by way of the familiar realm of everyday objects and works of art. Now let us glance at what is clearly genuine occult symbolism. This is the extraordinary image of the working of the higher world which was designed by Dionysius Freher according to the teachings of the

Rosicrucian Jacob Boehme (Figure 21). Even before we begin to examine this, we should observe that with all great works of art (especially with those steeped in occult lore) it is rarely possible to treat the symbolism exhaustively. However, even after a short study of the picture we may see several principles represented by standard occult symbols which occur again and again in art; by means of such great works we begin to learn something of the secret and sacred language of occult symbolism, a language which has been called 'the language of the birds'.

The topmost circle of Figure 21 contains the famous Seal of Solomon, a six-pointed star made up of two interpenetrating triangles ✡. It is a more sophisticated version of the star of Venus in Figure 5. The Seal of Solomon represents the Godhead. The fact that it is made up of two triangles is intended to symbolize the fact that it contains an element which is eternal and an element which is natural. The artist has adopted the method we saw in Raleigh's title page of Figure 10, for he has introduced a certain amount of labelling to make his symbolism clear. In this meeting of the spiritual and the material we are immediately reminded of Botticelli's painting of the contrast between the Etheric and the physical bodies.

The unity of the Godhead gives rise to two 'outpourings' (the word used by Boehme himself), one of which is labelled 'Eternal', the other of which is labelled 'Nature'. In the corresponding circles below these names we see the inverted triangle (left) explored in terms of the planets, and the upright triangle (right) also linked with the planets but bathed in darkness. This is the 'darkness' or 'illusion' of nature. There are two results of this separation. The darkness and the light meet in a central explosion. The word used by Boehme for this explosion was *Schrack*, which can be translated as meaning 'lightning flash'. At the same time the darkness and the light pour into the cosmic model below. This may be called a 'cosmic model' because it is not really a hemisphere. The zodiacal band, or zodiacus, shows (from left to right) Taurus, Gemini, Cancer, Leo and Virgo. Beneath this zodiacus we can see the Stellatum, studded with stars. In the space within are the planets, and at the centre is the Sun. Not surprisingly this globe is named the 'Solar World'. The entire image is actually an occult study of the laws appertaining to the solar world long before its influences reach the realm of man.

If we turn back to Figure 10, we may note a few interesting parallels. The whole theme of Boehme's plate is that underlying the solar realm, or behind the appearance which we on earth call the Sun, is a mingling and conflict (*Schrack*) between light and darkness. The duality by which we see the world, as contrasts of light and shadow, of joy and pain, is established long before the creative power of the Sun is streamed to make life on earth possible. This same duality is expressed in the Raleigh plate of Figure 10. At the top of the plate we see Providence in the eye of God. This alone is undivided, a single staring eye. Below everything is expressed in dualities. To the left is winged Good Fame, to the right winged Bad Fame. Like the outpourings of the light and dark of the Boehme image, these two touch the world map, which itself is a duality, divided not only into continental masses, but also into hemispheres. Below is the human realm (none of the symbolic personages have wings). We have the duality of Experience (an old clothed woman) and Truth (*Veritas*, as a young naked woman), the duality of Death and Oblivion. Even the woman in the centre is a duality, for she is an occult androgyne, with the head of a man, the breasts being suggested ambiguously by means of a metal cuirass. The image indicates that, just as the world is created by the duality of dark and light, so it is supported by the dualities in the created realm

21 *Hand-coloured engraving designed by Dionysius Freher to represent the cosmic scheme expressive of the occult writings of the mystic Jakob Boehme. From William Law's* The Works of Jacob Behmen, the Teutonic Theosopher *(1764–81)*

below. The main difference between Figures 10 and 21 is that the latter deals with the entire cosmic frame, while the former deals only with the nature of the earth.

Each of these remarkable images was constructed to serve a different purpose and each was to some extent serviced by occult symbolism. What is important in both of them is the teaching that it is only in the spiritual realm that unity is to be found. In the lower realms, of which the world of man is part, there is only the law of contrast, the law of duality, what in occult circles is called the Law of Two. This is the fundamental idea underlying attempts made to present visions of the occult in terms which are understandable to the ordinary man.

In the next chapters we shall explore a few of the lines of thought which have been opened up by our examination of these very different images. We shall do this by looking more deeply into the visions of the hidden world in those areas which are associated with occultism – witchcraft, for example, and divination, astrology, alchemy and so on. We shall study something of the fascinating way in which artists have attempted to portray, in visible symbols, the invisible world which is the domain of occultism. There is an order in the chapters, as they follow the time-honoured occult method of presenting ideas by means of what is sometimes called 'occult incarnation'. This is to say that the order of the chapters is designed to carry us down from the heavens, from the realm of the stars, into the lower realms of the earth. We start with the stars, then move into what is called the 'astral', which occultists say stands between the stars and man.

Then we glance at the occult images of man himself: man has his origin in the stars, but during his lifetime he stands on the earth, so we then look at the use to which occultists have put the earth, by means of religious or magical practices, to help man. This raises the question of how man might be protected from the darker forces which occultists trace within the world, and we therefore look briefly at the tradition of amulets and talismans which so often make use of both sky images and demonic images to protect man in his journey through the world. The existence of amulets as magical devices raises the question of why such protection is required, and it is here that we reach the lowest point of the occult incarnation, for we touch the realm of demons. At this point we glance at black magic, which is concerned with using the lower forces of the earth, which the occultists place under the control of the demons. It is an easy path from witchcraft, and from such divinatory methods as were once linked with the earth forces, to the demons themselves, who have built around their hellish centre a whole battery of fearsome images and sigils. It would be inappropriate for us to leave the subject of occult images with the demons, so we finally take a look at that important branch of occultism which is now called alchemy. A study of the strange images of this 'gold-making art' will soon show us that it is really one of the methods which occultists use to redeem the inner darkness in which the demons prefer man to dwell. Alchemy is the secret art which enables man to see the world aright, and offers an inner redemption which permits him a vision of the light of those stars from which he came.

1 The Star Wisdom of the Occultists

Modern astronomers tell us that the star Betelgeuse, one of the so-called red giants, has a diameter of over 300 million miles. If we were to imagine a football to be our earth, then the City of London would probably be equivalent in diameter to this enormous star – and yet Betelgeuse, for all its gigantic size, is far from being the brightest or largest of the stars in our heavens. So vast are the distances involved in this galactic realm that even such a star as Betelgeuse looks to us like a pinprick of light in the dark blue of the sky. It is somehow easier to imagine a pinprick of light than it is to imagine a sphere of incandescent gases 300 million miles in diameter; our minds do not easily assimilate information of this kind, our imaginations become numb in the face of such vastness. The world of astronomy seems somehow closer to science fiction than are the notions of the ancient astrologers who tell us that, when Betelgeuse is prominent in a person's horoscope, it will bring great wealth and honours in war. Such a view of the stars, however far-fetched it may seem to the modern mind, is at least human and quite literally down to earth.

The medieval astrologers drew images of the cosmos which profoundly influenced the occult visions and images still used in certain magical and astrological circles. However, these men did not conceive of such dehumanized vastness as is commonplace in the modern world; the ancient model of the universe was a less grandiose affair than the modern mechanical model, and it was somehow more homely. For the early astrologers the cosmos was no vacuum of intergalactic spaces, but a place inhabited by celestial beings and gods. This idea of the cosmos as a living entity is almost lost in the modern view of the world, yet it is fundamental to the occult vision. In most cases occultists would visualize the entire spiritual and material cosmos as a living being, sometimes in the image of man, at other times in the image of a tree. In either case, what was important in such an image was the notion that the entire cosmos was a living unity, in which all the individual parts (whether they be limbs and fingers or branches and leaves) were interdependent. It is this vision of unity, populated by spiritual forces and spiritual beings, which lies at the root of all the

valid occult images of the cosmos and the stellar world. The image of the celestial tree in Figure 22 is typical of this occult vision: it contains within its roots, trunk and leaves the spiritual forces which maintain the harmonious and just working of the cosmos. It is interesting to observe that this tree is actually upside down, with the roots in Heaven and the branched leaves reaching down into the material plane (into what are called the ten Sephirah in the Jewish occultist system of the Qabbala). This image of an inverted tree is often used in occult circles to show that the manifestations of the world (that is, the leaves and flowers which are the fruition of the activity of the tree or

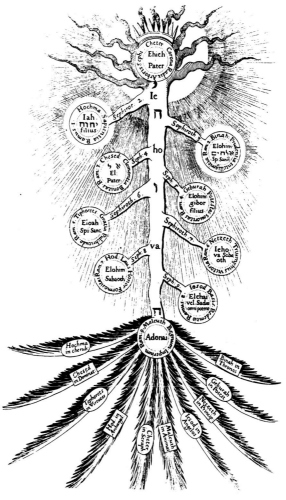

22 *Diagram of the Qabbalistic Sephirothic Tree, from the 1621 edition of Robert Fludd's* Utriusque Cosmi . . . Historia

23

אום קדמון שני

עתיק יומין

אנפין

אריך

אבא

23 *Qabbalistic diagram of the cosmic Adam Kadmon, from the 1684 edition of Rosenroth's* Kabbala Denudata

a diagram of the spiritual realm which cocoons and protects man during his lifetime on earth. This outer spiritual sphere they called the Stellatum or the Firmament. Figure 24, which is derived from an early model of the universe, shows the sphere of stars as the Firmament, one of the outermost of the concentric rings. For those who were not aware that the Firmament is the realm of stars, the artist drew in this concentric a series of twenty-eight stars. Inside the sphere of the Firmament are contained the spheres of the planets, starting with Saturn and ending with the Moon; below the Moon are the elemental spheres of Fire, Air, Water and Earth. Above the Firmament are marked the Crystalline Heavens and the *Primum mobile*, the 'first mover', which, it was believed, gave motion to the whole of the cosmos.

For the ancients the space between the earth and the furthermost planet, which was the cold, dark Saturn, was filled with the spheres of the other planets. These were not empty spaces, but rather the realms of spiritual beings, who were responsible for maintaining the planetary movements, sounds, music and life. The movements of the spheres, like the music made by the movements of the spheres, were derived from the first mover, the outer *Primum mobile*, yet these movements needed to be regulated or adjusted from time to time – sometimes speeded up, sometimes slowed down. The mighty spiritual beings who were responsible for this adjustment were called the Intelligencies or the Regulators, and each of the planetary spheres was said to be under the control of a particular Intelligency. For example, the sphere of the Sun was said to be under the control of the Intelligency Michael, while the sphere of the Moon was under the rule of Gabriel. It is this idea which accounts for the fact that in medieval painting and sculpture one sometimes finds archangels linked with planets or signs of the zodiac. In Figure 25, for example, there is an image of a crayfish, which was one of the two symbols used to denote the zodiacal sign Cancer. The tail of this crayfish runs into the halo of an archangel below. This sign Cancer is ruled by the Moon, which leads us to the conclusion that the archangel in this wall painting is Gabriel.

This lovely image of the zodiac is high on the wall of the baptistry in Parma, Italy. We should not be surprised to find that the Archangel Gabriel and the sign Cancer are emphasized in such a place, for in occult symbolism the sign Cancer is linked with water (the element of baptism), while in theological symbolism the Archangel Gabriel is the one who brought the news of the coming birth of Jesus to the Virgin Mary. This is one reason why so many occult pictures show the Moon

plant) are derived from the spiritual realms inaccessible to man, yet above him.

Occultists go further than merely portraying an upside down tree as an image of the cosmos – they insist that man himself is really an inverted tree, with the treetrunk his backbone, and the nerve endings which gather in such prolixity beneath the skull the roots tapping the spiritual forces within the head. The 'fruits' of the man's life therefore are to be found in the activity of his limbs, in what man does, in what he creates and leaves behind. This occult idea which locates the 'roots' of man's spirituality in the head is hinted at in the Qabbalistic image of the macrocosmic man (celestial man) in Figure 23, for the trepanned skull shows an interior which is intentionally drawn in such a way as to evoke roots as part of the brain structure. The notion that the brain of man is linked with the world of stars, and that man is really a sort of upturned vegetable or tree, is expressed in very many occult texts, but it is only rarely that one sees such a clear exposition of this in diagrammatic form.

When the ancient occultists portrayed in simple images the structure of the cosmos, they viewed the whole world of stars as being contained within a single broad sphere which stretched in a vast concentric sphere around the earth. The semicircle above the celestial man of Figure 23 is really

24 *A sixteenth-century illustration of the Ptolemaic universe. Note the* Primum mobile *of the outer sphere, which translates motion to all the lower spheres, and the Firmament in which the fixed stars are embedded*

PRIMVM MOBILE
CRISTALLINE
FIRMAMENT

FIER
AER
YEARTH

CŒLIFER ATLAS

Hic canet errantē Lunam, Solisq; labores
Arcturūq;, pluuiasq; hyad. gēinosq; triōes

ID.

25 (right) *Cancer and Leo, fifteenth-century bas-reliefs and frescoes in the baptistry at Parma, once an arcane centre of astrological lore*

26 (below) *Victorian cradle with zodiacal decorative tiles. The sequence of tiles, from Scorpio (left) to Sagittarius (right) through Leo, is not in the zodiacal order. Victoria and Albert Museum*

connected with the womb or private parts of woman (Figure 79). In this symbolism the pagan astrological symbols are harmoniously linked with the imagery of theology. Water is seen by both occultists and theologians as the material by which initiation and baptism take place (see p. 40).

The occult notion that man is born from the whole cosmos and is linked with the cosmos for the whole period of his earthly life is beautifully expressed in the Victorian cradle of Figure 26, which has tiles bearing the images of the twelve signs of the zodiac inset around the wooden sides: on the side shown here are the images for Scorpio, Leo, Virgo, Libra, Cancer and Sagittarius. This order is not directly related to the order of the signs or constellations in the skies, but it is possible that it was intended to place Water signs (Scorpio and Cancer) near the foot and head of the child, a further deepening of the birth symbolism. Such a cradle is really the earthly symbol of the cosmos from which the newborn child has lately come. The child within this cradle is symbolically nourished by the zodiac, just as it was prior to its incarnation in a physical body. Such designs proclaim the occult truth, which insists that man is an eternal being, a spiritual being, who dwells in an earthly body for a short period, yet remains a part of the entire stellar world which embraces the earth.

The idea of birth, which is linked by occultists to the notion of initiation (which is the birth into the higher world inaccessible to normal individuals), is of course reflected in the occult symbolism of the personal horoscope. A personal horoscope is actually a plan of the heavens, drawn for a certain place and for a certain time. This horoscope is usually the 'birth chart', in which case it is cast for the place and time of birth. Simple as the horoscope chart is, it contains within its symbolic form many of the spiritual ideas set out in Figure 24. Indeed, the horoscope figure is the most profound occult symbol in ordinary use in the West today.

The outer circle of the horoscope (Figure 27) represents the idea of pure spirit. The next concentric represents the limit of time. The ancient occultists claimed that time ends with the outermost planet, which in those days was believed to be Saturn, ruled by spiritual beings called Thrones. In Greek astrology Saturn was often called Chronos, a name which means 'time' and which has survived in English in the word 'chronology'. Astrologers were fond of depicting Saturn in the curious image of one who eats his own children (for this is one of the stories told of him in Greek mythology) as this was a symbolical reflection upon the nature of time, which seems to be the devourer of its own 'children' (the world below, including all humanity), as well as of itself. The majority of images of Saturn show him as an old man with a white beard (Figure 28), usually standing alongside, or over, the two signs of the zodiac, Capricorn and Aquarius, over which in traditional astrological systems he was said to have special rule. In other images, however, he is portrayed holding a serpent which is biting its own tail (literally eating itself). In some occult systems this serpent (Figure 206) was called Ouroboros. It is therefore likely that the curled snake is the origin of the notion that a circle represents the end of time, and it is certain that the occultists regarded the sphere of Saturn as marking the end of what was often called 'duration in time'.

The spheres beyond Saturn were 'out of time' or 'eternal'. We see, therefore, that the zodiac itself (beyond Saturn) was believed to exist out of time, out of duration; it was part of the eternal world, and this had profound importance in the development of astrological imagery. The astrologer maintains that the human spirit descends to the earth from the outer realm of the zodiac, which is timeless or eternal. The human spirit was visualized as leaving the timelessness of this outer circle and emerging into time at the centre of all the concentrics of spheres, at the earth itself. Because of this it is now usual for astrologers to draw into the outer concentric band the sigils (graphic symbols) for the signs of the zodiac, and to regard the very centre of the horoscope as marking the point at which the eternal

spirit of man emerges into time, in the temporary clothing of a physical (earth) body. This is the secret symbolism contained in the simple image ⊙, which shows spirit emerging into time as a dot. This dot is sometimes called the 'soul', and it represents the emergence of spirit into the realm of time and space.

The emergence of the human soul at birth into the flow of time is usually represented in the horoscope chart as a horizontal line, stretching in the horoscope chart from the centre out towards the west and the east ⊖. The east point of this

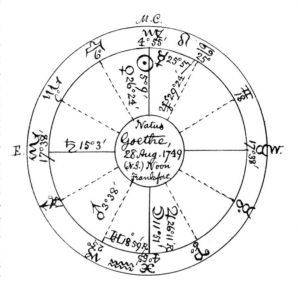

27 (left) *The horoscope of Goethe, who was born on 28 August 1749 according to the modern calendar. His Ascendant is given as 17 degrees 38 minutes in Scorpio*

28 (below) *Woodcut showing the opposition of Jupiter and Saturn, which are supposed to be in Taurus and Scorpio respectively. Note how Saturn (right) is represented as an old, lame man, wielding a sicle (itself symbol of time) After Johannes Lichtenberger,* Die Weissagungen von J. Lichtenberger, *(1527)*

Jupiter.   Saturnus.

As ist eine namhafftige Constellation fast wol zu mercken vnd zu betrachten / der schwerwichtigen grossen planeten des Saturni vnd Jupiters/ wilcher Coniunction vnd zusammen lauffung / er

horizontal actually marks the moment of birth, according to star time, expressed in terms of degrees of the zodiac. It is a convention of Western astrology that the east point should be placed on the left-hand side of the horoscope figure. The technical term for the east point is the 'Ascendant', and it marks the most important single factor in a personal horoscope. It is the Ascendant degree which really determines the zodiacal type of the personality. Figure 27 shows the horoscope of the German poet and philosopher Goethe: if you look at the Ascendant point you will see the sigil $\mathcal{m}$ and degrees 17° 38', which means that Goethe had 17 degrees and 38 minutes of Scorpio arising on the Ascendant when he was born.

It is this eastern point, the Ascendant, which is regarded by astrologers as marking the deep inner nature, or type, of the individual for whom the horoscope has been cast. Popular notions of astrology have failed to give the importance due to this point, and have embraced the erroneous notion that the type is determined by the position of the Sun. According to this idea, all people born in the same period of thirty days belong to a single zodiacal type: Goethe, for example, who was born when the Sun was in the sign Virgo, would be considered to be a Virgoan type, which is wrong. According to the true doctrine of astrology, Goethe is a Scorpionic type, and this may be seen from the subjects he takes for his great drama of *Faust*, since Scorpionics are given to probing into the hidden nature of things, which often means that the type is interested in occult matters, such as demonology, magic, astrology, and so on. *Faust* is, of course, one of the great demonological and magical dramas of all time.

Birth is often described by occultists as the emergence of the spirit into the confines of space as well as into time. The emergence into space is usually represented by a vertical line, stretching in the horoscope chart from the centre out towards the south and the north $\ominus$. These two directions symbolize the place of birth, marked by the lower end of the vertical (sometimes called the 'home' or the 'mother'), and the ambitions, marked by the upper end of the vertical (that is, the place where one aspires to be), sometimes called the place of 'career'. In Figure 27 it is marked 'M.C.', which is an abbreviation for the Latin term *medium coeli*, meaning 'middle of the skies'.

The four directions of space and time make a cross. The cross itself is a very deep esoteric symbol, for it not only carries all the Christian associations, but is also linked with the four elements of Earth, Air, Fire and Water. We have noted something of the Quintessence, or fifth element, of course, and may therefore recognize that this life force is visualized in the horoscope as emerging at the centre of the cross and expanding in the materialization of the physical world, as though it were crucified in space and time: $\oplus$.

Within the horoscope figure, the area between the point which marks out space and time and that circle which marks the end of time is regarded as the soul sphere. It is within this 'soul' area that the astrologer places the symbols for the planets, which are said to represent different aspects of the soul life. The planets must always be seen against a part of the zodiac, so the astrologer is careful to make sure that, when he draws up a horoscope figure, he places the symbols for the planets in appropriate places, against the correct signs of the zodiac. In Goethe's chart (Figure 27), for example, the planet Venus ♀ is in Virgo, while the planet Mars ♂ is in Capricorn.

The above notes on the symbolism of the horoscope by no means exhaust its occult meaning in connection with the idea of birth or the emergence into the cross of space and time. However, by now it should be evident that the esotericists who devised this symbolism left very little to chance: indeed, they attempted to invest every dot and line of their symbols with deep and subtle meanings.

Our view of the cosmos has changed since medieval times, when men believed that all the created world was a living being. The ancients imagined that the vast sphere of stars swung in movement around the earth, and they called the stars 'fixed' only in comparison to the 'wandering stars', the planets, which were evidently free to roam the skies. The word 'fixed' is still applicable to our notion of the stars, however, even though we now know that planets are not stars at all. We may still call the stars 'fixed' because, at this great distance of space from which we view them, they appear to remain fixed in the same relationship to one another. We see that they move across the night sky, some of them rising and setting over the horizon, but we know that this nightly movement is a sort of illusion, for it is a result of the earth's movement, of the spin of the earth on its axis. Were we to speak accurately, rather than figuratively, we should not really speak of the 'sunrise' at dawn, but of the 'earthdrop'.

So far as the ancients were concerned, however, the stars did move and, like the planets, were regarded as living things. In fact, some of the early writers on astrology discuss whether or not the stars are really superior animals; even those who did not agree with this idea were certain that the stars were alive. It was quite usual for the ancient writers to insist that the bodies of the stars were made of the life force or Quintessence. Even the Greek philosopher Aristotle supported this idea.

As we have seen, the Quintessence is a notion derived from occult literature. The word comes from the Latin *quinta essentia*, meaning 'fifth element', and it points to a superior and invisible element which holds together the four lower elements of Earth, Air, Fire and Water. We shall look a little more closely at the Quintessence when we examine the occult imagery of alchemy (chapter 8, pp. 148–9); for the moment, however, we need only imagine it as a sort of life force, like the new life pouring into the crucifix of time and space at the centre of the zodiac. The stars on the outer edge of the horoscope were said to be quintessential because they were living things, the very essence of the invisible force of life which permeated the earth. The symbol of the Quintessence is linked with one of the most powerful of all occult symbols of interlinked triangles ✡, the Seal of Solomon. The idea lying behind this symbol is that the four elements (Fire, Earth, Air and Water) are united in a single form and held together by the power, the fifth element, at the centre of the figure. The Quintessence is regarded by occultists as the source of life.

The figure of this Quintessence is used in very many occult books to denote the binding power, the healing power and the life source behind all created things. A most striking example of this is in the illustration to the occult text by the German occultist Jakob Boehme (Figure 21, p. 21). When Boehme wishes to portray the source of life in the cosmos, or the life force in its primal stage before it descends into matter, he chooses to picture the Sun at the centre of the Seal of Solomon. The solar centre, linked in this way with the Quintessence, is itself a symbol of the undivided life source. The way in which this central power of life divides (approximately into negative and positive, into light and darkness) is expressed in the lower diagrams. It is this duality which pours itself into the created universe and gives rise to light–darkness, love–hate and all the other dualities by means of which we experience the outer world. The bottom image, submerged in this duality, is not merely the image of our world, but a picture of the cosmos – we, the spectators of this image, are on the outside of the zodiac, looking in at the world as though we were gods.

The illustration to Boehme's book is a complex model of how some of the occultists of his time viewed the universe and related this view to the quintessential power of the stars. A more simple example is found in a small detail on the façade of the thirteenth-century cathedral at Amiens shown in Figure 12. As we have seen, because of its position on a cathedral, we might be tempted to see this sculpture as a picture of the Magi, the Wise Men, who followed the star in their search for the newborn Christ. However, this is really an alchemical image related to the idea of initiation. The four men represent the four expressions on the human plane of the four elemental natures – in modern terms, these are the temperaments of the Melancholic, the Sanguine, the Phlegmatic and the Choleric (see pp. 67–8). Whenever one finds the four elements in a genuine occult picture, one should look for a symbol of the fifth, the Quintessence. In this sculptured relief the form of the star itself points to the Quintessence, for the six rays of the star echo the design of the Seal of Solomon. The hole which has been bored into the

BRACKEN HOUSE

centre of the star is intended to symbolize the invisible fifth element itself. The man to the right is pointing to the source of life which will bring healing into the world.

Even though they believed that the bodies of the stars were made from the Quintessence, and that the stars were living beings, the early astrologers made a careful study of their supposed influences and tried to establish the natures of the most important ones. They studied the stars from several points of view, but most of all they considered the stars in connection with the Sun. They imagined the Sun as moving along a path against the backdrop of the stars, the zodiacus. This word was derived from a Greek term meaning 'living beings', which also gave us the modern term 'zoology', the study of living things. Now, the zodiacus is not actually a part of the Firmament, the sphere of the fixed stars. The zodiac is not a sphere at all, but rather a band of influence within which the seven traditional planets run their courses. In Figure 24 it is seen in the band of images which runs almost vertically down the series of concentrics. If you look at it closely, you will see the images for Taurus, Aries, Pisces and Aquarius. The zodiacal roundels in Figure 29 show the traditional images of the twelve signs more clearly. The Sun was visualized as running continually along the band of the zodiac, sparking each sign in turn into activity through its contact. However, since the zodiac itself was set in the heavens, it was related to the patterns of fixed stars contained within it. This is why in Figure 24 the zodiac is imagined as being wrapped around the entire series of spheres, including the *Primum mobile*.

29 *Modern zodiacal clock on the façade of Bracken House in Cannon Street, London. The device is some 2 metres wide, and the clock (installed in 1959) was designed by Thwaites and Reed. It is without doubt the most impressive large-scale zodiacal clock in Britain*

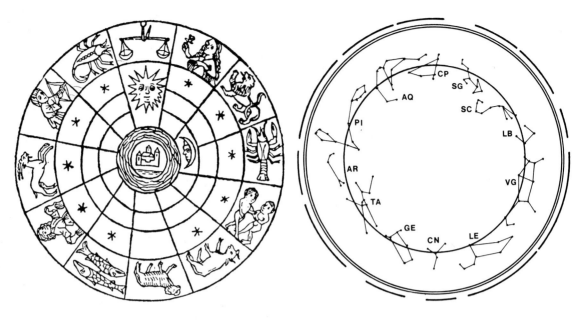

From what has been said, it will be realized that it is possible to measure the movement of the Sun in two ways. First, it can be measured in terms of the zodiac, and, secondly, it can be measured in terms of the fixed stars, the Stellatum. This simple fact gave rise to an idea which was later misunderstood by those not specialized in astrology. It gave rise to the idea that there were two zodiacs – one of equal arcs (as in Figure 30), and another of unequal arcs which were derived from the constellations. It is possible to see how the twelve images for the constellations in Figure 31 are of different lengths in relation to the ecliptic, the apparent path of the Sun against the stars. The fact that the twelve constellational images which bear the same names as the twelve zodiacal signs are part of a large number of constellations may be seen from Figure 33, which is a traditional constellational map. The twelve constellations are all strung out along the ecliptic in this coloured figure (the yellow graduated circle): one sees, for example, how much of the ecliptic is occupied by Virgo (in the blue dress, bottom left) in comparison with the ram of Aries (the yellow ram, at the top of the circle). It is instructive to compare this map of the sky images with the diagram in Figure 34, which picks out the twelve constellations which bear the zodiacal names: this enables us to identify the important twelve and to see just how different in size they are. The constellational twelve are obviously very different from the zodiacal twelve of Figure 30, which are visualized as consisting of twelve equal arcs of 30 degrees each. The twelve signs, as these are called (to distinguish them from the unequal constellations), are each associated with an image, itself derived from the constellation pictures, and

33 *Constellation map showing the twelve asterisms which bear the same names as the twelve zodiacal signs interpenetrating other constellations. For a clarification of this relationship, see Figure 34 below. A hand-coloured print of the woodcut by Albrecht Dürer made according to the specification of Heinfogel and Stabius in 1515. Private collection*

with a symbol known as a sigil. Figure 32 portrays the images of the signs, along with their modern sigils.

As the Sun moves approximately 1 degree each day, it will be obvious that it travels through a full sign of the zodiac in approximately thirty days. This movement, with one or two adjustments, has for many centuries formed the basis for our calendrical system in the West. This explains why the European calendar, derived from that of ancient Greece, has twelve months averaging approximately thirty days each. The notion was portrayed in some of the loveliest zodiacs found in Europe – in the medieval clocks and calendrical instruments designed to measure the passage of the hours, the days and the months. One of the most beautiful of these is to be found on the astrological tower in the medieval centre of modern Bern, Switzerland (Figure 35). The clock has the signs of the zodiac painted in gold against a blue band.

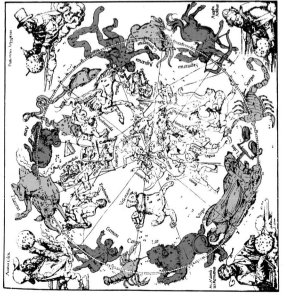

34 *Analysis of Figure 33 above to show the twelve asterisms which bear the same names as the twelve zodiacal signs*

The signs of the zodiac are, of course, twelve in number. As will be evident by now, these are quite different from the twelve constellations of the same name. Both the zodiac and constellation maps are presented as circles, however, and, in terms of occult symbolism, these circles represent the highest levels of spirituality known to man. This is probably why one finds the circle of the zodiac in some medieval cities, and why the circular star map of the constellations is placed in such a prominent position outside the Palace of the Nations in Geneva (Figure 36), as symbol of the spirituality involved in calling together all the nations of the earth into unity.

It is instructive to compare the star groups or stellar patterns as they actually appear in the skies with the traditional pictures derived from them. For example, in Figure 37 we have a direct photograph of the region of the skies said by astrologers to be dominated by the constellation Gemini. The image for Gemini is based on the notion of a pair of young boys (Castor and Pollux, according to one mythological version), who are usually presented in an image like that in Figure 38. How did the ancients link such images with specific regions of the sky? After all, it is quite possible to trace in the area shown in Figure 37 virtually any image merely by connecting together various stars.

Let us look at the problem from a different point of view. Let us take another part of the sky and trace only the main stars in that area. In Figure 39, for example, we have a diagram of the main stars in the constellation of Orion: this distinctive star group is called Orion after a giant hunter of classical mythology. It is difficult to understand how the ancients could trace into this pattern of stars the appearance of a hunter – it would be easier perhaps to trace into that configuration the image of a butterfly. This is one of the stumbling blocks to our understanding the ancient view of the stellar world, for we tend to imagine that the early astrologers projected images into the sky in such a way as to fit them over a framework of stars. This is not at all what they did. There is ample documentation to show that the early astrologers looked at the constellations and tried to feel what influences streamed from them. They then constructed symbolic images which expressed such influences. When they looked at the constellation which we now call Orion, they felt a powerful stream of energy which seemed to awaken something primeval in themselves. It was for this reason that they not only traced a giant hunter into the star pattern, but even created a complex mythology of interwoven stories to account for the presence of such a hunter in this part of the sky (Figure 40).

Some occultists trace the name Orion to an ancient Babylonian term *uru-anna*, which meant 'light of heaven'. Anyone who has looked at this wonderful constellation in the night sky will understand why it should be so called, for it is certainly one of the most brilliant and distinctive of the star groups. We can understand why the ancient Egyptians chose to name this constellation after their great sun god Osiris, who was also the 'light of heaven'. Whatever the origin of the name, however, the ancient Greeks imagined that the giant Orion had been created from earthly material by the gods, but he had become somewhat too big for his boots, continually boasting of his great strength. Forgetting that he had been made of earthly material, and was therefore only mortal, he had claimed that he could kill any earthly creature he chose. Weary of his boast, the gods brought forth the constellation Scorpius, the deadly-tailed scorpion, who promptly stung Orion to death. Then, at the request of the goddess Diana, whom he had often helped with her favourite sport of hunting, Orion was placed in the sky. Naturally he was put in a position directly opposite the constellation of Scorpius, so that he would never forget his fateful boast.

The point which is difficult for a modern mind to grasp is that when the ancient astrologers looked to that part of the sky occupied by the stars which they called Orion, they felt something of the nature of this hunter, of his human aggression and pride. To express these qualities they constructed a suitable myth and hung upon the loose

37 *Photograph of the actual stellar area corresponding to Gemini, for comparison with the image said to be derived from this part of the sky shown in Figure 38 below*

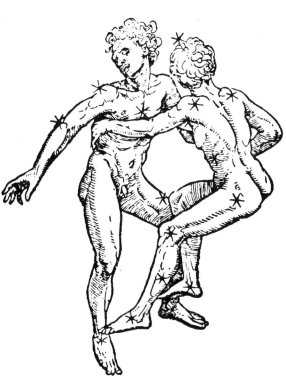

38 *Fifteenth-century woodcut of Gemini, traced from the stellar pattern of Figure 37 above. From the 1498 edition of Albumasar's* Introductorium in Astronomium

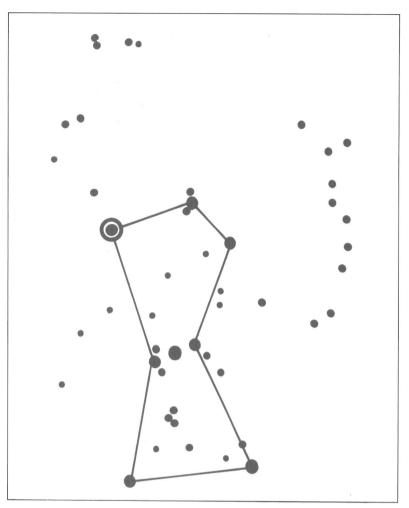

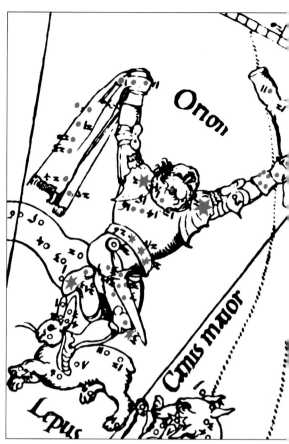

39 *A modern representation of the constellation of Orion. In modern times the projection is based on the assumption that we look up towards the stars from the earth, and trace the figure by joining together the important stars by straight lines*

40 *A detail of the representation of Orion from the Dürer map of Figure 41, to show how the figure of the giant (and of the Hare or Lepus at his feet) was visualized against the backdrop of stars. In medieval times it was common for the designers of star maps to assume that the onlooker was in outer space, looking down into the stars, as though the stars were spread out on a globe or on the Stellatum (Firmament). This accounts for the difference between the orientation of this Orion and the diagram in Figure 39*

structure of star patterns an image (in this case, of a hunter) which expressed their feelings. In this way the feelings engendered by the stars were set out in a huge picture book. Our own way of looking at the stars is different in modern times, and we therefore find it difficult to read this stellar picture book. It is for us much more of a mystery than it was to the ancients, even though it is perhaps no less a wonder.

What is even more difficult for the modern mind to grasp is that the ancients linked the stellar world with the human brain. The occultists of ancient times believed that the stars of the skies were imprinted upon the human brain, that the grey matter of the brain was a small image of the skies. We have seen this idea already expressed in the notion that man's being is really like an inverted tree, rooted in the brain (Figure 22). It is from the brain, or by means of the brain, that man makes images or imaginations of the world. It was therefore almost inevitable that the ancient

astrologers and occultists should trace archetypal images in the skies. These archetypal images were really an expression of human thinking, for it was really believed that all human thinking began, not in the physical brain, but in the ideas spread out in the sky, of which the human brain was merely a reflection. For the ancient occultists the sky was the realm of thought, where all images or imaginations had their origin. Without the sky, man would not have the ability to think or imagine. This view of the world, and of the role of the stars in human life, is now so far removed from our modern concepts, however, that it is difficult for us to grasp the occult origin of the constellational images.

The main forty-two constellations which have come down to us from ancient times have similar corresponding images and mythological legends attached to them as we trace in Orion. One who is conversant with the stories of the stars sees the night sky as a vast book, filled with adventure

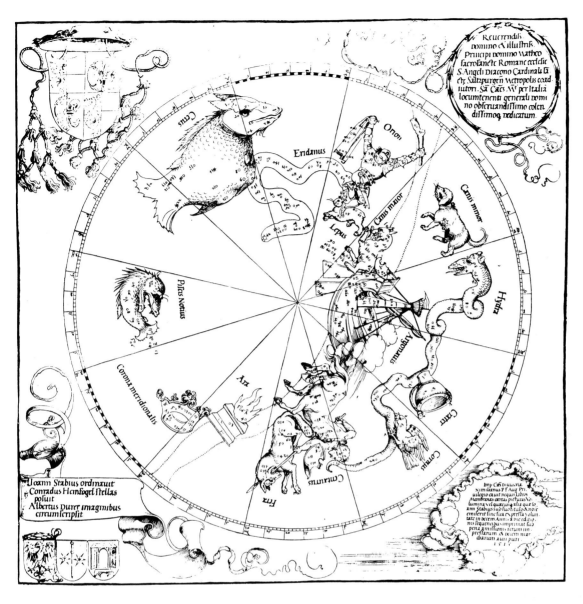

41 *Visualization of the southern hemisphere of stars. Woodcut by Albrecht Dürer made according to the calculations of Heinfogel and Stabius in 1515*

stories and secret symbolism. There is a story for each of the images in the Dürer woodcuts in Figures 33 and 41, the northern and southern star maps. These stories need not detain us here, however, since our main interest lies in seeing how some of these were used by occultists in their study of the world and in their symbols.

To understand something of the occult basis of the astrological images, we should look at them from a slightly different point of view. The Sun was visualized as passing through the equal arcs of the zodiac and marking off the passage of time. The most commonly used of all zodiacal imagery is concerned with the passage of time, which is sometimes called the 'images of the seasons' or the 'labours of the month'. Since the Sun moves through one sign of the zodiac in approximately one month, and since a sign of the zodiac was believed to exert a particular influence on the world, it was considered reasonable to imagine that each month should have a corresponding

labour or agricultural theme attached to it. Figure 42, from a fifteenth-century French manuscript, portrays the image of the sign Leo, through which the Sun was passing in the month of August, which was the month associated with harvesting. This is why a lion, standing against a backdrop of stars, is placed alongside the picture of a man reaping corn.

As the Sun moves through the zodiac it passes very close to certain of the fixed stars. Curiously enough, although this fact was observed, and sometimes even used, by the ancient astrologers, they preferred to think of the Sun mainly in terms of the zodiac. It was to the Moon which they looked when they wished to study the pathway through the individual fixed stars.

The Moon appears to move more quickly through the heavens than the Sun. While the Sun takes twelve months to move through the zodiac, the Moon moves the same distance in approximately twenty-eight days (four weeks of seven

42 *The lion of Leo and the corresponding labour of the month during which the Sun is in this sign. From a fifteenth-century manuscript in the Bodleian Library*

days). This means that it was possible for the ancients to divide the circle of the skies into twenty-eight divisions, each division relating to the average movement of the Moon in a twenty-four-hour period. This division into twenty-eight segments was linked, not with the zodiac, but with the fixed stars, with the Stellatum.

This division of the skies into twenty-eight compartments, the lunar mansions, was sometimes called the 'lunar zodiac'. Astrologers were fond of pointing out the main stars which marked these twenty-eight divisions and called these stars, or stellar areas, the 'stations' of the Moon. Figure 43 is a diagram derived from ancient star maps which show the stations of the Moon. In that part of the skies between Taurus and Gemini there is the small group of stars which forms the constellation Orion (Figure 39). This group of stars is the fifth of the twenty-eight divisions of the stars according to the lunar mansions (the word is from the Arabic *manzil*, and refers to a twenty-eighth division of the zodiac). This group

of stars, and the entire constellation of Orion, plays no part in the division of the skies connected with the movement of the Sun. It is not really possible for an astrologer to speak of the Sun 'being in Orion'. This alone should show that there was both a solar division of the skies and a lunar division. The solar division is linked with the number twelve, and the lunar division is linked with the number twenty-eight. It is a fact that the Moon is used to denote the fixed stars, which accounts for the reason why the artist placed exactly twenty-eight stars in the Firmament of Figure 24.

By now it must be clear that the signs of the zodiac are different from the images of the constellations. Because of this there are two different sets of symbols used to denote the signs and the constellations, even though these are often confused in popular thinking. When we see an image of a constellational figure which is superimposed upon a backdrop of fixed stars, then we may be sure that we are looking at a constellational image,

43 *A segment of the ecliptic, from 0 degree to 180 degrees, showing seven of the main constellational patterns to which the movement of the Moon was related in the lunar zodiac. The top numbers list the lunar stations, of which there are thirteen in this section of the zodiac; there are twenty-eight mansions or stations in the full lunar zodiac. Based on a medieval manuscript*

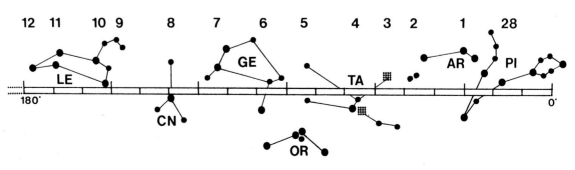

as in the medieval example of Gemini in Figure 38. When we see a zodiacal symbol (properly speaking, a sigil), then we may be reasonably certain that we are looking at a zodiacal sign, as, for example, in the sigil for Virgo in a sculpture from Bruges (Figure 44). However, when we see an image which is either a zodiacal sign or a constellation, yet without the telltale stars in the background, it is not always certain to which of the two traditions the image belongs. For example, the medieval painting of Pisces (Figure 45) and the fresco of Aquarius, the water pourer, from the Salone in Padua (Figure 46) could be zodiacal or constellational images.

The Latin word *aquarius* means 'water pourer' but, as is so often the case with occult symbols, the word hides the true symbolism of the figure. In both the constellation image and the zodiacal sign, the 'water pourer' is not really pouring water from his vase at all. He is pouring out the stellar Quintessence, the Waters of Life. In the true Aquarian spirit (which is the expression of a universal love for mankind), he is making this magical healing power available to all mankind.

We see now that, in some cases, if we wish to determine whether a sky image is zodiacal or constellational, we must have a more detailed knowledge of the context in which it is placed.

44 (above)   *Detail of a symbolic celestial globe, showing the zodiacal band with the sigils for Leo, Virgo and Libra to the front. The star is probably Spica, the main star of Virgo*

45 (below left)   *Pisces, from a fifteenth-century manuscript version of a book on astrology by the Arabian Albumasar, Bibliothèque Nationale, Paris*

46 (below right)   *Aquarius, the water bearer, from the fifteenth-century astrological frescoes in the Palazzo della Ragione in Padua*

There are only twelve signs of the zodiac, of course, so it is possible to confuse with these only twelve images of the constellations. This leaves well over thirty traditional constellations which cannot reasonably be confused with the signs. For example, the image in Figure 47, which is that of Centaurus, carrying in its hands another sky creature, usually called the Beast, is clearly constellational. Although there may be some slight resemblance to the sign of the zodiac Sagittarius, also half man, half horse, the latter always carries a bow and arrow (Figure 48).

There are far more constellational images than zodiacal ones, and in the majority of cases there is no problem in identifying them – the images have survived reasonably intact from very ancient times. It is in minor changes that the occultist will read the hidden meanings contained in such star images. Let us examine such an image more closely to see what this means.

Figure 49 is a detail from a rather grandiose constellational scheme painted on one of the vast ceilings in the Chiericati Palace in Vicenza. There should be no difficulty in recognizing the two constellational images of Scorpius and Libra in the central panel, and we should not confuse the Sagittarius to the upper right with Centaurus, as this horse–man carries a bow and arrow. However, we may not be able to identify with the same ease the naked woman to the upper left, nor the image of the crocodile contained in the small square panel. The naked woman is Andromeda.

She is chained to a rock, a reference to ancient Greek mythology with which so much of our stellar lore is concerned. Andromeda was the daughter of Cepheus and Cassiopeia, and she was punished (like Orion) because of a boast. This time the boast was made by another person, however, for it was her mother Cassiopeia who claimed that the beauty of Andromeda surpassed that of the Nereids, the lovely nymphs of the Aegean Sea. In punishment the sea god Neptune sent a sea monster (the Cetus of the constellations) to lay waste Ethiopia, of which her parents were rulers. The only act which could lift this curse was if Andromeda was offered as sacrifice to Cetus. Accordingly the tearful Andromeda was chained to a rock to await the coming of the monster. The story has a happy ending, however. She is seen by Perseus, who happens to be riding by on the flying horse Pegasus. He slays the monster with the aid of Medusa's head, which was so horrible that it turned to stone anyone who gazed on it. Having rescued Andromeda, he made her his wife.

The story has been interpreted on many different levels by occultists. For example, the medieval amulet makers would use images of Andromeda on stones and gems designed to bring love between husband and wife. This was perhaps a fairly straightforward interpretation of the myth, for Perseus and Andromeda became husband and wife after many difficulties. A deeper level of occultism, however, is that connected

47 (below)   *Centaurus and Bestia, from a fourteenth-century manuscript in the British Library*

48 (right)   *Sagittarius, from a fifteenth-century manuscript on astrology, Bibliothèque Nationale, Paris*

38

with the association drawn between this constellation and the Tarot card called 'The Star' (Figure 50). The significance of this connection is that every person carries within himself or herself an image of their ideal person – in modern psychological terms this ideal might be called the *anima* (in the mind of a man) or the *animus* (in the mind of a woman). Occultists insist that there is really only one perfect ideal embodiment for each human being, and that the wisdom of the soul is such that it will seek out this other person in the world (no matter what the difficulties involved) to find fulfilment, usually through marriage. This notion is to some extent reflected in mythology. Andromeda, through no fault of her own, finds herself chained to the earth. She is rescued by a man from the stellar realm, riding a winged horse. There is a sense in which all humans are chained to the earth and are rescued by their ideal partner, who comes into their lives as though from some mystical place, merging with their own space and time, which is their lifetime. In occultism this ideal partner, the healer of life's tribulations, is often symbolized as a star. As we have seen, the star is far more than merely a reference to the heavens – it is a reference to the healing, life-giving power of the Quintessence. In the Tarot card of 'The Star' we see a weak reflection of the old occult notion that the images traced in the

49 (above)   *Detail of the seventeenth-century astronomical ceiling in the Palazzo Chiericati, Vicenza, showing the images for Sagittarius, Libra, Scorpius and Andromeda*

50 (left)   *'The Sun' card of the Tarot pack. An eighteenth-century version from the Marseilles series*

39

51 *Images of the constellations Nothius (Southern Fish) and Ara (Altar), from the twelfth-century imagery on the zodiacal portal at the top of the Stairs of the Dead in the monastery of Sacra di San Michele, Val di Susa, Italy*

stars are archetypal thoughts or imaginations which live within the brain or thought processes of man: the star is shining upon the two children, who (within the astrological lore at least) symbolize Gemini, which has an intimate connection with human thought processes and ideation.

What about the mythological sea monster Cetus? What is this creature in the occult psychology of the ancient myths? In a sense Cetus is the dark side of the self, that part which prefers to turn a blind eye to the spiritual demands within ourselves. It is that part which clings to the material and devours the material realm (literally, devours the flesh of Andromeda). In modern terminology we might be inclined to call Cetus a materialist. When we study the images of Cetus we begin to see some of the deeper levels of esoteric symbolism. It has been suggested that Cetus was the ancient Tiamat of the astronomers of Babylon. Tiamat is a kind of watery demonic

being, once a mass of bitter water contained within a bottomless pit. The later Cetus was the embodiment of this bitter water, swimming in the seas of our world. In occultism 'seas' relate to the unconscious, hidden psyche of man, so to appreciate the Greek myth properly we have to visualize Cetus as swimming around in the hidden depths of our own being.

Cetus is, in a sense, the opposite of the sweet waters of the Quintessence (though the Babylonians called the sweet water by the name Apsu). From this ancient legend there developed an imagery of Cetus which portrayed it as a monster, sometimes as a grotesque fish or whale (it appears in such a shape in the Chiericati ceiling). In this level of symbolism the monster may be linked with the dark and bitter monster which lurks inside all humans. One wonders if this mythology of waters and a dark, fish-like creature is associated with later Christian imagery. Is it possible that this demon–fish may be opposed to the Christ–fish which is concerned with redeeming the darkness inside all men? The truth is that the fish was the most frequently used occult symbol for Christ (see p. 119).

In medieval art it was a commonplace for the image of the fish as a symbol of Christ (or three interlinked fishes as a symbol of the Trinity) to be placed at the bottom of fonts, beneath the water. Thus this symbolism points to the baptismal water as being the sweet waters of Christ, with the power to heal the bitter waters in the soul. The occult significance of the fish is perhaps among the deepest levels of symbolism derived from the lore of stars. Early star maps show another fish, the Southern Fish of our modern constellational maps, which the medieval astrologers called Nothius. The word 'nothius' is derived from the Greek for 'south', and was originally used to denote the Southern Fish, but the origin of the word is of interest to us here only in so far as it points to the idea of a fish, and therefore to water. Sometimes this fish is depicted as drinking the quintessential waters which flowed from the urn of Aquarius. Surely it is no accident that, when the star maps were Christianized in the thirteenth century, the occultists took this same Nothius and associated it with the constellation Ara, the pagan altar, which in the hands of the medieval occultists became the altar of the Christian Church, with the fish Nothius above it, as symbol of the living, healing power of the Christ–fish (Figure 51)?

2 The Astral World: The Invisible Sea

The casual observer might think that the old woman in Figure 52 is a witch. However, this is not so – she is actually one of the Fates of ancient mythology, spinning the thread from which the garment of life is made. In ancient times it was believed that there were three Fates, each one intimately involved in the life of man. What is of particular interest to our study of occult vision is that this old crone is portrayed in the midst of three worlds. She stands on a block of stone or rock which is shaped in the form of a cube. The solid cube (like rock itself) is one of the symbols of materiality, of the physical world.

The woman is surrounded by a luxuriant growth of flowers, brambles, creepers and ferns. Such an interweaving of plants is linked in occult symbolism with the etheric plane. The word 'etheric', which is derived from the Latin *aether*,

has almost the same meaning as the word 'Quintessence', the secret fifth element which the ancients believed to be the spiritual body of the stars, the life force on the earth. On reflection we see that it is entirely satisfactory that the life force should be symbolized by growing plants. In medieval times, when an artist wished to indicate events which were supposed to take place on the etheric plane (where time itself is different), he would fill the background area with swirling forms or plant-like growth, as, for example, in the sculpted detail of Figure 53 or in the alchemical symbolism of Figure 187.

Besides standing upon a stone in the midst of this symbolic growth, the old woman is carrying upon her shoulders a globe which reminds us of the cosmos held on the shoulders of Atlas in Figure 24. However, if we look more closely at

52 *One of the Fates working at the material from which destiny is woven. From the 1537 Augsburg edition of Boethius's* Consolation of Philosophy

53 *Detail of arcane bronze door on the west front of San Zeno, Verona*

54 *Wolves and astral symbols. Detail of a ceramic mosaic on the exterior schoolhouse wall at Mehren, West Germany*

this globe, we shall see that it is not a diagram of the cosmos at all: it is not meant to symbolize the heavens. In this semicircle there are a number of stars (each one in the now familiar Seal of Solomon form), as well as the humanized crescent Moon. To the extreme top right of the picture is a flash of flame, containing what might be hailstones or meteors, bursting in on the picture. This higher realm of fire and of the Moon is called the astral. The word 'astral' is from the Latin *aster*, meaning 'star', which is almost certainly why the artist has portrayed a number of stars on the lunar globe. When the medieval artist wanted to suggest that the events he was depicting belong to the higher astral plane, he would set them against a background of pure gold, or against a background of stars, to indicate the 'astrality' of his subject.

What precisely is this astral realm and how does it relate to the old woman below? In occultism the astral world is a realm which is normally invisible to ordinary men, but which is really a domain proper to the emotional life. Clairvoyants tell us that the astral plane is filled with emotional qualities, and to their higher vision it appears as a seething mass of coloured forms, all moving at different speeds, many of them changing shape with remarkable agility. In this astral world things which are invisible on our own earth plane have an independent existence of their own. For example, pure thought, which is quite invisible on the earth, takes on a form and colour special to itself on the astral plane. Similarly, human emotions (invisible on the material plane) have curious forms and colours peculiar to their own natures. Later in this chapter we shall see how some occultists have attempted to portray these invisible qualities of thinking and feeling as they (with their specially trained vision) perceive them on the astral plane.

In the occult image of man we find that the physical body corresponds to the world of minerals. This world has neither life force nor emotions. For this reason the artist who made the woodcut in Figure 52 has portrayed the physical realm by means of a symbolic cube of stone.

The life force within the plant world is that which lifts the material elements of earth into the beautiful organization of flowers and plants – it is the etheric force which pulls from the seeds in the darkness of the earth the variety of forms and colours. Such living organisms as plants have no astral within their natures.

However, the minute a living organism is penetrated by the astral world, it becomes charged with emotional life and desires, rather like an animal. All animals have an astral part to their being, for they exhibit strong emotional lives. The most used of all symbols for the astral world in medieval art is an image of a dog or wolf (Figure 54), which often seems to quiver with emotional intensity, life and energy. Sometimes, however, a lion is used to symbolize such astrality or the Astral body; such a lion symbol is derived from astrology, for the lion of Leo was linked with the heart of man (Figure 77), and it was once believed that the human heart was the seat of the emotional life. In yet other symbols the lower body was linked with the serpent of temptation, for it was believed that the strong desires within the Astral body were the forces which drove men to sin. In late medieval times the Astral body of man was called the 'Desire body', and it was usual for artists to show those who had succeeded in controlling their own astral natures standing upon an animal or serpent. A coiled serpent is often used as a symbol of the 'desire realm' of the astral world – that part of man's invisible being which must be controlled. The religious images which portray the saints or Christ standing upon a serpent (Figure 55) are really pointing to the idea that human sin (which must be overcome) is linked with the invisible realm of the astral.

The human being has a physical body, an Etheric body and an Astral body. Every man or woman is therefore capable of living and feeling. In addition to these three bodies, every healthy human being has also an individuality (sometimes called an 'Ego' in occultism) by means of which he controls the impulses in the emotional Astral body. With this Ego he is capable of making decisions, of controlling the appetites of the lower body. This is why it is perfectly possible to think of man as a spirit when his higher Ego is in charge, as well as little more than an animal, or at least 'subhuman', when his lower Astral body is in control.

Figure 56 is an occult image of what is sometimes called the Scale of Being. It shows a sort of ladder, reaching from the lowest part of the material world up to the heavens (here symbolized as a castle). Each of the steps symbolizes a level of being higher than the one below it. The man to the left of this picture has his foot on the lowest step, which is marked with the Latin *Lapis*, which means 'stone'. Already we see a link with the old woman in Figure 52, for she too stands on a stone.

The second step is marked *Flama*, which means 'flame', and is derived from an old notion that fire is actually the highest expression of the earthly nature – in the medieval view of things fire is really a refined sort of earth in rapid motion. We see such a fire in the flash of flame to the right of Figure 52.

The next step is marked *Planta*, which is related to our word 'plant', but which in its Latin meaning contains the idea of growth and propagation. This obviously corresponds to the abundance of plant life in Figure 52 – it is a symbol of the next stage of being, which is the etheric.

The following step upward is marked *Brutus*, which means 'animal-like' – the line from this step points to a lion, in confirmation that the king of the animals is an excellent symbol for this stage of

being. This corresponds, of course, to our astral world of the emotions.

Only at the next step do we see the word *Homo*, which means 'man'. The symbolism here points to the truth that man is in a sense a completion of the world of minerals, plants and animals.

What is the next step? It is marked *Celum*, which means 'heaven' – beyond is the realm of angels and God (*Deus*). The step marked *Celum* is joined by a line to the star-spangled clouds. We have already noted in chapter 1 that occultists link the star realm with the origin of human thought, and that they see thought as something higher than man, yet accessible to him.

The step marked *Deus* (God) leads into the palace above.

Each of these elements in Figure 56 is contained within the symbolism of Figure 52, had we but eyes to recognize them. The world of angels is traditionally linked with the Moon, so the moon face at the top of the picture points to the sphere of the Angels. The *Celum* or Heaven is also symbolized in the stars above the head of the Fata crone.

55 *Detail of stained glass showing Christ standing in triumph over the Devil. From the parish church at Mehren, West Germany*

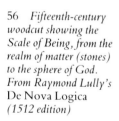

57 (above)   *Victorian wood engraving showing a deathbed scene as visualized by the occultist A. J. Davis*

58 (right)   The Sixth Palace of Hell *(1945) by Fay Pomerance. Lilith on the shoulders of Lucifer, appearing to a dying man. Private collection*

56   *Fifteenth-century woodcut showing the Scale of Being, from the realm of matter (stones) to the sphere of God. From Raymond Lully's* De Nova Logica *(1512 edition)*

And, if you look closely at Figure 52, it will become apparent that the steps of Figure 56 are also symbolized in the inclined distaff in the hand of the woman. This distaff is quite enormous: it is obviously intended to symbolize something of great importance. Like the steps of Figure 56, it begins on a stone and, like these steps, it also finishes in a most curious form which resembles a castle. The old crone, whom we know to be one of the Fatae, is the equivalent of the human being who stands between the inert lifeless stone below and the City of God, symbolized by the castle, above.

A full survey of the occult symbolism in Figure 56 would take us well beyond our present limits, so we should concentrate on looking more carefully at one line of symbolism, which is that connected with the lion. As we have seen, this lion represents the emotional life of man and the related astral plane. It is that plane within which man lives, as though within an invisible sea – much as fish live within water. Occultists tell us that, while the astral plane is certainly invisible to

ordinary people during life, it becomes visible after death. After the physical body has been left behind like a worn glove, the human spirit enters into the astral plane. The Victorian deathbed scene in Figure 57 may be just a little mawkish, yet it proclaims this idea that the soul of the newly dead old woman leaves the body with all the beauty and freshness of a young girl, and rises to the astral realm. The artist has shown the mourners around the bed looking down at the body, unaware of the beautiful spirit above. This spirit is the Astral body of the departed: the artist has drawn the edge of the picture frame through the spirit to indicate that it is transparent and invisible to those below.

The modern painting of a deathbed scene in Figure 58 is also a portrayal of the astral plane. The man is dying, and because of this the astral beings which have been invisible to him during his lifetime are now crowding around his bed, making themselves all too apparent to him. The astral demon Lilith presents herself to him in the form of a beautiful woman in the hope that she will per-

44

When the time comes for an evil man to die
LILITH appears to him and induces him to sin with her
and during his sin she kills him

59 *Detail of an astral symbol from the mosaic in Figure 54*

60 *Detail of lamb with seven-rayed star. The entire Mehren mosaic, which depicts St Francis with the animals, contains many arcane symbols*

the painting of Lilith in Figure 58 is related to the lower plane of the astral world. However, both levels are said to be flooded with colours, and it is inevitable that those who have seen the plane and have the ability to paint have tried to represent it mainly in terms of colour. Some very interesting occult images have been produced as a result of this. Some images used in religious symbolism are really derived from occult notions, and there is no area of religious art which is more closely linked with occultism than this astral realm. One of the deepest beliefs in the Christian religion is that the untamed power of the lower astral may be redeemed, or tamed, by the love of Christ. As we have seen, some Christian works of art attempt to symbolize the untamed emotions (which are proper to the lower astral sphere) in terms of the snake; others use the symbol of flames. The idea behind this flame symbolism is that, when such wild tongues of flame are controlled or tamed, they become the soft fire of stars. The detail in Figure 59 is from Figure 54 and shows that the three-tongued flame is intended to symbolize untamed emotions. The whole picture from which this detail is taken shows St Francis confronting the savage wolves. Behind him stand a number of sheep, already by nature quite tame. The symbols above the heads of the ferocious wolves look like flames, burning in anger towards St Francis. The symbols above the heads of the sheep are six-pointed stars (Figure 60), which recall the ancient tradition that the stars on the edge of the cosmos were made from the soft life warmth of the magical Quintessence. The entire image proclaims that the love of Christ, as represented by Francis, will convert the anger of the lower astral into the star-like love of the higher astral. Although these symbols are used in a Christian work of art, they are none the less derived from occult sources.

One of the earliest attempts to portray the Astral body of man (as seen by a clairvoyant) emphasizes the beauty of the colour, and it is this which has been the keynote of the majority of astral illustrations ever since (Figure 61). Many occultists point out that the Astral body differs according to whether or not man's lower passions are controlled or tamed. Those people with chaotically arranged colours (especially those with large areas of dull red or violent movement) betray an emotional life which lacks discipline, while those with relatively harmonized areas of colour (Figure 62) are themselves disciplined and well balanced.

One important group of occultists attempted a systematic programme of research into the appearance and colour of the astral plane, and their findings profoundly influenced the theory of colour in modern art. This group worked at the end of the nineteenth century and was connected with the then recently formed Theosophical Society, which had been founded in the United States

suade him to sin with her. She knows that, if she succeeds in this, she will gain part of his soul.

What may we learn from this picture of pre-death temptation? Occultists speak and write of the astral plane with such familiarity that we may be sure that, while normal people do not have the ability to see it, those with special insight or with a clairvoyant training may see the plane easily. This is confirmed by a vast literature of occultism and spiritualism which describes the astral plane in great detail. Occultists say that parts of the astral are extremely beautiful while other parts are quite ugly – there are, in effect, higher and lower levels in the astral plane. We may be certain that

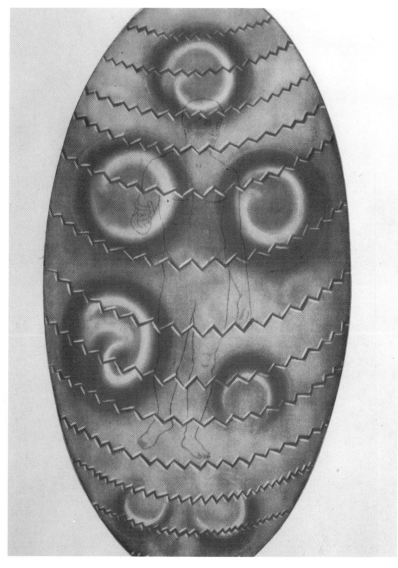

at the instigation of the great occultist Madame Blavatsky. Among this group was a clairvoyant called Leadbeater, who had free access to the astral plane. He made it his practice to look into the astral, by means of clairvoyant techniques, and to dictate to artists what he saw. These artists would then attempt to interpret his visions in colour; after detailed correction by Leadbeater, they would paint finished pictures to represent what he had seen.

A very large number of these curious paintings have survived and among the most remarkable are what Leadbeater called 'thought forms'. These thought forms were described by him as being the forms produced on the astral plane by human thinking. He claimed that every human thought, no matter how slight or unimportant, created a pattern or image in the astral, and he attempted to portray the most interesting of them by dictating detailed descriptions of them to his artists. He even published commentaries on what these thought forms represented. The images in Figures 63, 64 and 65 show that these range from un-

formed, chaotic structures, which represent undisciplined or unclear thoughts, to very precise balanced formations, which represent thought arising from clear meditation.

The two thought forms in Figure 65 are ones which Leadbeater claims to have seen at a funeral. The one to the left shows a spiritual thought form, which was a result of the highest meditation in the face of the loss of the loved one. The form to the right, on the other hand, shows the materialistic grief emerging from the mind of one who is unable to accept that death is a liberation into a higher world. The proboscis-like feeler which runs from the base of this thought form is said to be reaching into the grave, as if to bring back the dead body, as though the dead body were itself the departed human. In studying such paintings as these one cannot help observing that they do not really relate to thought so much as to feeling – they are really emotion forms rather than thought forms. This is perhaps understandable, for the realm of the astral plane is the realm of the emotions, rather than of thought.

61 (left) *Late-nineteenth-century portrayal of the astral body of man as seen on the higher plane by the clairvoyant C. W. Leadbeater. From the 1908 German edition of Leadbeater's* Man Visible and Invisible

62 (above) *Another example of a portrayal of the astral body as seen by Leadbeater*

63 (right, above and below)   *Thought forms indicating 'vague intellectual pleasure', as seen by Leadbeater on the astral plane. From C. W. Leadbeater and Annie Besant's* Thought-Forms, *(1897 edition)*

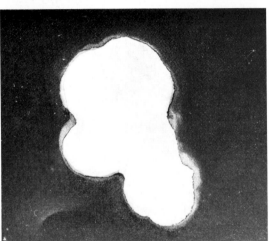

64 (far right, above and below)   *Clearer thought forms seen by Leadbeater, representative of (above) a determination to solve some problem and (below) 'explosive anger'*

65   *Thought forms seen on the astral plane during a funeral. The one on the left is issued by a spiritually minded person, while the one on the right is from a materialistic person, its form expressive of the wish to lift the dead body from the grave*

Among the most interesting of the pictures derived by Leadbeater in this way was a series of paintings of music forms – the forms built in colours on the astral plane from earthly music. Figure 66 shows 'a ringing chorus by Gounod', which Leadbeater saw spreading into the astral realm for over 600 feet above the church in which the chorus was being sung. One observes that the forms within this vast cloud are built entirely out of colour, and the forms as a whole really represent the first completely abstract art. It is not surprising that the Russian artist Kandinsky, who possessed a copy of Leadbeater's book with its many coloured illustrations, should have been

67 *'Tanga Woman'*
(1982),
silkscreen print by
Michael Adams

enthused by these to paint the first abstract pictures in Western art.

In later books Leadbeater took the study of the astral colours even further and classified them according to their spiritual meanings. Inevitably such a view of the astral world had a considerable influence on the development of painting, and the influence of such teaching about the colour and movement of the astral, of how colours may be used to depict abstract things like sound, is still an important factor in art, so that many painters who find themselves interested in occultism are inclined to attempt to incorporate into their work elements which point to this hidden realm. A good example is to be found in the prints and paintings of Michael Adams, who has often attempted to paint the 'sound' which is the constant background to his subjects. In Figure 67, for example, he is much more interested in painting the astral atmosphere – the noise of street music, birds, the chatter of people – than in depicting the street itself. Although the subject matter is immediately identifiable, there is a level on which one might say that Michael Adam is really pointing to the astral realm behind the familiar world of everyday experience. 'It is not enough to paint a cicada, you must paint his sound. A cicada is much more sound than something seen,' says Adams. As he speaks, he points in his painting to an area of scribbled sigils, above the central umbrella, which contains the sigil for Aries γ, an occult symbol for the inpouring of the spiritual world into the realm of man. To the right of the picture, above the head of the man with an upraised hand, is a star burst of yellows and reds that one might take to be an umbrella. It is not an umbrella, however, for it is as much 'abstract' as the Aries sigil: 'That's the sound of birds – quite deafening, even louder than the disco music!' explains Michael Adams. Such a picture, and such comments, indicate how deeply some artists have been swayed by the wish to paint the world hidden behind visual experience.

It is one thing to see, or to sense, the astral forms which lie behind the appearance of a busy, animated street, and quite a different thing to see, or sense, such astrality in inanimate objects. Some clairvoyants can see the astral forms which emanate from lifeless material. This is not because material forms have Astral bodies, but because all things are bathed in the astral plane, and therefore to some extent influence this plane. It is interesting, for example, to compare the image of a human Astral body (Figure 61) with the astral emanation from an ordinary horseshoe magnet (Figure 68). What is communal to these two pictures is that both artists chose to illustrate the astral forces in terms of colours. Although the two artists belonged to different occult groups, they both experienced the same difficulty, which was that the colours which are available to us on the earth plane are not sufficiently beautiful to describe those seen on the astral plane. 'The beauty of these colours,' writes the artist who painted the astral emanations of the magnets, 'cannot be represented to the outward eye.'

In previous centuries artists and occultists often attempted to show something of the appearance of the astral world. Some concerned themselves with showing the appearance of entities of the lower astral plane, while others attempted to show the Astral body of man on the higher plane. The lower astral plane is sometimes called the 'demonic' in popular lore, and we might therefore say that any of the demons which are represented in chapter 7 on demonology (Figures 169, 172 and 176, for example) are really astral beings or astral appearances. It was always recognized by occultists that those who sought to conjure demons or ghosts could only do so by persuading these creatures to appear on the material plane. This plane is by no means their normal habitation, for they are really inhabitants of the lower astral realm, but traditional occultism claims that sometimes it is possible (by means of magical spells) to persuade spirits or demons to penetrate the

material so as to become visible. It was because the conjuration of spirits demanded the merging of the astral and the material in an unlawful way that the old magicians would draw protective circles in order to keep the harmful influences of the astral beings they conjured at a distance. In the eighteenth-century engraving in Figure 69 we see two magicians conjuring the spirit of a dead person in the traditional manner of black magic. The astral being stands in front of them, and they look aghast at the emanation, protected from that forbidden lower realm only by the conjurer's circle.

Occultists maintain that when a person dies, it is possible for him to leave behind a non-physical shell. These shells have many different names in occultism, but in popular thought they are called ghosts. Like all etheric and astral phenomena, ghosts are not normally visible, but there are times – for example, under the influence of the heightened state of sensitivity which accompanies bereavement, or when one is frightened – to see ghosts. Far too many personal records of the ghost experience have been left by people for this to be denied. Perhaps more remarkable than the fact that people have seen the invisible realm of ghosts is the fact that this realm has been photographed time and time again. Of course, the majority of photographs which pass for spirit pictures are forgeries; there are said to be well over eighty different ways of producing a more or less convincing image which might be taken for a spirit picture. However, in spite of this, there is abundant evidence to show that from time to time the appearance of ghosts and related psychic phenomena has been caught on film.

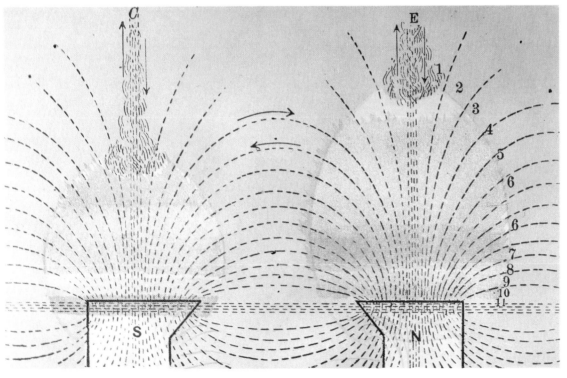

68　One of the earliest examples of an attempt to portray the invisible aura of the etheric or astral plane. In this case the artist is showing how the magnetic field appears to clairvoyant vision

69   *Hand-coloured engraving showing a historic attempt to evoke the spirit of a dead
man in the churchyard of Walton-le-Dale in Lancashire. In the seventeenth century
Edward Kelly and his friend Waring attempted to raise the spirit with a view to learning
the whereabouts of a treasure they supposed he had left behind*

In a sense there are two different kinds of spirit photographers – the professional who specializes in taking pictures of etheric or astral beings, and the amateur, who takes a picture which accidentally captures the appearance of a ghost or some related phenomenon. The professional spirit photographer is usually either a medium himself or works in close collaboration with a medium. In this way it is possible for the photographer to see (either in a trance or through clairvoyant ability) the spirit he is photographing and to pose his picture accordingly. The picture in Figure 70 was taken by one of the best American spirit photographers of the last century, Wyllie. It is a rare picture, not only because both the dog and the woman are spirits, but because it was taken in a specially conducted trial. The story was recorded by the psychic investigator W. T. Stead, who tells us that Wyllie took the picture for J. Wade Cunningham of Los Angeles. A medium had observed that Cunningham was often followed around by the spirits of a beautiful lady and a dog (both of them invisible to Cunningham himself). It was arranged for Cunningham to stand alongside an empty chair in the hope that the spirit dog would jump on the chair to have its photograph taken. However, at the first attempt it was the lady who appeared in the picture, her head in a halo of light above the empty chair. Two days later a further attempt was made to photograph Cunningham against the empty chair, and this time the lady appeared again, along with 'the coveted image of the dog that Cunningham recognized as the distinctive animal he had owned many years before!'

In contrast with this mediumistically directed photography is the more simple photograph in Figure 71, which shows a cat, which a moment or two earlier had been sleeping on the mat in front of the electric fire, watching in astonishment as a curious kitten (or is it a large rat?) runs across the mat, as though scurrying for the safety of the chair. The photographer who made this strange picture was merely attempting to take a photograph of his pet. He did not develop the roll of film immediately, and shortly afterwards he died, so he never saw the extraordinary picture he had taken.

Images which appear in this way in pictures, and which were not visible at the time when the photograph was made, are called 'extras'. Some of the strangest pictures incorporating such extras are those made in seances, where serious attempts are often made to break through the ordinary barriers which prevent men and women from seeing into the higher realms of spirit. However, it is in mediumistically controlled seances that

70 (above)   *Spirit photograph of a woman and dog, by the American spirit photographer Wyllie, 1897*

71 (right)   *Photograph of a live cat with a curious 'extra', taken by Alfred Hollidge in 1974*

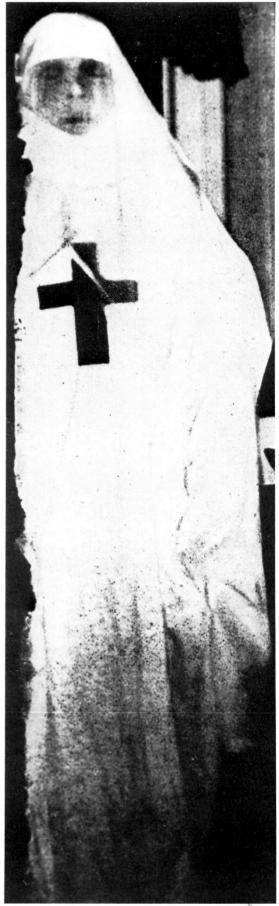

72 (above) *The medium William Eglington supporting an ectoplasmic materialization of an Arab, London, 1878*

73 (right) *Incomplete materialization of the spirit of a nun photographed by the medium Castelwitch in a seance in Lisbon, 1918*

such phenomena occur and permit photographers to take pictures which are of spirits materializing in an almost physical form. It is claimed by spiritists that under certain circumstances spirits may build up a sort of imitation body from a semimaterial substance called ectoplasm. There are many remarkable records of whole groups of people, sitting in a circle in the darkened room during a seance, watching a piece of ectoplasm, originally no bigger than a ball of wool, gradually build into a form closely resembling a human. Many photographs of such complete (or partly completed) forms have been taken, among which the most interesting are those in Figures 72 and 73.

Figure 72 shows a famous, perhaps even infamous, medium called William Eglington (in a state of trance) being weighed down by the huge materialized figure of an Arab. Eglington's biographer was present when this picture was taken and has left an interesting account of the events leading up to it in the seance:

[Eglington's] breathing became increasingly laboured and deep. Then, standing in full view, by a quick movement of his fingers, he gently drew forth, apparently from under his morning coat, a dingy white-looking substance. He drew it from him at right angles and allowed it to fall down his left side. As it reached the ground it increased in volume and covered his left leg from the knee downwards. The mass of white material on the ground increased in bulk and commenced to pulsate, move up and down and sway from side to side. Its height increased and shortly afterwards it quickly grew into a form of full stature, completely enveloped in the white material. The upper part of this the medium then drew back and displayed the bearded face of a full-length materializing spirit, considerably taller than himself.

Figure 73 was also taken in a seance, held in Lisbon during 1918, but in some ways this is a far more frightening image, for the nun is only partly materialized and her face is almost subhuman at this stage of development 'We saw at first a kind of vapour, through which it was possible to distinguish the picture on the wall,' writes one of those present.

This vapour grew a little longer, became thicker, and took the form of a spirit which gave us the impression of being a monk dressed in white. It advanced and drew back three times towards the red light, on its way it knocked on the table. Three times it disappeared and then reappeared, making the same movement.

It is significant that the figure never sufficiently developed for those present to determine whether it was a monk or a nun, and the psychologist who described the phantom noted that the whole of the right side (including the right ear, shoulder and arm) was entirely missing, 'as if this part had, from top to bottom, been ripped off a life-sized portrait.' Such phantoms, be they etheric or astral, are certainly not from our own familiar world of experience.

Not all appearances from the astral realm are so hideous, however. Indeed, occultists insist that the higher realm of the astral is inhabited by the angels. We saw this to some extent when we examined the symbolism of the star, linked with the refined astrality of the Quintessence (Figure 60), for the step marked *Angeli* in Figure 56 is joined by a line to a picture of an angel in a cloud of stars. This is an association of great importance, for in Christian theology the angels were said to be the spiritual hierarchies immediately above man. They were invisible beings, yet even so they played a great part in the life of the individual. Of course, there were several ranks of angels, from the Angels proper to the Cherubim and Seraphim on the very edge of the world, and it was the lowest of this rank which was most intimately

74 *Engraving by Albrecht Dürer of the Virgin and Child standing on a crescent Moon. The symbolism is usually explained as representing the Assumption of the Virgin, but its origin is involved with arcane matters*

connected with man. In some occult systems it was claimed that every human being had an attendant angel and devil, and that both of these lived in the next plane of being, which was the astral realm. The sphere of the Moon was the sphere proper to the Angels and to the demons. This in itself probably explains why the clairvoyants speak about there being two levels to the astral plane, one of which is highly refined and one of which is rather gross. It is likely that the horns so often portrayed on demons are a throwback to this idea of the lunar sphere, for the horns are really linked with the crescent Moon. So intimately connected with the lower passions and the astral realm is the image of the crescent Moon that we find many religious images in which saints, or even the Virgin Mary, stand upon the crescent of the Moon, as though trampling down a vanquished demon or snake (Figure 74). Such images are reminiscent of the trampled serpent of Figure 55.

The two groups of symbols behind the Cherub in Figure 75 are probably intended to point to the two extremes in the ranks of the angels. The lowest of the ranks are Angels themselves, linked

75 *The six-winged Cherub, symbol of the highest of the spiritual hierarchies near the throne of God. Several of the symbols in this manuscript indicate an arcane intention on the part of the artist. From a thirteenth-century manuscript in the British Library*

with the Moon, while the highest are the Seraphim, linked with the Quintessence. In the two main divisions of the background behind this Cherub, divided into red and blue, we find whole groups of the two main symbols for the astral and the Quintessence. These are the crescents of the Moon and the six-pointed stars with a central hole derived from the Seal of Solomon (see p. 29).

This image of the Cherub standing in front of these important occult symbols is interesting for several reasons. Clairvoyants often claim to have seen the beings of the astral plane, whether these be the demons of the lower levels or the angels of the higher levels, or even the living thought forms in between. But few ever claim to have seen the higher ranks of the angelic choir, such as the Cherubim or the Seraphim, for these live in spheres far beyond the astral. If no one has seen

them, then how do we know what they look like? The inscription to the left of the Cherub in Figure 75 seems to be very much aware of this problem, for, in discussing the numerology behind the image, it admits that this Cherub is depicted in the form of a man with six wings. The implication is that, while this is a traditional symbolic form for the Cherub, no one knows what the being really looks like.

One of the most beautiful of all occult designs is that made to illustrate a manuscript by the visionary Hildegarde of Bingen, a nun who was blessed from a very early age with the ability to see into the higher realms which lie behind the world of phenomena. The illustration in Figure 76 is from this text and is capable of many levels of interpretation. Hildegarde herself (who may be seen in the bottom right of the picture looking up at her vision) wrote that such pictures as she used were intended to be seen by the 'inner eyes' as much as by the outer ones. However, we may trace in this design elements which are of profound importance to our study of the astral.

We have already noted that the occultists say that the human being has an Etheric and an Astral body, which may be regarded as sheaths for his physical body. The etheric is often portrayed in terms of plant life, but sometimes, because when they are seen the etheric forces look like a kind of moving light, the colour white is used to depict this body. This is a good choice of symbolism, in fact, as the Etheric body is itself pure and sinless, having none of the animal nature proper to the astral. The true etheric is in constant movement, however, as it is a 'living' thing. We may see how Hildegarde (who gave detailed instructions to her artists in much the same way as Leadbeater was to do seven hundred years later) ensured that the part of her design which was intended to represent the Etheric body of her cosmic man was both white and moving. Of course, it is impossible to represent movement adequately on a still picture, but the tonal gradations and the lines traced across this pure area of white are certainly sufficient to indicate Hildegarde's intentions. Beyond this area of white we see an early attempt to portray the nature of the Astral body. Hildegarde has resorted to picturing in this area the heads of animals and fish, in order to show that this part of the cosmos in man is linked with the animal world, where the desires reign. This concentric of colours is also linked with the four elements. The innermost circle represents Earth, centred on the sexual parts of the cosmic man. This sphere of Earth is wrapped around by the life-giving etheric forces to show that it is, like man, a living being. After this comes the realm of Water, symbolized by the waving white lines on a background of blue. Then comes the realm of Air, symbolized by a starry blue sky, followed by the realm of Fire, symbolized by tongues of flame against a black

background. In comparison with the peace and dignity which one feels in the central area of moving white, these coloured concentrics are restless and jarring. They catch to perfection the nature of the Astral body of man. Naturally one must speculate on the outer concentric of red. Is this merely a continuation of the Fire element or is it a symbol of man's own inner selfhood, the unique human Ego? The single human face to the extreme left of the design might suggest that this is indeed the case.

76 *Arcane illustration of the macrocosmic man in the thirteenth-century 'Liber Divinorum' of Hildegarde of Bingen. Public Library, Lucca, Italy*

3 The World of Man

It is one of the basic teachings of occultism that man is a miniature image of the whole cosmos – 'Man is a microcosm' proclaim many of the esoteric texts. Perhaps the most well-known image of this teaching is found in the curious diagrams which are called officially 'melothesic man', the 'zodiacal man' of popular astrology. These figures show the body of man linked with each of the twelve signs of the zodiac. The head is ruled by Aries, the neck and throat by Taurus, and so on, right down to the feet, which are ruled by Pisces. The most famous of medieval images of melothesic man is from a lovely manuscript painted by the Limbourg brothers for the Duc de Berri (Figure 77), which portrays man inscribed within an almond-shaped form, a magical structure which is called a *vesica piscis*, with the zodiacal signs covering his body.

A comparison of this painting with the simple woodcut in Figure 78 shows that, while the parts of the body are associated with exactly the same signs (for example, the ram of Aries has rule over the head, the fish of Pisces over the feet, and so on), there are sometimes slight differences in the images themselves. For example, in the Limbourg picture Capricorn is painted not as a goat–fish (which is the usual image for this sign), but as a curious shell–goat. Again, the crude woodcut shows Gemini, the ruler of the arms, in the image of two small children, while the Limbourg plate shows Gemini as a naked man and woman, arm in arm. There are important reasons behind such deviations from the tradition, but these reasons need not concern us here – it is sufficient for us to observe that, even in such seemingly unimportant pictures, the occult tradition points to new ideas which are important in the medieval period. For example, the developing notion of the spiritual relationship between man and woman, who are to be visualized as equals in the Gemini image, is one which was being developed in the new romance literature of the medieval period, especially in connection with the Grail legend.

Those who are not aware of the importance of such details of symbolism, and who fail to note the significance of minor deviations from the norm in such images, may be tempted to see astrological and occult diagrams on a superficial

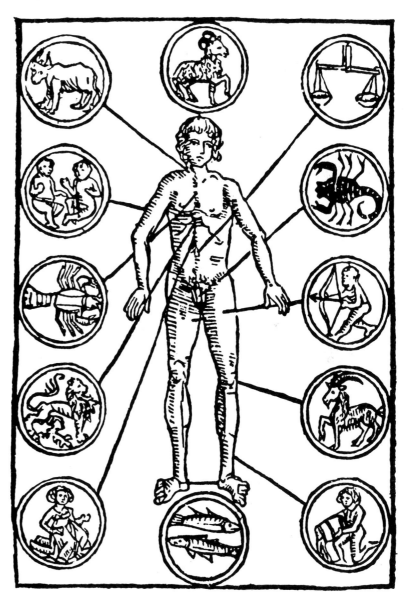

77 (left)   *Zodiacal man from the Limbourg brothers' 'Très Riches Heures du Duc de Berri', one of the most arcane astrological documents painted in the early fifteenth century. Musée de Chantilly*

78 (above)   *Zodiacal man. This fifteenth-century German woodcut evinces no esoteric content, but merely records the astrological link between the parts of the body and the twelve signs*

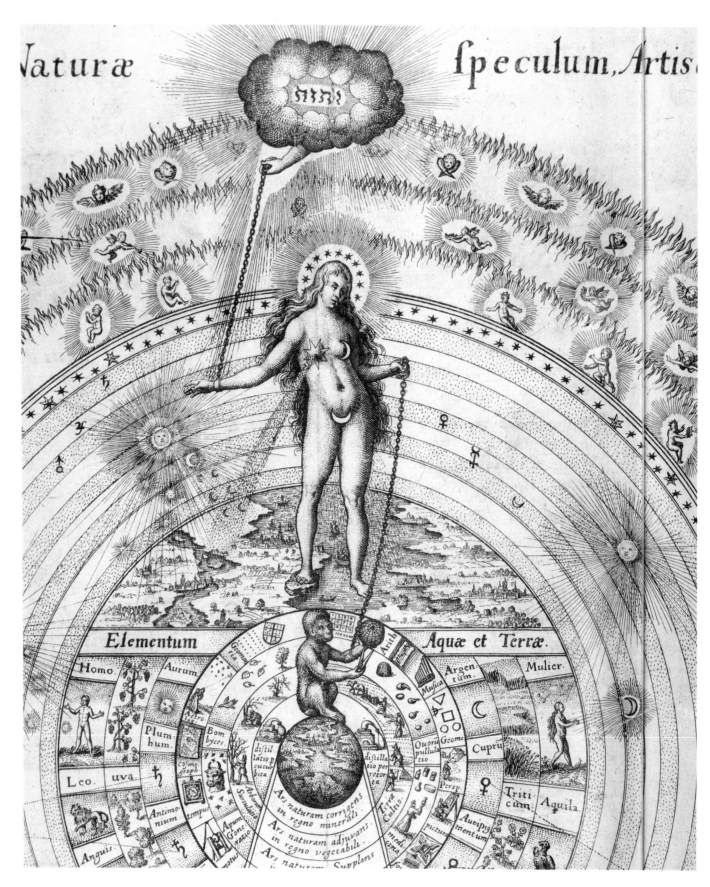

79   Anima mundi *(the Soul of the World) linked to the heavens and the earth and set against a background of planets. Detail from an engraving by Johann de Bry in Robert Fludd's* Utriusque Cosmi . . . Historia *(1617)*

level. For example, such people may consider the image of Aries the Ram and see it as pointing to the inner nature of man as a sort of battering ram, to that part of the human being which relates to courage, and which makes the person impulsive and headstrong. Such associations alone may be taken as accounting for the link drawn between this sign and the human head. However, as with most occult images, zodiacal man contains deep hidden meaning within its symbolism. Aries is represented by the sigil ♈, which some claim is a drawing of a ram's horns – for Aries is linked with the image of a ram. However, it is said by occultists that this is not really a drawing of horns at all, but a diagram of what might be called a cosmic funnel which allows the forces in the spiritual world to pour to a single point.

This simple diagram is used to denote a most important thing about the human being, which is that we are all carrying within us the ability to draw down from the invisible realms above the life forces of spirit and of thought. It is as though our brains (located in the head, ruled by Aries) are the receiving mechanisms which take thought from the spiritual realm above. This may appear to be a strange notion to modern man, who is accustomed to believe that humans think with the brain. However, occultists teach that thinking is an operation by which we open ourselves up to receive thoughts from the cosmos, from the realm of stars. In a sense the pictures by which we think are floating invisibly in the air around us, and we have the magical ability to take these pictures into our own brain and to turn these invisible things into imaginations or visualizations. This esoteric idea is contained in the simple sigil for Aries, which shows the head of man opening itself receptively to an upper invisible world.

Each of the twelve modern sigils for the twelve signs of the zodiac may be considered in a similar way, for they all relate to similar occult properties of the human body. They each reflect the way in which the microcosm is linked with the cosmos.

Thus, zodiacal man might be described as the twelvefold model of man. There are, however, other models with different numerological bases. There is, for example, the occult image of man which is called the threefold model. Figure 79 shows a woman standing against a background of astral symbols. She is called the *Anima mundi*, the Soul of the World, and, as every human being is linked with this world soul, we may see within the symbolism certain things which point to the nature of man. Her right hand is chained to the Hebraic name of God in a cloud: this is a symbol of man's link with the spiritual realm. In her left hand she holds a chain which is shackled to a monkey: this is a symbol of her link with the lower material realm.

What the occult symbolism of Figure 79 reveals is that man (or woman) is caught between two worlds, both of which are usually invisible. One

80 *William Blake's print* The Ancient of Days *from his occult poem* Europe: A Prophecy *(1794)*

world is linked with the higher spiritual realms normally associated with God and with the choir of angels. The other world is linked with the lower, demonic realm normally associated with the bestial and the demons. In this picture the monkey is used as a convenient image of the lower world. In fact, the monkey is not really demonic in the accepted sense of the word. He sits on the earth and measures a small model of the cosmos with calipers. This is not the activity of the demons, of course. The monkey really represents the scientific outlook – that is, the attitude to the world which concentrates on its physical nature and is concerned only with what may be measured. The symbolism is perhaps more concerned with the occult principle of the calipers than with the monkey, for a pair of calipers unites the centre and the periphery of a circle at one and the same time. The calipers remind us of a remarkable definition of God as a being who is a centre and circumference at one and the same time. Such a symbolism is echoed very graphically in an engraving by the occultist William Blake, which shows God with his own head at the centre of a circle, measuring or creating the world below (Figure 80). His mind is at the centre and his attention is at the periphery of the circle. There is an echo of this idea in the modern symbol for the Sun ☉ which occultists say is a drawing of the soul (the inner centre) emerging into space and time from the circumference.

It is no accident that the globe which the monkey measures in Figure 79 is contained exactly within a series of concentric bands, which lists (alongside traditional symbols) such things as arithmetic, geometry, time, motion and so on: these are the disciplines concerned with relating the earth (or earthly things) to cosmic laws. These earthly matters are visualized as the concern of the scientist, who is often hypnotized by earthly matters; one notes the intensity with which God leans over and looks towards the earth in order to make his measurements. The monkey, then, is an image of a propensity within all men – a propensity to study the earth without real concern for the larger spiritual cosmos. It is an early symbol for what we would now call materialism.

We must observe that the woman is not actually chained to this monkey – she holds the chain freely and might, if she chose, let go. However, the diagram implies that it is necessary for her to hold the chain, just as it is necessary for God to hold the chain which binds the woman. Occultists would claim that, were God to let go of the chain, the whole cosmos would wither – the cosmos needs man, just as much as man needs the cosmos.

This remarkable diagram contains so much occult symbolism that a full analysis would certainly reveal many of the important trends of occult thought. However, we shall merely note within the image the idea that man (or woman) is to be visualized as being poised between two invisible worlds, the spiritual and the material. The body of man, so firmly rooted in the physical, consists of a separate third realm.

This idea of man as the interpenetration of three worlds finds its most interesting images and symbols in alchemy. The alchemists were fond of describing the realm of man's thinking as the world of Salt. This term is a curious one, for it deals not so much with the operation of thinking as with the end product of thinking. Perhaps one reasonable explanation for the choice of salt as a symbol for thinking is that ordinary white salt may be imagined as a whole realm of tiny stars

fallen to earth – in terms of the occult notion of the origin of thought this is not at all a far-fetched analogy. Man has the capability of drawing into his own world spiritual ideas in the form of thoughts, and of turning these into pictures which are, to some extent, material things. These material forms are the alchemical Salt. One of the alchemical symbols for Salt is the inverted triangle ∇, which suggests the idea of descent into matter. From what we have learned about the occult view of the stars as the archetypal realm of thinking, we may understand why an inverted triangle, which points down to the earth, may be used as an occult symbol of thinking. It is clear that the triangle ∇ may be linked with the sigil for Aries Υ, which is drawn as a straight-edged angle in Figure 81.

The alchemists symbolize the lower world in terms of Fire. As we have already seen, the triangle resting on its base is one of the most frequently used of all symbols for the element of Fire. In occult imagery the flames of Hell, burning upwards, are linked with this notion of Fire. Sometimes the same hellish world is symbolized as Sulphur. The sulphurous fires of Hell are often used to symbolize the lower nature of man – that which is intimately involved with the earth. The monkey of Figure 79 measures the earth and is distracted from cosmos beyond. The fires burning in the lower half of alchemical man in Figure 82 are intended to show that inner burning which results from a lack of concern for the cosmos, from selfishness. Selfishness, which leads to spiritual isolation, is often presented in occult imagery as a burning or flaming condition. In a very direct sense the flames represent what the ancients would have called 'the roots of feeling', which in modern times may be linked with the unconscious element in man, the source of his primal energies. The flames of the inner hell are carried by all men who are concerned only with themselves and are hypnotized by material illusion. Since the flames of fire burn upwards, most occult systems symbolize Fire as a triangle $\triangle$ resting on its base, its apex pointing to the skies.

There is an interesting parallel between the image of *Anima mundi* in Figure 79 and the image of man in the alchemical diagram of Figure 82. In Figure 79 the woman stands on Earth and Water (the map of England and the sea), but her upper part is silhouetted against a backdrop of planets and stars. In the same way the upper part of the alchemical man of Figure 82 is symbolized by a circle of stars. Both diagrams in their own way denote the idea that man is caught between the demonic realm and the spiritual realm, both of which are contained within his being.

If we return to the alchemical words Salt and Fire, and see these as symbols of 'the result of thinking' and 'the roots of feeling', then we shall be able to understand more fully some of the most profound alchemical images of man. Figure 83 – the title page of an alchemical text – shows two

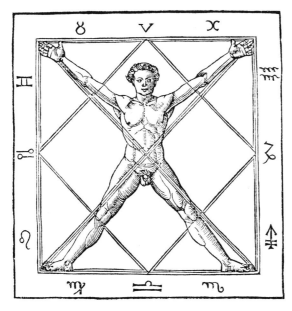

81 *Occult emblem with sigils for the zodiacal signs, from Henry Cornelius Agrippa's* De Occulta Philosophia *(1532)*

triangles meeting against a background of floral motifs. This floral background is one of the symbolic devices used by occultists to indicate the life force or Quintessence (see p. 41). Fire and Salt are visualized as meeting against the life force: this is actually an occult image of man. The Salt of thinking pours downwards and meets the upward streaming of willing Fire. The space between these forces is the realm in which man himself has his existence, between the two worlds of thinking and willing. If the movement down of the Salt triangle ▽ and the movement up of the Fire triangle △ are continued, then the two will eventually form the occult symbol of the Seal of Solomon ✡ (see p. 21).

It may be difficult to see the full occult implications of a diagram as simple as Figure 83. Let us therefore examine another view of threefold man. The alchemists visualized the human being as threefold. The upper part of man (generally iden-

tified with his head) is where the Salt process takes place. This Salt is a result of thinking, of making pictures in the brain. To put it another way, Salt is really the precipitation which is a result of the spiritual activity of image making. As we have seen, one of the possible reasons why Salt was chosen as a convenient symbol of the product of thinking is that the grains of salt may be said to resemble the inert forms of stars, like little specks of light which have fallen to earth.

The alchemists visualized the lower part of man as the seat of the will, in which all the undisciplined, animalistic forces and selfish urges are gathered, burning in a sea of flame. This part of man is almost a volcano, for the darker forces of the will sometimes erupt into the conscious world of man and induce him to do things which he would not normally do. The alchemists call this part of man Sulphur or Dark Fire, or sometimes just Fire.

82 *Engraving from William Law's edition of Boehme's mystical writings. The engraving is ingeniously designed to incorporate overprinted 'doors' which open to reveal 'inner consequences' and spiritual developments. A comparison with Figure 202 will indicate how, below the fires which stream up the legs of the man, is a doorway which reveals the demons of Hell*

63

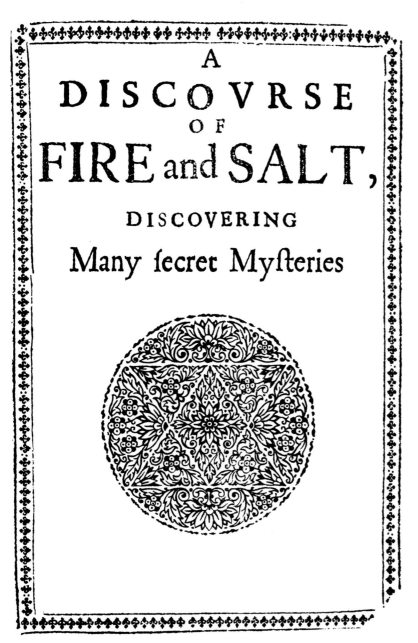

A DISCOVRSE OF FIRE and SALT,

DISCOVERING

Many fecret Myfteries

83 *An arcane device on the title page of an alchemical text on Fire and Salt. The floral background to the occult figure is intended to show that it is a diagram of an etheric relationship*

The third part of man is said by alchemists to be linked with his emotional life. The middle part of man, linked in a direct way with the lungs and with breathing, is that part in which man is most harmoniously related to the outer world. In breathing man takes into himself the outer air and from this abstracts the oxygen which he needs for his own life-support system. This area of breathing, or of emotional balance, alchemists called Mercury. Mercury is that impulse which tries to reconcile the two extremes of man – the thinking process and the willing process. When the thinking process forces its way too deeply into the feeling sphere, Salt is produced, for this gives rise to human tears, which taste of salt. When the willing process bursts into the feeling sphere, we have a sort of wild hysterical laughter, which the ancients associated with the untamed nature god Pan. In the perfectly balanced man the three parts

of Salt, Mercury and Sulphur work harmoniously within their own spheres.

This alchemical image of threefold man permeated much of medieval alchemy. The alchemists called these three, when they manifest in man or in the cosmos outside man, the Three Principles and gave them special symbols: ⊖, ☿ and ♀. In the Rosicrucian diagram of Figure 84 these three symbols appear above the circle containing the Seal of Solomon. They also appear on the breasts of the silver and golden double-headed eagles, which are the Eagle of the Moon and the Eagle of the Sun respectively. One interesting difference between this latter group of sigils and those above the seal is that the sigil for Salt does not have its cross – it is in the form θ. In fact, this is a most interesting occult symbol, for it is derived from one of the late Graeco-Roman astrological systems as a symbol for death. The form is really the Greek letter theta, and was the first letter of the ancient Greek word *thanatos*, meaning 'death'. What is the connection between the Salt of the alchemists and death? What, indeed, is the connection between human thinking and death?

According to occultists, the realm of thought is filled with spiritual life forces. When these life forces are channelled down into the limiting realm of the human brain, they to a certain extent die, for they cannot live within such a small prison. The human being receives the spiritual energies as mental imags and there is a precipitation of Salt, said to result from the meeting of the pure spirit of thought with the physical realm. Salt is therefore the symbol of dead images, of a stellar power which was once alive, but which has been sacrificed to make pictures in the mind of man. Just as man breathes in oxygen from the material world and breathes out carbon dioxide, so he 'breathes' into his brain spiritual images and gives back only Salt. This is why the principle of Salt is symbolized by an ancient image of death.

The unrestrained Fire forces are located in the lower part of man, as we have seen in the occult diagram of Figure 82. We have also noted that the volcanic life force seething in this lower part of man was linked in ancient times with the god Pan. We may now begin to understand why, in classical images, Pan is depicted as having animal-like lower parts, with the legs of a goat and cloven hooves (Figure 171). The unrestrained nature forces in man (located by the occultists in the lower part of man) were from very early times seen as a powerful energy which only required discipline to become a great power for good. Without such discipline these energies could only run wild and become a power for evil. This notion almost certainly explains why the image of Pan was a source for many of the medieval pictures of the Devil or demons, as will be seen in chapter 7.

A full appreciation of the Three Principles in man shows that human beings are visualized by occultists as carrying within them fragments of

MYSTERIVM MAGNVM STVDIVM VNIVERSALE.

TINCTURA

TINCTURA

alba.

rubra.

LO VE

MAGISTER IESUS CHRISTUS
D. et H.

This is the golden and rosy Cross, which is carried by each

made of pure spiritual gold, and brother upon his breast.

Benedictus Dominus Deus Noster, qui dedit nobis Signum.

FAITH.

HOPE

Hear, O my son, and receive my sayings, and the years of thy life shall be many. I have taught thee in the ways of wisdom; I have led thee in the right paths. When thou goest, thy steps shall not be straitened, and when thou runnest, thou shalt not stumble. Take fast hold of the instruction, let her not go; keep her, for *she is thy life.—Prov. IV. 10.*

Frater Rosæ et Aureæ Crucis

PATI ENCE

TINCTURA

Those who have the Spirit of Christ, will find wisdom in the teachings of Christ and receive the heavenly Manna and the Philosopher's Stone. Many hear the words of wisdom, but do not desire wisdom, because they do not possess the Spirit of Christ. He who desires to understand the words of the wise and the doctrines of Christ, must become Christ-like himself.

"Call unto me, and I will answer thee, and shew thee great and mighty things."—*Jeremiah xxxiii.*

84 *A nineteenth-century hand-coloured engraving using alchemical symbolism. The three sigils between the double-headed eagles represent Sulphur, Salt and Mercury. Private collection*

dog-headed (Figure 85), a form which reminds us of the Egyptian god Anubis (who participated in postmortem trials and experiences). Though dog-headed he has a human body, and over his heart he holds the caduceus which is the emblem of Mercury. In late occult symbolism the Anubis element of Mercury was lost, but the form of his caduceus was preserved (Figure 86).

Old fairy stories often contain hidden truths which were later adopted into occult symbolism, and this realm of threefold symbolism is no exception. In fairy stories we find that the hero or heroine is constantly encountering representatives of the inner self in the form of dwarfs or giants. The symbolism is fairly transparent, for the dwarf is (among other things) a symbol for human cleverness and the power of thinking – very often in the old stories the dwarfs forge magic rings or other amulets from gold. This is a fine symbol of the way man makes thoughts from the starry realm. Gold itself is a symbol of the spiritual world; this explains why the medieval painter so often used a golden background to his biblical illustrations and paintings. The things made from this gold, such as rings, are human thoughts. The secret ring, by which the owner can make himself invisible or omniscient, is a symbol of the link which may be made with the invisible realm of spirit above. The dwarf works in the earth, in a dark cave; this is a symbol of the cavern of the head, where picture making takes place.

One of the most frightening images of the activity of the dwarf is that told in the story of Sindbad and the Old Man of the Sea. Here, of course, the sea is the astral realm (see p. 125), one of the levels of the invisible realm of spirit from which thinking proceeds, and the Old Man is the dwarf. The Old Man sits on Sindbad's shoulders and eventually grips so tightly that Sindbad can no longer feel free to do the things he wants to do. Eventually the Old Man is almost in control of Sindbad and turns into a vicious tyrant. This is a symbol of the extent to which thinking which loses contact with the spiritual realm (and, like the monkey of Figure 79, is concerned only with the outer world) becomes obsessive. Sindbad is no longer free to think, but must do the bidding of the cunning Old Man. There is a distinct relationship between the Old Man of the Sea and the monkey.

The giant, on the other hand, is usually stupid. He has none of the adroit cleverness of the dwarf or the Old Man, though what he lacks in intellect he makes up for in strength. The giant is a personification of the dark fires which burn in the will realm of man. If such deep powers were to be unleashed without control, then the whole world would be destroyed.

The symbolism of the fairy story places man (usually symbolized as a prince, a princess, a boy or a girl) between the dwarf and the giant. The

85 *A Roman representation of Mercury, derived from the Egyptian imagery of the dog-headed Anubis, who presided over the dead. From the Roman* Mosaic of the Months, *formerly in Thrysdus (El Djem), but now in Sousse Museum, Tunisia*

the power which is linked with the stars, as well as the darker powers which are linked with the earth or with the demonic part of the earth over which the Devil has rule. The reconciling force in the human frame is breathing, the harmony of the heart, which is linked with Mercury. It is no wonder that the sigil for Mercury ☿ has a crescent at the top – this crescent is a sort of chalice, which carries the liquid spirituality of the individual. Whether this liquid is of a highly refined spiritual nature or of a dark demonic nature is up to the individual concerned. Perhaps this duality is expressed in the symbol of Mercury which is linked with the death cult of the ancient Egyptians: some early Roman images of Mercury show him to be child has to learn how to be more astute than the dwarf, and if not actually stronger than the giant, then at least able to outwit him. Only when this lesson has been learned may he or she find the treasure or the loved one. The fairy-story symbolism is here an older layer of esoteric imagery which was later changed by occultists to the Three Principles.

So far we have glanced at occult imagery relating to man in the abstract. What about the personality of man – what about those things which help make man into an individual? When we turn to the occult symbolism concerned with the personality of man, we are faced with a variety of different systems. There is a system of classification connected with the number twelve, in which man is described in terms of the twelve signs of the zodiac. There is also a system by which man is described in terms of the influences of the seven planets. Perhaps more directly related to the occult system, however, is the ancient system which is called the fourfold model.

From the very earliest historical times man has been visualized as containing within himself a balance of four qualities. These four qualities are linked with the occult elements of Fire, Earth, Air and Water. According to occultists (who inherited the basic ideas from the Greek philosophers), these four elements are found within all men and women, manifesting through the four humours, or four temperaments. What makes each individual unique, at least in terms of these elements, is the mixture of the four within the personality. An individual with more Fire than someone else is certain to be more 'firey', which is to say that he will be more impulsive, aggressive and active. A person with more Earth will be more practical, perhaps slower, but more dependable, and so on.

The way in which the four elements interact within the human psyche were studied in great depth by occultists, who gave special names to the personalities derived from them. The Fire element was said to give the Choleric temperament. The Earth element was said to give the Melancholic temperament. The Air element gave the Sanguine, while the Water gave the Phlegmatic.

The Choleric was active, impulsive and belligerent. It was usual for occultists to portray this type carrying a sword or dressed as a soldier. In Figure 87 the man on the extreme left is Choleric (flames can be seen behind his cloak), while in Figure 88 the woman at bottom right is the Choleric type. Above her head is a roundel with a salamander, the traditional Fire being, basking in the flames. The Melancholic temperament is slow, pensive, careful and practical. Occultists would often portray the type dressed in a thick cloak (to indicate that the personality was cold) and carrying religious symbols, for the Melancholic temperament was said to be the best one for monks or philosophers. The woman at bottom

left in Figure 88 is dressed as a nun. She is looking down to the roundel in which there is a pig, a symbol of Earth. The pig is seen also at the foot of the man to the right in Figure 87. The Sanguine temperament is volatile, changeable and often very clever. The type is often portrayed as a beautiful woman, as in Figure 88, where she is semi-naked, pointing to the skies (a symbol of the Air element). The changeability of the Sanguine type is symbolized in the image of the chameleon in Figure 88 (top centre). In Figure 87 the symbol for the Air type is the bird or the monkey. The Phlegmatic type is slow, sensitive and unstable, and is often portrayed holding a bow or an arrow (as in Figure 88 – the Phlegmatic in Figure 87

86 *An eighteenth-century engraving of Mercury with his caduceus, which in this case has the two intertwined snakes topped not by a dove (as is more usually the case) but by a pair of wings, which reflect the notion of the heavens in much the same way as do those on his feet*

87 *Personifications of the four humours or temperaments. From left to right: the Choleric (Fire), the Sanguine (Air), the Phlegmatic (Water) and the Melancholic (Earth). From a fifteenth-century German 'Shepherd's Calendar'*

appears to be holding an arrow flight) and is associated with the fish. In Figure 88, below the Phlegmatic woman is a roundel depicting a dolphin, the archetypal symbol of water and spirituality.

Of course, the four elements and their corresponding temperaments were rarely seen in isolation, as temperaments, but rather as the manifestation of the zodiac on the edge of space. Occultists linked the types with the twelve signs of the zodiac, and we find that each of the twelve zodiacal personalities exhibits one or other of the four temperaments, according to the schema:

Fire (Choleric): Aries, Leo and Sagittarius
Earth (Melancholic): Taurus, Virgo and Capricorn
Air (Sanguine): Gemini, Libra and Aquarius
Water (Phlegmatic): Cancer, Scorpio and Pisces

By this means the four become twelve, and the four elements, which essentially belong to the inner nature of the earth, are projected into the twelve signs which really belong to the heavens. With such a projection we are returned once again to the image of the melothesic man in Figure 77. Occultists have given the twelve signs of the zodiac an incredibly rich symbolism, and it might be worthwhile glancing at how these relate to the personality of man.

Aries is the ram (Figure 89), with the sigil ♈. We have already glanced at one strain of occult symbolism in this strange sigil, but we should also observe that the ram is linked in occultism with the notion of butting (with its horns, of course), suggesting the conflict or impact which takes place each time the spiritual realm meets the physical in the human activity of thinking. The ram brings down the pictures of the spiritual realm and makes them earthly. This is probably why the ram is so often depicted as looking towards the following sign Taurus, which is an Earth sign. The 'fire' of the stars, from which thinking proceeds, descends to the earth plane by way of the Fire sign Aries into Taurus. The sigil for Taurus ♉ may be seen as a receptacle for this spirit. Some occultists trace the receptive crescent of this sigil to the bull's horns and point out that the horns of Aries bend downwards at the tips since Aries is trying to draw the fire from the skies, while the horns of Taurus (Figure 90) reach upwards as though to receive the images made by Aries.

88 *Emblems of the four elements, humours and temperaments on the title page of* Septem Planetae, *a book dealing with the relationship between the planets and the seven ages of man*

AER

PHLEGMA

AQVA

SANGVIS

IGNIS

SEPTEM PLANETÆ
Septē
Hominis
ætatibus respondentes scilicet
1. INFANTIAE
2. PVERITIAE
3. ADOLESCENTIÆ
4. IVVENTVTI
5. VIRILI ÆTATI
6. SENILI ÆTATI
7. SENECTÆ DECREPITÆ
Cum eorundem in eafdem operationibus
et effectibus elegatiffimis figuris
depicti
Homo natus de muliere breui uiuens tem:
pore repletur multis miferys
Job.14
Dies annorum noftrorum in ipsis
SEPTVAGINTA āni eruit
psal. 89
Gerardus de Jode excu.
ao 10. 1581.
Mar. de vos uen.

TERRA

MELANCOLIA

CHOLERA

♈ Aries

of man's thinking, as may be seen in Figure 91. The old images of Gemini show the twins arm in arm, as symbol of their harmony, as an outward sign of their ability to communicate. It is also a symbol of the fact that all artistic activity is rooted in love.

There is a deeper occult significance in the traditional image of Gemini, however. Very often the twins are drawn as mirroring each other – as though each was a reflection of the other. This notion is concerned with the idea of thought. In Aries thought is taken from the spiritual realm and made into pictures. These are materialized in the realm of Taurus, which is concerned with the earth and with receiving. The result is that in the following sign (Gemini) the spiritual realm may be said to find a reflection on the material realm. The pictures of the heavenly world have come down to earth. This is why the twins face each other (Figure 92), for one represents the spiritual inflowing of ideas and the other the earthly reception of these ideas (though of course, being twins, they cannot easily be separated). In the mythology which accounts for the origin of the constellation Gemini we find that one of the twins is immortal while the other is mortal – which is to say that one belongs to the realm of the gods while the other belongs to the realm of the material world. Some see these children as being Castor and Pollux, the twin sons of Leda and Jupiter, while others see them as Apollo and Hercules. In each case, however, the important thing is that one is a god and is therefore immortal, while the other is linked with the earth.

In Gemini the spiritual and the earthly meet in unison. We find this idea expressed in the two-snake image of the caduceus which Mercury, the planetary ruler of Gemini, usually carries in his hand (Figure 93). These two snakes are mirror images, in much the same way as are the twins of Gemini. The Tarot card of 'The Sun' (Figure 50) is linked by occultists with Gemini, and it is now easy to see why. The Sun represents the outpouring of spirit energy into the material world, in which the twins stand as symbol of the union established between spirit and matter.

How can this descent of spirit be traced into the fourth sign, Cancer? Cancer is nowadays often called Cancer the Crab, but in earlier forms of astrology it was more usual for it to be represented as a crayfish, as in Figure 94 (though it is in the familiar crab form in Figure 77). Both the crab and the crayfish have in common the idea of the shell, and it is in this that we begin to see the occult significance of the sign in relation to the model of man. The first two signs, Aries and Taurus, have horns – it is as though their connection with the spiritual cosmos is concerned with how these hard structures may be used to receive and channel the spiritual forces from the heavens. The third sign, Gemini, has nothing hard in its imagery – the twins are naked, dwelling openly and without

89 and 90 Hand-coloured woodcuts of Aries (above) and Taurus (below), from a 1496 edition of Hyginus, Poeticon Astronomicon

Gemini is the first sign to express the condition of Air, which is the medium of communication. In modern astrology Gemini has rule over such things as the media, advertising and so on. In the traditional forms of astrology the planetary ruler of Gemini (Mercury) was given rule over all artistic activities, letter-writing, sculpture and so on – over those forms which were a direct result

♉ Thaurus

91 (above)   *French fifteenth-century print of Mercury and the human activities over which he has rule*

92 (below)   *Gemini as the twins – one mortal (with the scythe), the other immortal. From a 1504 edition of Hyginus,* Poeticon Astronomicon

shame in the light of the Sun (Figure 50), totally receptive and open to the influx of the spiritual. The sign Cancer represents the occult notion that what has been received is now inside the human being, locked within the shell of the crab body. This is one reason why in the zodiacal man Cancer is given rule over the ribcage. The ribcage is a sort of protective covering around the heart, a defensive system for the emotional realm. In Cancer it is as though the hard horns of ram and bull have been turned inside out, so that they are no longer pushing aggressively into the world, but are turned into a defensive, protective armour around what has been received from the spiritual. Cancer the Crayfish is really a symbol of a treasury of forces and ideas which have been given to man by the invisible spiritual world. Perhaps this is one reason why many astrologers link Cancer with the unconscious realm of man, with that part in which all hidden knowledge may be found.

There is a sense of completion about this descent of spirit which may be traced in the Fire, Earth, Air and Water of the first signs of the zodiac. The completion is to do with the fact that the spiritual realm has succeeded in reflecting itself in the material realm. This notion of completion is

93 (left) *Mercury and his rulerships. From the fifteenth-century manuscript 'De Sphaera' in the Bibliotheca Estense, Modena*

94 (below left) *Cancer as a crayfish. Hand-coloured woodcut from a 1496 edition of Hyginus,* Poeticon Astronomicon

expressed also in the sigil for Cancer ♋. This sigil is sometimes said to represent the form of the female breasts (for Cancer is linked with the idea of nourishment, and milk is one of the symbols of the power which streams down from the spiritual realm). It may well be that this is cne level of occult meaning within the sigil, but a much more profound level is to be found in connection with the preceding sigils. The three sigils for Aries, Taurus and Gemini – ♈, ♉ and ♊ – are each drawn on a symmetrical vertical axis – one half of each is reflected to make a whole. It is only with Cancer that we first meet a sigil which is not a mirror image. The form ⌒ does not reflect itself as though in a mirror – were it to do so, then the sigil would be written ⌒⌒.

The fact that it is the first sigil to escape from a simple vertical symmetry is an important part of the occult symbolism of Cancer, of the Water nature on earth. It is in Cancer, when the spiritual powers have been, so to speak, personalized, enclosed within the human breast, that a sense of duality arises. What was formerly outside, and the gift of the spiritual realm, is now inside, so that the individual is convinced that it belongs to him. The first three signs of the zodiac portray in occult symbolism how the spiritual world becomes available to man and becomes visible in the material plane of Taurus and Gemini; it is only with Cancer that we find man making this spiritual energy into something personal.

This points to one of the most profound notions in occultism, which is that everything that man has – his thoughts, words, deeds and emotions – does not really belong to him, for it is in a sense only on temporary hire from the spiritual world. For the duration of a lifetime (passed within the isolating shell of Cancer, which is an image of the shell of the physical body and perhaps explains why the sign Cancer is linked with birth) man takes for granted this spiritual gift and considers it to be his own. He no longer reflects perfectly the idea of the spiritual, but has taken from that realm a power which gives him the sense of being able to live independently of the cosmos. Of course, the truth is that no man is an island – no man may live a life independent of the cosmos. This is one of the themes developed in the image of man as the *Anima mundi* in Figure 79.

Our glance into the relationship of the first four signs of the zodiac to the life of man has shown that the zodiacal images are part and parcel of a deep strain of occult symbolism. A thorough analysis of the twelve signs, along with the images

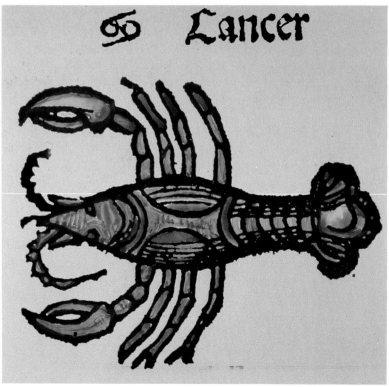

ℭ Cancer

and associated sigils, would show that each reflects a deep connection between man and the cosmos. It must be evident already that anyone who looks at the melothesic man of Figure 77 and considers it only as a list of arbitrary correspondences is failing to see the deeper levels of symbolism into which occultists reach. It must also be evident that, the moment one begins to look at man through the symbols of occult lore, one finds that it is impossible to separate man from the cosmos as a whole.

This is perhaps most clearly illustrated in the occult diagram of Figure 95, which is replete with esoteric references. Man is depicted as a duality – as a being of light and a being of dark, the lower being a sort of demonic reflection of the higher. The heads and arms of the two figures are arranged in such a way that they together form a Seal of Solomon, which may be viewed either as the meeting of Sulphur and Salt or as the meeting of the four elements. Half hidden within the centre of this seal is a cross, itself half white and half black, a symbol of the internal fight between darkness and light which is one of the conditions of the earthly life in which the Quintessence struggles to emerge in material form, within the limitations of space and time. Of course, this Quintessence, figured here as a cross (rather than merely as the dot of soul), is placed at the centre of an elliptical circle – but in this case the circle is presented in the form of the Ouroboros snake biting its own tail, a symbol (as we have seen) of the limitation of time. The triple crown on the head of the upper countenance is topped by a cross to indicate that, in the man of light who eventually emerges from the struggle with the lower darkness, the inner light (the central cross) emerges as an outer form in the visible light of day. Crude as it is, this diagram is worth considerable attention, for in presenting in this particular form the meeting of the higher and the lower, demonic elements in man it makes use of several of the occult symbols which we have examined so far. It is rare to find symbols of the cross, the Seal of Solomon, darkness and light, the Ouroboros, and the demonic and the human united in one single diagram.

95 The Great Symbol of Solomon, *from Eliphas Levi's* Transcendental Magic *(English translation) of 1896, representing the God of Light and the God of Reflections*

4 Earth Magic and Earth Spirits

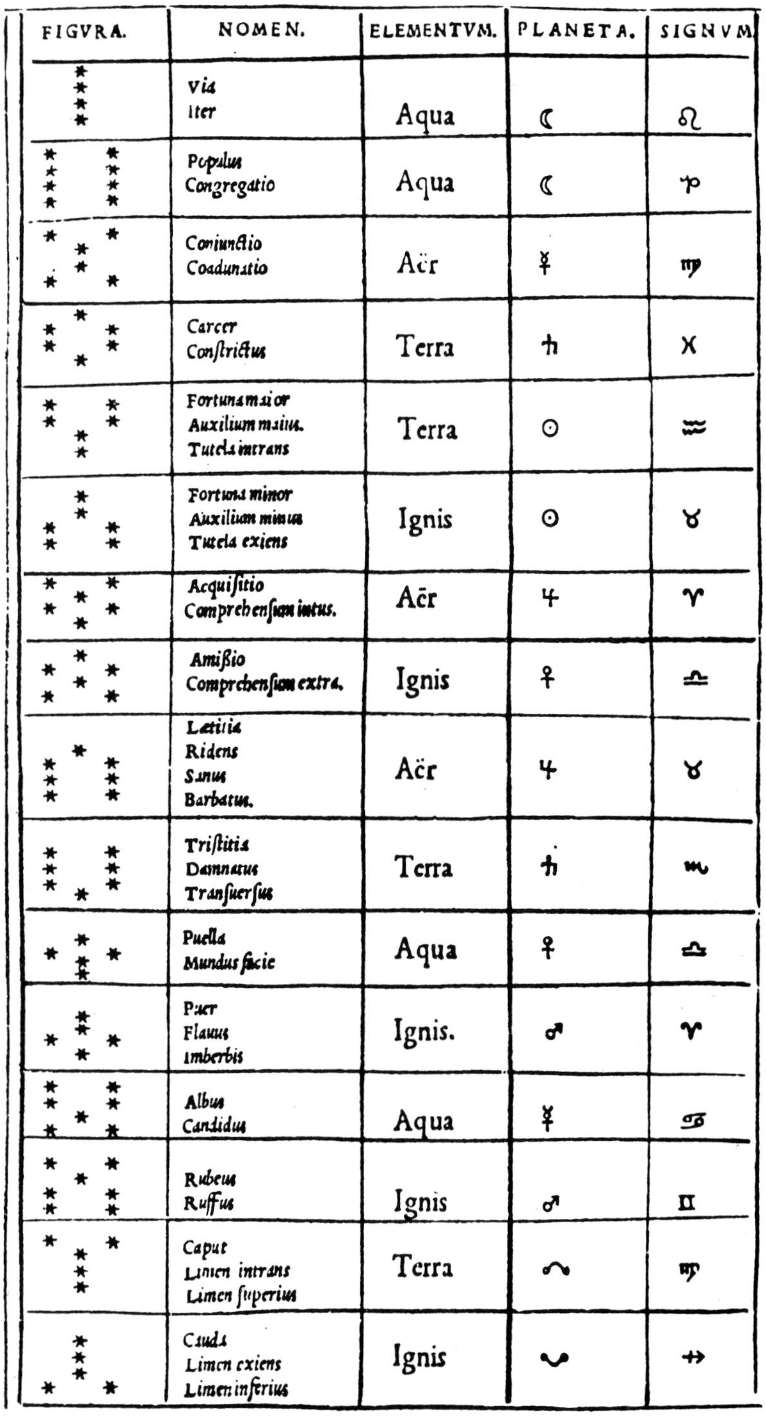

FIGVRA.	NOMEN.	ELEMENTVM.	PLANETA.	SIGNVM.
* * * *	Via Iter	Aqua	☾	♌
* * * * * * * *	Populus Congregatio	Aqua	☾	♑
* * * * * *	Coniunctio Coadunatio	Aër	☿	♍
* * * * * *	Carcer Conſtrictus	Terra	♄	♓
* * * * * *	Fortuna maior Auxilium maius Tutela intrans	Terra	☉	♒
* * * * * *	Fortuna minor Auxilium minus Tutela exiens	Ignis	☉	♉
* * * * * *	Acquiſitio Comprehenſum intus.	Aër	♃	♈
* * * * * *	Amiſſio Comprehenſum extra.	Ignis	♀	♎
* * * * * * *	Lætitia Ridens Sanus Barbatus.	Aër	♃	♉
* * * * * * *	Triſtitia Damnatus Tranſuerſus	Terra	♄	♏
* * * * *	Puella Mundus facie	Aqua	♀	♎
* * * * *	Puer Flauus Imberbis	Ignis.	♂	♈
* * * * * * *	Albus Candidus	Aqua	☿	♋
* * * * * * *	Rubeus Ruffus	Ignis	♂	♊
* * * * *	Caput Limen intrans Limen ſuperius	Terra	☊	♍
* * * * *	Cauda Limen exiens Limen inferius	Ignis	☋	♐

96 *Table of geomantic correspondences from Henry Cornelius Agrippa's* De Occulta Philosophia *(1532)*

In ancient times it was believed that the earth was a living being, with a soul and a spirit, like the planets and stars. The earth was a sort of animal, permeated with spiritual forces running through it and over it. It is this belief, perhaps more than any other, which separates modern man from the ancients, for now few people believe that the earth is itself alive, and so it is very difficult for us to understand many of the rituals and practices which men of earlier times indulged in with the aim of making use of the earth spirit or earth forces.

There are so many different forms of earth magic that it is not feasible for us to examine all the many ways in which magicians and occultists have attempted to use earth forces for their own ends. We shall therefore content ourselves with looking at some of the ways in which men have used earth forces, such as earth spirits or underground spirits, to see into the future; at the way in which medieval artists used the symbolism of mazes in cathedrals; and how these linked with the secret Quintessence which was said to keep the earth alive. We shall also glance at those most remarkable survivals of prehistoric earth magic, the stone circles and standing stones, in Britain.

In earlier times there were two main forms of earth magic used for predicting the future. One made use of what was later called natural magic, while the other made use of what can only be called demonic magic. Natural magic attempted to use the virtues or secret powers of things visible in the material world, while demonic magic, as the name suggests, was concerned with using those secret powers possessed by earth spirits or demons.

The most popular of the methods of prediction involving earth magic of the natural kind was what is now called geomancy. This was a method of answering questions (usually questions about the future) by means of stones or earth. There were several different ways of doing this, but the most usual was for the magician to listen attentively to the question being asked of him, and then to mark a circle in the ground and throw a number

of stones into the circle from a distance. If an odd number of stones fell into the circle, then the magician regarded this as being equal to the number 1. If an even number fell into the circle, then he regarded it as being equal to 2. After repeating this operation four times he was able to build up a symbol called a 'geomantic figure'. If he had obtained in four throws a 1, a 2, a 2 and a 1, then his geomantic figure would look like:

The method of geomantic prediction rests upon this simple device of constructing figures from four throws of a set of stones. All the possible permutations of four throws give a total of sixteen geomantic figures, each of which has been given a Latin name (Figure 96). In order to answer the question, the geomancer throws the stones four times, and then inserts the resultant figure into a special formal pattern which sometimes closely resembles a horoscope figure, but with geomantic figures taking the place of the planets, or even the zodiacal signs. By repeating such throws, he constructs an entire figure, or formal order, and then interprets it according to special rules.

By the medieval period the sixteen figures had been linked with the four elements, the twelve signs of the zodiac and the planets (Figure 96), as well as with a number of geomantic spirits which were supposed to dwell in the earth and to aid in the interpretation of the patterns. In Figure 97, which is from a fourteenth-century illustration to a book on astrology by the magician Michael Scot, we can see two geomantic figures on either side of the female who represents the Moon. One of these is called *Via* or *Iter* (Road), and the other is called *Populus* or *Congregatio* (Crowd). As the drawing suggests, each of these figures was linked with the lunar nature and with the zodiacal sign Cancer, which was said to fall under the rule of the Moon.

A far more dramatic and far less therapeutic form of earth magic was that used to predict the future directly by means of demons or earth spirits. Since it was taken for granted that demons lived within the earth, it was believed that by means of certain rites connected with earth magic it would be possible to compel demons or earth spirits to appear and reveal to the conjuring magician the answers to questions about the future. It was also assumed in ancient times that Purgatory and Hell were in the earth, and so some magicians used occult methods designed to compel not only demons but also the shades of the dead to appear as ghosts, to demand from them knowledge of the future.

In Greek and Roman times there were many religious centres where such forms of prediction were undertaken. The most famous and beautiful was without doubt that at Delphi, where a mediumistic pythoness, or priestess, was consulted on all matters, from affairs of state politics to highly personal questions. In those days Delphi was supposed to be at the very centre of the earth, and in the museum at this famous site there is still a huge stone called an *omphalos* which was regarded as marking the 'navel' of the earth, located at a particular point in the religious centre or *temenos* of Delphi. The centre of the earth was a very special place, and there, from a crevice in the earth, magical fumes were said to rise, by means of which the pythoness would go into a state of trance. This trance was sometimes called a mantic fury, because it gave her the ability to look into the future (the Greek word from which we have the modern 'mantic' means 'predicting the future').

Even before the Greeks took over the hillside of Delphi for their religious purposes, the area was regarded as sacred, and the traces of sacrifices found on the spot indicate that it was used even in prehistoric times for the worship of an earth spirit. Legend has it that the sun god Apollo

97 *Drawing showing a personification of the Moon with geomantic symbols on either side of her head. These two geomantic figures fall under the rule of the Moon. Illustration from a magical text by the thirteenth-century Scottish astrologer, mathematician and magician Michael Scot, Bodleian Library, Oxford*

arrived in Delphi and killed an earth monster on the spot where the temple was later built to his honour. In popular accounts it was said that the pythoness of Apollo's temple, who gave responses about the future to those who questioned her, was influenced (or even driven into her frenzy) by fumes caused by the decomposing body of the monster killed by Apollo. Be that as it may, the pythoness (usually an old woman, but in earlier times a young virgin) would go into a state of frenzy and her utterances would be interpreted by a priest for those who sought responses. The rock from which she is said to have made the original prophecies is still in place in Delphi, near the sacred navel stone and an exquisite treasury built by the Athenians to mark their gratitude for the way Apollo helped them in their public and military exploits (Figure 98). The responses to questions and the oracles given by the pythoness became legendary in ancient times, and there was scarcely a king of importance during the centuries while Greece and Rome were powerful civilizations whose messengers were not sent to Delphi in search of an occult oracle.

Delphi was the most famous of the earth oracles linked with a sun god. There were, however, equally famous centres where predictions of the future were obtained by darker means than a frenzied pythoness, and where, instead of a god of the Sun being evoked, the spirits of the dead were consulted. We are fortunate indeed that fairly recently a most extraordinary ancient centre for such consultations of dark spirits has been discovered and excavated by archaeologists. This, a necromanteion, is near Ephyra, in western Greece. The word *necromanteion* is, of course, Greek, but it has survived in a slightly different version in the English language in the word 'necromancy', which means 'prediction by means of dead spirits', a method which we shall look at on pp. 90–91 when we examine the ways in which magicians sometimes attemped to raise the dead. The necromanteion at Ephyra was probably the most famous place in the entire ancient world. Here men came to learn about the future (or the past) from the dead spirits which could be raised there, either through private sacrifices or by means of priests. It is the centre at Ephyra which is mentioned in the *Odyssey*, the great epic poem by Homer.

Homer tells us how his hero Odysseus is advised to consult the spirits of the dead at the entrance to Hades (the ancient underworld). This entrance was believed to be near the river Acheron, which still runs near the ruins of the necromanteion, and which in ancient times was believed to pour its waters into one of the rivers of the Underworld. He is told that he must dig a pit in the earth, and then pour into this milk and honey, followed by wine and water, sprinkling over the top of these liquids a light covering of flour. This is the offering to the dead. He is then to sacrifice a fine black ram and a sheep, and to promise further sacrifices on his return home. The dead will then rise from the necromanteion to devour the offerings of food and blood. Odysseus is ordered to keep back these shades of the dead with his sword, until the spirit of the blind seer Tiresias appears to answer his questions about the future. When Odysseus does as he is bid and makes the sacrifice, he gets more than he bargained for, as he meets the shade of his dead mother (whom he until then had fondly imagined to be still alive) and speaks with the ghosts of some of his close companions, killed during the historic battles outside the walls of Troy.

There are several historical records of people consulting the spirits of the dead at the mouth of the Acheron at the place which is even now called the Oracle of the Dead, and anyone who visits this remarkable place in modern times is rubbing shoulders with some four thousand years of history. The underground chamber of the necromanteion itself appears to have been partly restored in Roman times: it is immediately below one of the central courts in this maze of corridors and yards, through which modern archaeologists have built a stairway. Inside, the walls and roof are much as they were in ancient times, formed by enormous blocks of stone and arched vaulting (Figure 99), a drear and frightening place. Even though it is now lit by an electric bulb, rather than by torches or candles as in ancient times, something of the eerie quality of the underground chamber remains, as though the earth spirits of darkness and the shades of the dead are not far away, still longing for blood sacrifice.

Another form of divination popular in ancient times was geomancy. Although the word is from the Greek words *geia* and *manteia*, which together mean 'predicting by means of earth forces', it is nowadays used in a very different sense. It is used (wrongly, as it happens) to denote the study of earth patterns, or earth powers, which many occultists insist run across the surface of the earth, like invisible streams of power. It has been suggested that the ancient pilgrimage routes which spread across Europe were actually designed to follow such streams of power, and that the stopping-off points for the pilgrims, such as monasteries and cathedrals, were built on ancient magical sites where several earth powers meet. Chartres was such a centre, of course, but the most important in medieval times was the cathedral at Compostella in Spain, which marked the farthest important pilgrimage point to the west. People who followed the pilgrimage routes were consciously or unconsciously bathing themselves in refreshing and rejuvenating earth powers – this had little to do with geo-mancy (telling the future by means of the earth) and everything to do with geo-therapy (healing by means of earth forces). Often special anterooms were built to house pilgrims during their long (and often dangerous)

98 (above) *The Treasury of the Athenians and the Rock of the Sibyl in the temenos at Delphi, Greece. It was from this rock that the oracles were said to have been delivered in very ancient times, before even the Temple of Apollo was built above it*

99 (left) *The subterranean cell in the necromanteion at Ephyra, western Greece, where in ancient times the spirits of the dead were evoked from Hades*

journeys. Some historians suggest that the narthex of St Madelaine at Vezelay in France was such a place, and the fact that the symbolism on the inner door (which leads to the church proper) is concerned with the spreading of the Gospel and contains some of the earliest sculpted astrological images of medieval art would seem to confirm this (Figure 100).

Some of the most interesting survivals of earth magic are found in the medieval cathedrals. In the cathedral of Chartres, for example, on the central axis of the nave is a large marble design which is usually called a labyrinth (Figure 101). It was built into the nave at the same time as the cathedral was constructed, in the late twelfth century, and for a very long time it has been called a maze. However, it is not a maze or a labyrinth. The whole point about a maze is that one can get lost in it. One enters a maze or a labyrinth to try to find a way to the centre, but one is constantly faced with alternatives and choices. Having entered such a maze, and having unwittingly taken a wrong

turning, one usually gets lost. As the ground plan of the Chartres circle indicates (Figure 101), it is just not possible to get lost in this pattern: one starts at the beginning and, after following a curvilinear pathway for some time, finds oneself at the centre. Instead of the pathway being designed to lose a person, it is, rather, designed to lead him or her in a particular way towards the centre.

If this curious pattern is not a maze, what is it? The effect of following its pathway is that one does a sort of dance towards the centre, at one moment walking towards that centre, at another moment circling around it, at another moment moving away from it, caught in an elaborate marble choreography.

In modern times one arrives at the centre to find oneself standing in a flower pattern of six petals. The old records tell us that in the very centre of this floral design there used to be a brass plaque. Three figures were engraved upon its surface, those of Theseus, the Minotaur and Ariadne.

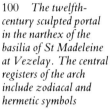

100   *The twelfth-century sculpted portal in the narthex of the basilia of St Madeleine at Vezelay. The central registers of the arch include zodiacal and hermetic symbols*

These three figures were the main actors in an ancient Greek myth connected with the earth. The story goes that the king Minos built a vast underground labyrinth in Crete, where he kept the savage Minotaur, which was a monster with the lower part of a man and the upper part a bull. Each year the Greeks of Athens were compelled to send to Crete a group of seven young men and seven young women for the Minotaur to devour. These young people were chosen by lot, and one year it fell to the son of the king of Athens himself to join the party. This young prince was called Theseus. When the ship bearing Theseus and his companions arrived at the main port of Crete, Ariadne, the daughter of King Minos, saw Theseus and fell in love with him. To help him, she secretly gave him a sword and a ball of thread, so that by unwinding the thread he would be able to enter the labyrinth den of the Minotaur without fear of losing his way and kill the monster.

The brass plate from the centre of the Chartres maze is now lost, but it is likely that the fight between man and monster was incised in one of the traditional forms derived from ancient times, as, for example, something along the lines of the Greek ceramic painting of Figure 102. We may be sure about this because, although the Chartres version is lost, the occultist Fulcanelli records that old drawings of the plate showed Theseus and the Minotaur in combat – a popular enough theme in ancient art, and often taken as a symbol of man fighting his own lower nature. No doubt the two lovers and the monster which almost came between them were visualized as Christian symbols by the architects who placed this image in the centre of the Chartres maze. No doubt Ariadne was seen as a pagan image of the Virgin Mary (to whom Chartres itself is dedicated). It is she who gives Theseus the means to kill the devil Minotaur, and we may therefore assume that Theseus was seen as a symbol of every good Christian, armed by the Virgin Mary to slay the Devil. It would not be very difficult for the medieval people who saw these three figures to recognize the Minotaur as the Devil, for they took it for granted that the Devil had horns, rather like a bull. Also, in medieval books on demons there is actually a devil called Morax, who is said to appear to magicians in the form of a bull-headed man. There are several other surviving fragments of mazes in other cathedrals, all of which seem to confirm this idea of the Christianized Minotaur.

There is a maze image remarkably like the circle in Chartres set in the external wall of the cathedral at Lucca. In this the medieval text (which is partly destroyed – Figure 103) does not actually mention the Minotaur, but it reminds us that the labyrinth was built by the Cretan Daedalus in order that anyone who had entered would be trapped inside – though Theseus found a way, thanks to Ariadne! This *laberinthus* is not really a maze, of course, for

101 *Drawing of the thirteenth-century 'maze' in the nave of Chartres Cathedral. As one cannot get lost in this formal pattern, it is scarcely a maze, but more of a ritualistic dance pattern. The central floral device is a magical symbol*

102 *Drawing from a fifth-century Greek vase showing Theseus killing the Minotaur. It would have been a design something similar to this which was once set in brass at the centre of the Chartres 'maze'*

it is exactly the same arrangement as that found in Chartres. Once again, the cathedral in which this stone is inset is dedicated to the Virgin Mary.

But what have these so-called mazes to do with the earth itself? Well, the Cretan labyrinth, with which the design at Chartres must be linked, was said to have been built beneath the earth. This in itself made it easy for people to associate the labyrinth with demons, for in medieval times both Hell and Purgatory were imagined to be inside the earth. When the medieval poet Dante climbed down all the levels of Inferno, he found at the very bottom of the pit of Hell, sunk in a lake of

frozen ice, the Devil himself. The medieval schema of the earth and its surrounding spheres in Figure 104 shows the Devil at the centre of the earth, in a schema which any medieval person would immediately recognize as a plan of the cosmos, with the zodiac on the outside and Hell in the middle.

In the Christian version of the labyrinth at Chartres we do not descend like Theseus (or Dante) into circles set within the earth. We dance (as it were) to a centre on the surface of the earth and, on reaching the centre, rather than the Devil in demonic triumph, we find the story of how the Queen of Heaven has rescued all mankind from the clutches of the Devil through the power of love. The labyrinth has been Christianized so that it no longer tells the pagan story about fear of an earth monster, but proclaims a story about the love of a celestial queen.

While this is no doubt how the ordinary members of the congregation might understand the symbolism of the maze at Chartres, the occultist would add one or two refinements to the symbolism. The occultist would point out that the six-petalled marble flower at the centre is to be seen as something more than merely a flower. Its struc-ture points to one of the ancient symbols of the earth, the Seal of Solomon (Figure 105). In the medieval view of nature it was believed that all created material forms were composed of the four elements, and that the differences between things were really the result of different proportions of these four. When the occultists searched for a series of symbols to denote the four elements, they chose the Seal of Solomon as the basic form. The triangle on its base represents Fire, because it tends to rise. The triangle resting on its apex represents Water, because it tends to sink. Earth, which was also a 'sinking' power, was linked with Water, because the two combined to make the earth fructify with plant and animal life. For this reason the symbol for Earth was linked with the triangle of Water $\bigtriangledown$. The symbol for Air, which tends to rise, was linked in a similar way with that for Fire $\bigtriangleup$, for it was recognized that Fire and Air work in harmony, the one feeding the other and both rising together.

104 *Medieval illustration of the Ptolemaic system, showing the fires and Devil in Hell* (Infernus). *Around this diabolic centre are the spheres of Earth (*Terre*), Water (*Aque*), Air (*Aeris*), Fire (*Igne*), followed by the Sphere or Heaven of the Moon (*Celum lune*). British Library*

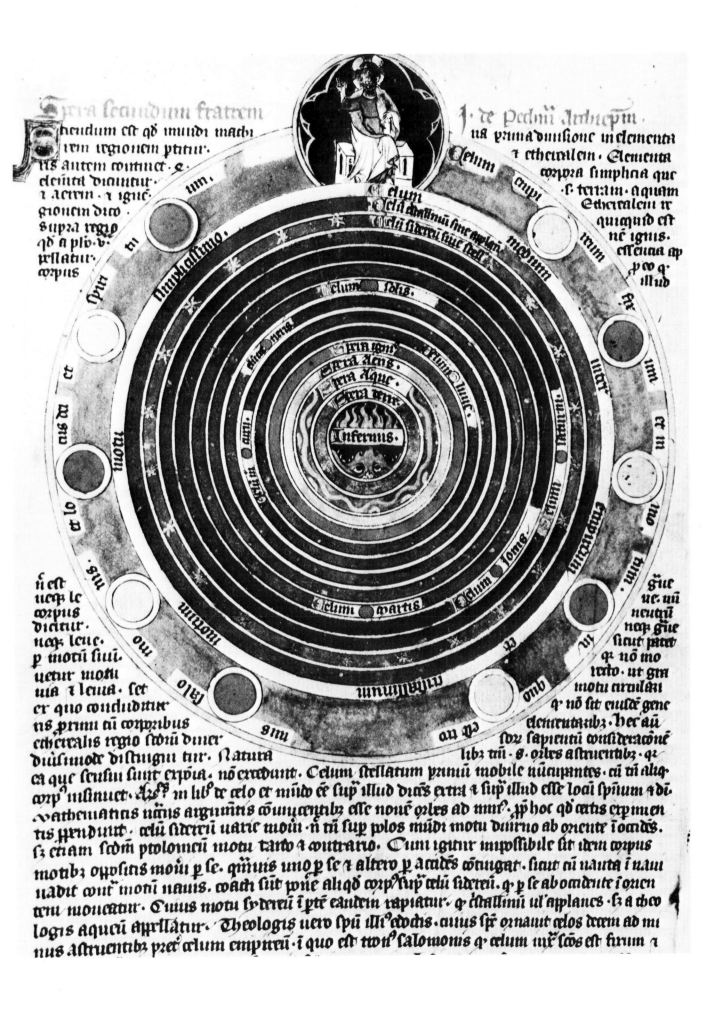

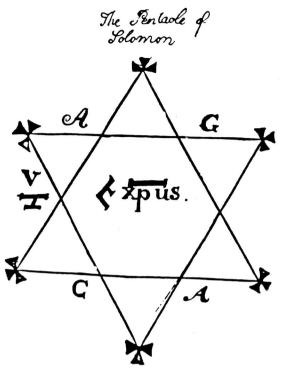

The Pentacle of Solomon

A G

V I

✠ xp̄us .

C A

105 *Detail from a grimoire, showing the Seal or Pentacle of Solomon. This six-rayed star would fit into the centre of the Chartres labyrinth of Figure 101*

In the medieval world plan it was imagined that the four elements spread out into space around the earth. The shell of the earth itself was made of Earth, beyond this was a layer of Water, followed by a layer of Air, the whole thing being sealed in by a layer of warmth, or Fire. This is shown in a medieval plan of the heavens in Figure 104. Now this plan is really a schema – no one really believed that the earth was entirely covered by water, of course. It was a schema of the natural place of these things, showing that if they followed their own natures, they would settle down in that order of stratification. What was it that mixed the four elements so that they intermingled? As we have seen, it was the fifth element, the Quintessence.

This magical and invisible Quintessence is also symbolized in the Seal of Solomon. One of the interesting things about this seal is that there is a space inside the two interacting triangles. It is in this space that the triangles meet, their centres overlapping. This is the place of the Quintessence, where each of the four finds a common point. In some cases, because the Quintessence is said to be invisible, those who draw the symbol leave the centre of the seal empty, and a six-sided polygon is sometimes used as a symbol for the Quintessence ⬡. In other cases a single dot or the symbol used for the Sun itself ☉ is placed in the centre of the seal, or ☼, to indicate that this is the place where all the four elements find unity.

When you follow the long pathway of the Chartres maze and arrive at the centre, you find yourself standing in the very place where the medieval occultists placed this powerful source of life, the Quintessence, as a symbol. In a way, therefore, the earth magic of this symbol at

Chartres is exactly the opposite of the earth magic of the labyrinth of Crete, which was a symbol of the descent into Hell by way of a perilous path in which you may get lost, and even be devoured by a devilish monster. You cannot get lost in Chartres: you are drawn to the saving power of the Virgin Mary; and although the journey is a long one, you at last stand at the centre, where the power of the Quintessence itself is felt. In a sense the labyrinth of Chartres is really the labyrinth of Crete, lifted from its dark earth and Christianized. Is this the reason why for centuries (some say since before the present cathedral was built in the twelfth century) the image of a mysterious Black Virgin has been kept in the underground crypt? This Black Virgin has been linked with Isis, and this fact reminds us that in ancient times such figures were kept in the subterranean chambers of pagan temples and were the subject of special veneration. It is said by some occultists that such statues were regarded as symbols of the earth, which would be fructified by the coming Christ.

One wonders if all the main churches and cathedrals on the pilgrimage routes had mazes linked with the Virgin? After all, the pilgrimages were themselves long and dangerous – people who undertook them did not do so lightly, and they must have realized that their journey was one of the soul as much as the body. There would be many twists and turns, as there is in the ordinary journey through life, but in the end the pilgrims knew that they would arrive triumphantly at the centre, that their journey's end would bring them to that state of grace linked with the Quintessence, symbolized by the six-pointed star.

The extent to which circular devices (such as the zodiac and the planetary spheres) were used to symbolize the heavenly powers, as well as the earth itself, should call to mind another most important realm of earth magic – ancient stone circles. It is said that there are still traces of over five hundred such circles in the British Isles to this day, and it is evident that a long time ago there were even more. What were they?

It is likely that they were built for a number of reasons – as religious centres in connection with a solar or lunar cult, as meeting places for the old mystery religions of the North, and so on. However, in recent times it has been shown that several, if not all, of these circles were designed to mark out on the earth positions by which it was possible to record and note the cycles of the Sun and Moon over a long period of time. The most complex of the surviving circles is also the most famous – the magnificent circle of Stonehenge which stands in vertical contrast to the flat plains of Salisbury around (Figure 106). This circle was built long before the Druids became a powerful religious force in Britain, and has been associated by many occultists with the surviving priests and magicians from the lost continent of Atlantis.

Occultists say that the last part of this continent was said to have been submerged by the sea about 16,000 years ago, and with it went the remains of a vast civilization which had covered a land mass approximately where the Atlantic is today.

In the past it was believed that the stone circles had been built by giants. The name used by the ancient Britons for Stonehenge was *choir-guar*, which means 'giants' dance', and we find a tradition that the huge stones were carried by giants, first from Africa to Ireland, and then by magical means from Ireland to Salisbury. The old myths which tell of the stones for such circles being lifted into place by giants or carried through the air by magicians are perhaps not quite so fanciful as we might now think. Serious occultists insist that the old earth magicians of the lost Atlantis knew of a secret earth power (which later occultists called Vril) which was so powerful that it could cancel the force of gravity. Occultists say that, although these huge stone circles and monoliths were not constructed by giants, they were at least built by priests working with a gigantic power. It has been argued that such a power, surviving from the occult schools of the lost civilization, was used to build the pyramids of Egypt and Central America, the stone circles of Europe, and the ancient walls of ancient cities of Greece, single stones of which weigh over 100 tons. Some occultists claim that the continent was destroyed by those who misused this terrible earth force for their own personal gain.

The stone circles, now merely so many tourist attractions, were really gigantic, permanent earth computers. The patterns of their stones, concentrics and outlying marker stones were designed to keep track of the passage of time and to determine the periods for religious festivals and other important religious activities. Yet these circles, which stretch from the northern islands of Scotland to the south of England at Stonehenge (Figure 106), and west to the farther coasts of Ireland, are more than just earth computers. Strange magical rites were practised there, stones were invested with secret powers of life, and entire sites became centres for the spiritual realm of the higher world to keep contact with the world of man. Even to this day, ruined as they

106 *Stonehenge, the most remarkable of the British stone circles, on Salisbury Plain, viewed from the south at sunset*

Some of the earth magic which was practised by the ancients was worked not on stone but directly onto the earth itself, in huge patterns. In Europe the most famous of these are the patterns dug through the topsoil to reveal the chalk below, as in the series of white horses, of which the most famous is the prehistoric dragon horse at Uffington (Figure 108). A most remarkable chalk image is that discovered by the modern archaeologist Lethbridge on Wandlebury Hill, near the Gog-Magog Hills in Cambridgeshire. From the air this appears as a huge goggle-eyed goddess riding a horse or a chariot; some say that this strange god is standing behind a dragon (Figure 109). Speculation as to what the figure represents has proved fruitless, but it has been linked with one of the two ancient giants, Gog and Magog, who were supposed to have come to live in Britain in ancient times. As with the stone circles, it is not at all clear what purpose these ancient figures were intended to serve. Like the huge sand drawings of the ancient Nazcas culture of Peru, of which the enormous monkey of Figure 110 is among the most interesting, these earth drawings in chalk remain a mystery. The monkey is over 100 metres across – so large that it cannot be seen from the earth itself and, while visible from an altitude of 1500 feet, is best seen from a helicopter hovering some 400 or 500 feet in the air.

Inevitably such figures have been the source of much imaginative guesswork, and one authority has been led to call the Nazcas desert figures 'the largest astronomy book in the world', though there is little indication that they are linked with astronomy at all. Some researchers emphasize the obvious fact that they were designed to be seen from the air (the illustrations for the Gog-Magog goddess and the Nazcas figure were both reconstructed from aerial photographs). This has led to hypotheses as to their origin as far-fetched as their being survivals from a lost age when air travel was known, reminding us that occultists insist that the ancient Atlanteans had flying machines. Another theory is that they were designed only to be seen by those who had developed the capability of astral travel, by which, in a body-free experience, they could 'fly' across vast distances at any height they chose. It is far more likely, however, that these monuments in chalk and sand really mark ancient mystery sites; they are almost certainly located in spots which were once venerated because of some earth power which could be sensed in the locality, the meeting point of cosmic forces on the earth.

The White Horse of Uffington (Figure 108) has with good reason been called a dragon rather than a horse, but, whatever its identity, it is almost certain that it was a tribal symbol impressed in the earth as a sort of personal signature of the tribe who lived in the vale and hills of this lovely part of Berkshire. Just as there is magic in the sound of

107 *One of the three monoliths known as the Devil's Arrows at Boroughbridge. Legend has it that the Devil hanged himself from this central stone*

. are, it is still possible to feel something of the ancient earth magic, a secret power, as one wanders and wonders among their surviving upright stones. It is perhaps not too imaginative to see the circles drawn by these stones as the permanent forebears of the temporary earth circles drawn by magicians when they sought to make contact with the spiritual or diabolical worlds; such an earth circle can be seen in Figure 69. It is surely no accident that so many of these stones and circles are linked with the Devil – as, for example, the 32-foot-high Devil's Arrow at Boroughbridge (Figure 107), which is part of an ancient stone alignment.

108 *Aerial view of the prehistoric turf-cut horse at Uffington, Berkshire. It measures 363 feet from head to tail. Originally the figure probably depicted a dragon*

109 *Reconstruction of the chalk-cut hill figure discovered by T. C. Lethbridge on Wandlebury Hill near Cambridge. Some say it shows a goddess riding a chariot pulled by horses, while others maintain that the figure is that of a dragon*

110 (above) *Aerial view of one of the vast sand animals constructed during the ancient Nazcas culture in Peru. Such figures are so large (this monkey is about 100 metres across) that they cannot be seen easily from the earth itself and only reveal themselves fully from the air*

111 (left) *The ruins of the church of St Michael on the tor at Glastonbury has become in recent years a centre of pilgrimage for those interested in earth currents and ley lines*

names, and magic in the words we write on paper, so there is even greater magic in the images which men spend months digging from the earth.

Certain natural hills on British soil have also been linked with this earth magic. The most famous is that called Glastonbury Tor (Figure 111), which is said to be part of a huge zodiac carved into the earth, with its lines marked out by earthworks, old road systems and especially constructed lines of trees (Figure 112). This zodiac was discovered in the early part of this century, and traced in a circle with a diameter of almost 9 miles, with the centre at the village of Butleigh (marked B in Figure 112), and with Glastonbury (G) to the northwest set in the image of what is supposed to be the fish. The village marked K is Kingsweston, located above the back of the lion.

112   *Schema of the vast Glastonbury Zodiac, 9 miles in diameter and said to be traceable in the countryside around Glastonbury (G), centred on the village of Butleigh (B). The back of Leo the Lion is marked by the village of Kingsweston (K) (the lion is the king of the zodiacal herd)*

113   *Two of the constellational figures which are said to be derived from the earth formations around Glastonbury. These are the only two forms which may, without too much stretch of the imagination, be said to resemble the constellational figures usually traced in the skies.*

114 *Pendle Hill in Lancashire, famous for its witchcraft legends, is also said to be the centre for an earth-drawn zodiac similar to that of Glastonbury*

115 *Prehistoric rock carving originally on Rumbolds Moor and now in the bus station in Keighley, West Yorkshire (see text)*

Only two of the images traced in this way are really satisfactory in terms of the tradition – these have been abstracted from the zodiac and marked with the appropriate sigil to show how closely they resemble modern images for Virgo and the horse–man Sagittarius (Figure 113).

The Glastonbury zodiac has gained a certain amount of notoriety since the earth map of Figure 112 was proposed, but there is still much argument among scholars as to why its images should reflect modern notions rather than the sky lore of the ancients who were supposed to have constructed this secret earthwork. In the north of England there is Pendle Hill (Figure 114), perhaps more famous for its stories of the witchcraft which was practised on its slopes (see pp. 108 and 109). This hill, too, is linked with ancient stories of mighty giants, who are said to have thrown the huge stones (glacial erratics) which litter its surface across the valleys from neighbouring hills, and its distinctive shape is also said to be the centre of a huge earth zodiac, but no one has so far succeeded in convincingly tracing out its form from aerial maps.

If the large stones of the ancient circles and standing stones are involved with earth magic, are also smaller stones which bear ancient carvings? It has been proposed that certain of the curious stone

116 *One of the two so-called Doubler Stones on the edge of Addingham Moor above the village of Steeton in West Yorkshire. Prehistoric carvings and the mysterious cup and ring marks are still clearly visible on the surface of both stones*

carvings which are found in parts of the British Isles were really linked with similar earth powers as the huge circles. It is quite remarkable how many of these carvings include circular designs – the one which consists of a series of concentric circles, in Figure 115, is said to be about 4000 years old. The two outlandish stones, known as the Doubler Stones, on the edge of the moors in Yorkshire (Figure 116) contain several incised circular patterns on their flat surfaces, and while many of these have been scratched over by vandals, it is still clear that they were intended to serve some magical purpose. Some specialists have suggested that such marked stones served as altars for blood sacrifices (a large stone a few miles away has been called the Druid Stone for some centuries). Others have suggested that the stones are really intended as markers to indicate the direction of the invisible flow of earth energy across the surface of the British Isles. In ancient times, when there were few roads and no maps, such markers would have been invaluable, even necessary.

Few of these carvings are now in their original place, of course, having been removed to museums in order to delay the erosion to which they were being subjected on open moorlands; a few have been removed for public display – that in Figure 115, for example, is set in a mound of stones in the pedestrian way around the bus station in the old wool town of Keighley. However, from one or two which survive in their original place it is possible to link their designs with earth magic, for they are usually placed in special alignments.

There are a whole series of such carvings on a huge rock just above Ilkley. This stone is itself something of a landmark and is popularly called the Pancake Stone, even though it does not look at all like a pancake. The stone appears to be a natural one, in the sense that it was not carved and put in its present location by man, as was the giant Devil's Arrow of Figure 107, and is located on the edge of a ridge, which makes it visible for miles around. When one examines the prehistoric carvings on its surface, one notices that the circles have axis lines drawn through them. The axis lines of the larger designs point in the same direction, which is towards the moors. If you follow this line across the moors, you eventually come to the remnants of a stone circle called the Twelve Apostles. Could it be that these ancient designs were intended to mark out the sites of ancient religious centres? Could it be that anyone who followed such signs would be bathed with the vivifying earth forces, such as were later adapted to form the pilgrimage routes through Europe?

5 Black Magic:The Use of Unseen Powers

As we have seen, occultism deals with the laws which proceed from an invisible world. One of the most widespread delusions about this invisible world is that it is a realm which is wholly beneficial for human beings, that it is inhabited entirely by kindly angels. However, this is far from the case. Occultists often call the invisible realm nearest to man the 'astral plane', and generally distinguish between the lower and higher levels of this plane. Those individuals and occultists who seek to make use of the higher levels of the spiritual plane for the good of humanity are often

117 The Resuscitated Rose, *an eighteenth-century illustration of the experiment in palingenesis conducted by the alchemist Vallemont. The rose was not a physical rebirth, but the 'spectre of the rose'*

called 'white magicians', while those who make use of the lower levels – usually to the detriment of humanity – are often called 'black magicians'. However, the distinction between the two is not always so clearly marked as one might imagine. A vast number of occult images are concerned with portraying the lower levels as being under the control of dark and demonic forces, with what in popular thought is known as black magic.

One often finds that in the realm of occultism (as in life itself) what starts out with good intentions does not always end as expected. What starts out as white magic sometimes ends up distinctly grey, if not black. In the history of occultism there are very many examples of this, but none quite so clear as in the story of what is now called palingenesis. This word (of Greek origin) was adopted by groups of occultists and alchemists during the seventeenth century in connection with their researches on plants. These alchemists were attempting to restore to life, or resurrect, the spiritual body of plants after the plants themselves had been destroyed.

The procedure they adopted was to destroy a plant completely by burning it, yet preserving the ashes. After a few alchemical operations, they extracted the 'salt' of these ashes, put it into a glass and mixed it with some (now unknown) chemical agency. The mixture was heated, and within the glass there grew the image of the destroyed plant. An image of such a successful experiment, marked 'Resuscitated Rose', is shown in Figure 117. It comes from a series of palingenetic experiments conducted by an alchemist called Vallemont. These interesting attempts to re-form the spiritual body of plants were part and parcel of alchemy, and were really linked with the stream of white magic which has flowed through Western occultism for many centuries. Those who succeeded in performing these experiments hoped to demonstrate from such alchemical operations the reality of the spiritual realm. However, these good intentions were soon forgotten, and certain men who were less interested in spiritual things turned their attention away from dead plants to a consideration of dead humans.

Such individuals were not averse to the practice of black magic and started experimenting with the ashes of dead people, which (they claimed) could be resurrected by palengenesis exactly in the same way as plants. The main difference was that, while the resuscitated spiritual bodies of plants were the same size as the originals, the resuscitated human spirits were much smaller. Now the fact is that in occult circles – at least in those circles concerned with white magic – it has always been regarded as harmful for human beings to call spirits (or astral shades) of the dead back to earth, and occultists regard those who do this, or attempt to do this, as dabbling in black magic. Those who follow the white path of magic insist that the dead have their own concerns in the postmortem realm and do not wish to be brought back to the material realm by such devices as seances or necromancy, even for a short time. Only those who are not aware of the true nature of the spiritual world will concern themselves with dragging the spirits of the departed back to the earth. The numerous images of human shades appearing to the command of magicians, whether in midnight conjurations (Figure 69) or in darkened seance rooms (Figure 72), are regarded by serious occultists as belonging to the lower levels of the astral world and involved with black magic.

It is unlikely that the alchemists who began these experiments in palengenesis knew where their experiments would take them. As we shall see in chapter 8, most alchemists were dedicated to the path of white magic and were deeply religious individuals. However, the history of occultism is filled with examples of people who set out to perform certain experiments, or to make contact with demonic beings, purely in order to do damage to other people or to the world at large. In occultism such people are said to follow the left-hand path. In popular lore those who follow this dark path are called witches or warlocks.

A witch is a female who has given herself to the Devil and agreed to be his agent of evil; the warlock is her male equivalent. In medieval times it was believed that because the demons had no physical bodies they themselves could not personally do physical damage in the world; for this reason they needed to persuade humans to do their evil work for them. The idea of witchcraft was bound up with this idea that humans would enter into agreement with the Devil to do harm in return for certain rewards. What these demonic rewards were is never very clear from the records that have survived, but the social or religious rewards are more obvious, as the savagery of the punishments for being a witch or a warlock (and even for falling under suspicion of this) have gone down in history as one of the darker periods in the history of the Church.

It is interesting that the early court records show that very many warlocks were arrested and put to death, yet the greater number of illustrations of witchcraft portray women as the

118 *A sixteenth-century illustration of a witch, from the title page of a tract* A Most Wicked Worke of a Wretched Witch . . . *(1592)*

offenders. This is almost certainly due to the scurrilous nature of the majority of illustrations used in even serious texts on witchcraft. The popular notion of the witch even in early times was of an old crone, with warts and all (Figure 118), and it is from this tradition that the modern Disney-like witch has emerged, complete with steeple hat and broomstick (Figure 119), which in the painting by Arthur Rackham is a goose. The reality was otherwise, however, for very often among the witches burned or hanged were even very young children. The famous Pendle Witches who were hanged at Lancaster in 1612, for example, included a girl of eleven years old. One hardly ever finds such facts illustrated in the witchcraft imagery. On the other hand, one does see the witchcraft lore and legends frequently being used as an excuse for sensual images which might otherwise be frowned upon by the Church. The magnificent engraving by Albrecht Dürer in Figure 120 is an example of this, for it is clear that what really interested Dürer was the sensuality of the female bodies. The only reference to the notion of witchcraft in this engraving (the title aside) is the half-hearted reference to the flames of Hell and the demon head, both of which may be seen through the doorway to the left, and the skull and thighbone on the floor. Take away these almost incidental references and the picture could be called something quite different.

Around the idea of the witch as a worker of evil grew all sorts of horrible fictions. If the witch had given her soul to the Devil, then it followed that she also gave her body to this master. From this simple proposition there grew a vast storehouse

119 *Old Mother
Goose in the guise of a
transvecting witch. The
original Mother Goose
was derived from the
initiation lore of the
medieval cathedral
centres, but her image
quickly degenerated into
the stock picture of an
evil-worker.
Illustration by Arthur
Rackham, from*
Mother Goose *(1913)*

Boguet omits to mention that at this point, when the woman began to tremble, she would have been shown the instruments of torture.

The confessions which he extracted in this way included such admissions that 'she had long since given herself to the Devil, who at that time had the likeness of a big black man'; that the 'Devil had four or five times known her carnally, in the form sometimes of a dog, sometimes of a cat, and sometimes of a fowl; and that his semen was very cold.' That 'she had countless times been to the Sabbat, an assembly of witches . . . and that she went there on a white staff which she placed between her legs.'

In these few confessions of a terrified woman (who had been imprudent enough to ask for lodgings in the home owned by the parents of the eight-year-old child) are contained all the germs of the witchcraft delusion. She admits sexual relations with the Devil, attending the assembly of witches – the Sabbat – and making night flight. In order to gain a clear idea of the medieval notions of witchcraft, and how these views influenced the images which were produced in connection with the belief, we should examine each of these three in some detail.

The witches were supposed to fly or transvect to the assembly of witches, usually at the dead of night. This idea of a witch flying on an animal or on a stick (the supposed witch questioned by Boguet spoke of a white staff), was developed fairly early in the growth of the witchcraft persecutions. Perhaps the first picture to illustrate such transvection is that from Molitor's book on witches, printed in 1489 (Figure 121). Few modern readers, used as they are to the idea of witches flying on broomsticks, would recognize a witch flight in this picture, for the two women and the man (distinguished by their clothes) are changed into diabolic forms and ride the cleft branch of a tree rather than a broomstick. It is even possible that the leading witch is on the back of a demon, itself riding the branch, but the details are not clear. However, the general idea of diabolical flight is well expressed in this picture, even if it is very different from the notion of witches flying on brooms which developed in later romantic art and popular fairy stories. When this picture of diabolic transvection was printed, it was believed that such night flight was merely a delusion of the supposed witches. However, the delusion itself was taken very seriously, so that someone who imagined such a flight to a Sabbat, or who even dreamed that he or she had made such a flight, was treated as though he or she was a witch and committed to trial.

The countryfolk of the fifteenth century believed that it was not the object used for such flight which was itself important. The 'magical' thing behind such strange flights was actually the ointment which was rubbed on the object or on the body of the witch intent on night flight. With this

of legends concerning the sexuality of witches and warlocks and their relations with the Devil or his demons, the so-called succubi and the incubi (see chapter 7, p. 124). In the courts and torture chambers established to stamp out witchcraft one of the standard questions asked of any female suspect was how many times she had carnal knowledge of the Devil.

A fairly typical story is told by the French witchcraft judge Henri Boguet of the trial, in 1598, of a woman suspected of bewitching a child of eight (whose claims were indeed the only evidence against the woman). The judge writes without any trace of compassion:

To look at her you would have thought she was the best woman in the world; for she was always talking of God, of the Virgin Mary, and of the Holy Saints of Paradise. . . . she was pressed to tell the truth, but without success. Accordingly it was decided to shave off her hair and change her garments, and to search her to see if she were marked in any way. She was therefore stripped, but no mark was found; and when they came to cut the hair of her head she submitted with the utmost confidence. But no sooner was her hair cut than she grew perturbed and trembled all over her body, and at once confessed, adding to her confessions from day to day.

120   The Four
Witches *(1497), an
engraving by Albrecht
Dürer. Other than the
title there is little in the
picture to suggest that
the women are witches;
however, the demon to
the left appears to have
an interest in their
welfare*

121 (right) *An early woodcut showing transformed witches transvecting upon a stick. The dog-like creature at the back may be a familiar. From Ulrich Molitor's 1489 edition of* De Lamiis

122 (below) *Drawing based on a rare pamphlet of 1589 depicting the hanging of three witches in that year at Chelmsford. The six familiars in the illustration are described as 'imps' in the trial records. Private collection*

magical flying salve it was possible to make almost anything into a suitable object for transvection. A large number of engravings and woodcuts are dedicated to illustrating this use of magical ointments or unguents (as they are usually called), mainly because of the sensual nature of such images. And this remarkable flying salve, which was such a boon to the illustrators – where did this come from? It was said, by those who took it upon themselves to explain the nature of witchcraft, to be a gift from the Devil himself, presented to each witch after she had kissed his posterior at the Sabbat. Many of those who condemned witches insisted that the ointments or salves were made from the thickened gravy of boiled children, murdered while unbaptized, and many of the early images illustrate the notion that only noxious things go into the witches' brew from which such ointments are made (Figure 123).

The flying salves were regarded by some as unnecessary, however. Even as late as 1608 one expert on witchcraft, an assessor in witchcraft trials, was insisting that witches flew to their Sabbats on brooms, black rams, goats, oxen and dogs, and that few witches had any need to use unguents. So far as this author was concerned, the nature of the diabolic carriage was fairly irrelevant, for in every case it was really nothing other than the Devil himself in disguise. By a similar species of reasoning, the witch's pets ceased to be pets and became devils in disguise – these were traditionally called 'familiars'.

The familiar was the witch's own special demon in disguise, the secret helper in her diabolical aims. Some say that the witch was given the familiar (that is, a demon in disguise) by the Devil at her first Sabbat at the same time as he gave her the flying ointment. As the French witch-hunter Boguet wrote: 'a witch's power is governed by that of the devil which is his (or her) familiar.' For very many centuries – even in pre-Christian times – it had been believed that every human being was accompanied through life by a good angel and a demon. If the human chose to avoid the beneficient influence of the angel, then the power of the demon grew stronger. Eventually, as the theory of demonic influences took a grip of European thought, it was believed that if the human being went so far as to enter into pact with the Devil and chose to become one of his servants, then that personal demon would appear in a visible form, first to the witch herself and later to other people. In this form it would accompany the witch wherever she went, persuading her to do evil. This idea of a single demonic helper was soon extended to encompass a number of such familiars, so that a typical witch was expected to be surrounded by a whole bevy of familiars in a variety of shapes. Like the broomstick of later witch legend, the familiar became a stock-in-trade of witchcraft, so that virtually any household pet of a suspected witch would be viewed as a demon.

Figure 122 shows three witches who were hanged after being found guilty of witchcraft at Chelmsford in 1589. The six familiars in the foreground are mentioned frequently in the trial records as having been the cause of the deaths of those bewitched.

Another name for the familiar was 'imp', and it was taken for granted that in return for its diabolical services such an imp would suck at the breasts of its owner. Later it was believed that the imp familiar would suck from any protuberance on the human body, so that those charged with discovering witches were told to search the entire body of a suspect to discover any spots or malformations which might be used to suckle an imp. They would even shave off (or burn off) the hair of the head and private parts to faciliate this search. It was to reveal such spots, or 'imp teats', that the judge Boguet had his unfortunate female victim stripped, shaved and searched; the possession of such a malformation on any part of her body would have been regarded as sufficient proof of witchcraft.

Although in the early centuries it was assumed that the imp familiars would suck at the teats of their witches, in a later stage of the witchcraft heresy it was believed that the familiars would suck blood from their mistresses rather than milk. One infamous witchfinder, Matthew Hopkins, who was sometimes called the Witchfinder General (Figure 124), claims to have seen several witches give suck to their familiars. Hopkins reports watching a number of imps visit one of his unfortunate victims while she was in prison. This was a defenceless old woman with only one leg, who had already endured some of Hopkins's torture. Hopkins later said that one of these imps was 'like a fat spaniel without any legs at all'. He relates that, when she saw the familiar, the woman 'clapped her hand on her belly, and said he sucked good blood from her body.' In Figure 124 this old woman is to the left of the picture, pointing to her supposed familiars, whom she names Holt and Jarmara. This latter familiar looks more like a dopy household pet than any bloodsucking demon, though Vinegar Tom below (with the head of an ox and the body of a greyhound) does at least have a fantastical quality about its form. These pictures of witch imps are from the notorious book written in self-defence by Matthew Hopkins himself, who stands in judgement above the two suspect witches as they name their familiars. It was Hopkins's own sworn testimony that he had seen these curious familiars ('in the forms of a white dog, a greyhound, a polecat and a black imp') visit the old lady in her cell that led to her being hanged as a witch. Hopkins died in his own bed in 1646, having sworn or hounded to their deaths almost a thousand men and women in the guise of witches and warlocks.

Imps and broomsticks, while synonymous

123 *Witches preparing a magical brew with the intention of poisoning people, animals and crops. The witch on the left is putting a dead cock into the brew, a reminder that some of the contemporaneous grimoires demanded the sacrifice of a cock in order to raise demons. From Ulrich Molitor's 1489 edition of* De Lamiis

with the popular image of the witch in modern times, are actually a far cry from the central theme of medieval witchcraft, the Sabbat. The Sabbat, a word which once struck terror into the hearts of churchmen and simple country people, was nothing other than a sort of sales conference held by the Devil to encourage his minions the witches towards further evil. This Sabbat, usually held in some remote or wild country district, was supposed to involve the introduction of new witches and warlocks to the Devil, the worship of the Devil in open mockery of Christian ritual, and a grand finale of a rowdy nature involving lewd and permissive sexuality.

Like the extreme form of witchcraft itself, there is much doubt as to whether there was such a thing as a genuine Sabbat. Perhaps it existed only in the minds of the monks and judges who were responsible for torturing their suspects into confessing details of these night-time rituals. The Sabbat was turned by such people, perhaps even by well-intentioned monks, into a nightmare parody of Christian ritual. They said that whatever was practised in a church in honour of God was reversed in the Sabbat. Instead of good Christians meeting together in the daytime to worship an invisible god, evil witches and warlocks gathered together at night-time to pay homage to a visible devil and to participate in lewd dances to his honour.

Matthew Hopkins Witch Finder Generall

My Imps names are

Holt

1 Ilemauzar
2 Byewackett

Sacke & Sugar

Jarmara

3 Pecke in the Crowne
4 Griezzell Greedigutt

Newes

Vinegar tom

124 *An illustration from the tract* Discovery of Witches, *written by the soi-disant* Witchfinder General Matthew Hopkins (1647). *Hopkins represents himself in judgement over two suspects (subsequently hanged) and a whole bevy of familiar imps, from cats, rabbits and 'newts' to a legless dog, mentioned during his interrogations*

Although there was nothing very new in the idea of evil-workers and witches meeting together in order to practise evil, the concept of the Sabbat as a systematic desecration seems to have been invented by theologians during the fourteenth and fifteenth centuries. The very idea of the Sabbat was unknown in previous centuries and the word itself was not on record until round about 1450. Even the famous *Hammer against Witchcraft* (better known by its Latin title of *Malleus Maleficarum*), printed in 1486, scarcely mentions the Sabbat, though it dwells on almost every other iniquity which might be practised in the name of the Devil.

Yet in spite of the newness of the word – which implies that the idea was itself new – within a few years it was believed that the Sabbat was raging almost like a contagion through Europe. One farmer of the seventeenth century notes that he cannot catch sight of a hare running across his own land without taking for granted that it is a witch who has changed her shape on her way to the Sabbat! The hare was indeed supposed to be one of the favourite disguises of witches and

warlocks, and this may have its origins in the curious May dances which the creatures are supposed to do, and which were seen as Sabbat dances by the credulous. By the following century it seems to have become the main duty of the Inquisition – established much earlier to combat heresy in general – to root out witchcraft and stamp out the abomination of the Sabbat. What was this awful thing which disturbed the waking lives of the medieval monk and layman alike?

It would be very easy to quote at length one of the witchcraft trials, for these all too often list with unrestrained abandon all the horrors of the diabolic happenings which were supposed to take part in the Sabbat. However, as is so often the case, a single picture will tell the story far more poignantly than words. Figure 125 is by no means an exceptional image of a Sabbat: it is of a crude nature, meant to illustrate one of the innumerable accounts of witchcraft which appeared in the seventeenth century, yet it contains hints of many of the practices supposed to be followed by witches in the course of their gatherings.

As one may see from this picture, there is a concentration on the idea of sexual promiscuity – it was this which seems to have occupied the attentions of the witchcraft judges and the Inquisition more than any other single factor. In the bottom left a demon, with a lower body remarkably like the nature god Pan (Figure 171), is embracing a witch. A bawdy circle of witches, warlocks and demons dance around the Devil, who is in the traditional shape of a goat, with a witch bending to kiss his posterior. In this circle of dancers a demon may be seen holding the breasts of a naked woman, and behind him another demon reaches for the private parts of a clothed woman. In the air to the left is an image rare even in such salacious prints, for there we see a woman lying on her back, with her legs raised, her dress pulled up over her body, and the devil goat leaping off with all signs of satisfied desire. The instruments of transvection are also worth noting, for in the bottom right a woman rides a sort of pitchfork, while in the skies a naked woman rides what appears to be a branch and a partly clothed woman is astride a goat. For all its lewdness, this print is fairly typical of the images which were circulated in the sixteenth and seventeenth centuries as portrayals of the Sabbat.

From an examination of such a picture we see that a Sabbat was viewed more as an orgiastic meeting than anything else. It seems to have been seen as almost incidental that those who had sold their souls to the Devil would pay homage to their master (Figure 126). No wonder that, in a world filled with such images and ideas, the judge

125 (right) *An eighteenth-century engraving intended to show the Sabbat which was supposed to take place on the Brocken in the Harz Mountains – a Sabbat later popularized by Goethe*

126 *Four woodcuts from Guazzo's* Compendium Maleficarum *(1608 edition). From left to right: (top) witches riding to the Sabbat on monstrous goats; the Devil ordering witches to trample the cross; (bottom) witches being 'baptized' by the Devil; a ritual of public pact*

Boguet could set down in astonishment his disbelief that there were still people around who did not believe that there were witches; as he says:

their transvection to the Sabbat is astounding; we can but marvel at their oblations, their dances, their obscene kisses, their feasts, and their carnal couplings with their Master; it is beyond comprehension how they cause hail and tempests to spoil the fruits of the earth, and again how they cause the death of a man or the sickness of an animal.

The curious image of a demon with burning hands in Figure 125 is probably a reference to something which a witch-hunter as infamous as Boguet had claimed or invented about the Sabbat. This man was Bodin, a judge who seems to have derived much pleasure from the torture of his victims, and who actually wrote: 'a person once accused of witchcraft should never be acquitted, unless the falsity of the accuser or informer is clearer than the sun.' Bodin mingles myth with fantasy when he writes that, once the orgies of the Sabbat are over, the Devil 'consumes himself in flames'. He burns to ashes, and these the witches and warlocks collect and use for personal acts of evil afterwards. The demon with burning hands behind the worshipped goat in Figure 125 may be another form of the Devil, having set himself

alight to burn to ashes, like the phoenix of classical mythology (see chapter 8, p. 150).

Bodin, who tortured so many men and women into confession and had a deserved reputation for ensuring that his victims died in the flames rather than being put out of their misery before the flames engulfed them, was well aware that the Sabbat, besides being an occasion for devil worship, was also a breeding ground for further witchcraft. In his eyes the Sabbat was more than merely an opportunity for demons and witches to make mockery of Christian virtues – it gave the opportunity for the Devil to recruit new staff. A large number of prints illustrate what is usually called 'the induction' of a witch – which is to say the introduction of a novice (by established witches) to the devil religion by means of the Sabbat (Figure 127). At this first Sabbat it was imagined that she would be required to mock the Church and God by administering diabolic sacraments in place of the holy wine, and to allow the Devil to indulge in her body.

Witchcraft itself did not begin with the terrors of the Inquisition, for it was older than the Christian Church. Even that most distinctive ritual of witches – the demonic Sabbat – has roots in practices much older than Christianity. These roots have been traced by some historians to a very ancient Roman festival called the Lupercalia,

127 *A seventeenth-century engraving by Jasper called* The Abomination of the Sorcerers. *The scene is littered with flotsam and jetsam of the satanic lore and with items gleaned from the diabolic grimoires, so that virtually every line of the engraving is symbolic of evil and death, from the crossed bones in the foreground to the burning house seen through the window (witches were held responsible for incendiarism)*

which was held on 15 February each year. Some historians say that it was held in honour of Pan, the goat-footed god of nature, but others have suggested that it was held in honour of the wolf which gave suck to Romulus and Remus, the mythical founders of Rome itself. In any event, the Roman festival was held at the foot of the Palatine Hill near the cave in which the bronze statue of the wolf was kept, and here the priest sacrificed goats and dogs. It is said that the blood

of these animals was smeared on the foreheads of two youths, to be wiped off afterwards with wool dipped in milk. The bloody skins of these sacrificed animals were cut into long strips, which were then used in random whippings in the streets of Rome. Women believed that to receive such lashes (some say, given by priests, others by naked youths wearing only a girdle of goatskin) was a sure cure for barrenness and certain other illnesses.

Perhaps it is too imaginative to associate the Sabbat of the witches with this rite of the Lupercalia, for the Sabbat itself was openly dedicated to the worship of the Devil; it is perhaps only the connection between the Devil as a monstrous he-goat and the sacrificed goats of the Roman festival which links the two gatherings. In addition, the Lupercalia was held once a year, while the Sabbat was supposed to take place each week. The Sabbat may originally have been derived from pagan nature cults or from fertility cults, but by the time it was described by those responsible for the witch-hunts in the sixteenth and seventeenth centuries it was little short of orgiastic.

If the actual existence of Sabbats is in doubt, should we then not ask if there were such things as witches? In the medieval period, as in every period, there were undoubtedly people who were evil-minded, and there was clearly the usual number of sick individuals who wished to bring disorder into the world, but it is doubtful that more than a handful of people were consciously involved in the exercise of evil. There can be little doubt that the prosecution of supposed witches was big business in the later Middle Ages, and very many judges, court officials and witch-finders gained a well-paid living from their sordid work. Equally such things as the trial of Joan of Arc and her subsequent burning were signs that witchcraft trials had become involved with state politics. It is possible that there were people who imagined themselves to be in league with the Devil, and perhaps there may have been groups of people (especially in country districts) who found themselves still linked with the pagan gods and worshipped them in secret. And yet again there were undoubtedly surviving heretics (like the Albigensians) who chose to worship in their own way, even though this was contrary to the edicts of the Church. There are many records of such dissident Christians, who were doubtless moral people, being smeared by the priests of the Inquisition and, under the pressure of unendurable tortures, confessing to the most awful parodies of Christian ritual, such as the naked worship of the inverted cross, the slaughter of children for ritual purposes, and sexual orgies around the altar. The pagan gods and the images of the heretics were all too easily made into demons by the medieval monks, who had a vested interest in showing that the Christian god was the one and only God. The most horrendous stories of witchcraft were born in the torture cells of the witch-hunters themselves, who had a financial interest in discovering witches and putting them to death. After a careful sifting of a great deal of medieval witchcraft material, one might reasonably come to the conclusion that, while the belief in witchcraft was almost universal in those days, it is unlikely that there was any practice of witchcraft in the forms described in the torture rooms and trials of the witches. The notion of witchcraft appears to have been born of fear, rather than of any wish to aid the Devil.

The organized terror against witchcraft appears to have had its roots in twelfth- and thirteenth-century theology. Up to this time it had been one of the strongest views of the Church that even telling the future was a devilish art. Because of this, one of the occult arts which we might nowadays deny is occult in any sense at all was condemned by many important theologians: this was astrology. Astrology was a most curious subject in the twelfth and thirteenth centuries, mainly because Europe was seeing the reintroduction to the West of ancient Greek and Roman astrology by way of Arabic literature which was flooding into Italy, France and England at that time. The result of this explosion of interest in the ancient art of astrology led to many conflicts within the Church. On the one hand, the practice of astrology was still forbidden by canon law, yet, on the other, the symbols of astrology were being used as important symbolic themes in cathedral building – zodiacal images and entire zodiacal circles were being constructed as part of the very fabric of Christian churches (Figures 14 and 15). The main reason why this intriguing subject should have been banned by the Church is linked with the early history of Christianity, with the time when the Church was trying to distinguish its own beliefs from those of the Gnostics, who taught their own system of beliefs in terms of astrological and magical symbols. By banning astrology the Church was attempting to reject the Gnostic views. In addition it was believed that all attempts to reach into the future were immoral, since only God knew the future. Against this simple view there rose the notion that demons could also pretend to know the future, and thus anyone using the occult arts to peer into the future was actually consulting demons. This is why so many of the occult systems which we now regard as being relatively harmless were frowned upon by the Church – the use of horoscopes, playing cards and geomantic figures (see chapter 4) were ways in which the Devil could exercise his power over man.

An interesting occult image which reflects this notion may be seen in the hilltop monastery of Sacra di San Michele in the Val di Susa. At the top of a steep flight of stairs within the monastery (stairs ominously called the Stairway of the Dead) there is a zodiacal arch. On either side of this arch are a number of zodiacal and constellational images (Figure 128) carved in the early thirteenth century. We shall not concern ourselves here with the occult basis of this astrological material but will examine a small detail to the side of the column which carries the twelve images of the zodiac. At the bottom of this column is the head of the Devil (Figure 129), from whose mouth protrudes a long floriated tongue which stretches up the entire column, enclosing a

128 (above)   *Twelfth-century images of Sagittarius and Scorpius from the constellational arch at the top of the Stairs of the Dead in the monastery of Sacra di San Michele, Val di Susa, Italy*

129 (below left)   *The head of the Devil at the bottom of a decorative column on the constellational arch of Figure 128. The tendril which emerges from the demonic mouth terminates in the body of the human being in Figure 130*

130   *Detail of man near the top of the decorative column mentioned in the caption for Figure 129, showing how the demonic tendril is inserted into the man's anus*

large number of animal and plant symbols. Near the top of the column is a human being hanging in the floriations. One of the tendrils passes into the body of this man (Figure 130), in order to show that the Devil has him in his power. Almost certainly the intention behind this symbolism is to hint that the adjacent astrological images are dangerous, a fertile field for the diabolical intentions of the Devil.

Astrology, like all the predictive arts, was linked in ancient times with black magic, involving the agencies of the demons. This is the reason why, when Dante was allowed to visit Hell, he found those who had predicted the future (by whatever means) consigned there, with their heads twisted around so they might now only see behind them. This was the punishment for being involved in the diabolic practice of seeking out the future, which was (theologians supposed) known only to God. Among those so tortured in Hell Dante saw spirits he recognized as astrologers.

The notion that the predictive arts are themselves dangerous or involved with demonic agencies is still not entirely forgotten. Those who practise the art of divination by means of earth (see chapter 4, pp. 74–5) usually admit that the future is made known by means of earth spirits.

Within the geomantic tradition (as within the astrological tradition, for that matter) we find occult lists of the names of all the demons linked with the geomantic figures and the planets.

The Chinese occultists, who have developed very many different systems of divination, insist that all methods of looking into the future are involved with contacting the demons. They say that only one system of divination is protected, for it was given to man by the higher gods – this is the system which has come to the West under the name of the *Book of Changes*, the Chinese *I Ching*. This system of prediction involves a ritual designed to allow chance to determine the nature of a six-lined figure ☷, the hexagram. Each of the six lines of the hexagram is either broken (yin) or unbroken (yang). The combination of such lines gives rise to sixty-four different hexagrams, and to each of these has been appended a special interpretation. Each of the individual lines has also been given a particular value and reading. The aim behind the operation is for a person to ask the *I Ching* operator a question, which is then put to the *I Ching* text (or, more accurately speaking, to the spirits who control the text). By means of a special operation a particular hexagram is obtained, and this is regarded as the answer to the question, which may be interpreted by reference to the book and in the light of a complex system of symbolic readings known to the Chinese diviner.

According to ancient Chinese texts, the *Book of Changes* should only be consulted after complex religious rituals have been conducted and under no circumstances should one merely toss coins. To break either of these rules is to offend the spirits who protect this system. The correct way to consult the text of the *I Ching* in order to obtain answers about the future is by means of yarrow stalks, or specially prepared sticks (Figure 131), which are manipulated by means of a complex ritual. Nowadays, especially in the West, many people consult the *I Ching* by means of coins, which they toss a number of times to determine the appropriate hexagram in response to their questions. The Chinese texts insist that this is the wrong procedure and point out that anyone who is anxious to use the spirits to obtain the answer to a question should be prepared to put into the divinatory procedure the time and effort which the use of plant sticks demands.

In the West there is no divinatory technique which is said to be free of the influence of the spirits, and many occultists insist that most of the methods of looking into the future invite the attention of the lower levels of demons. This is particularly true of such practices as the ouija board, by means of which groups of people attempt to spell out messages which they presume come from the dead. Ordinary cartomancy – fortune-telling by cards – is also said to be controlled by demons. It is argued that what appears to be the random fall of cards into a formal pattern

131 *The ritual described by the Chinese* I Ching *for using yarrow sticks for divinatory purposes. The manipulation of the sticks gives rise to a figure (a hexagram) which is interpreted according to certain rules. Although now many people throw coins to consult the* I Ching, *the ancient texts claim that this is unwise*

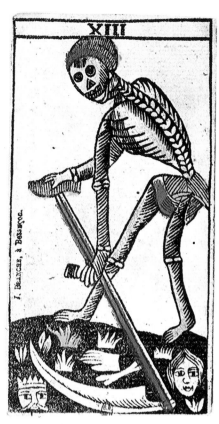

suitable for a reading is actually determined by spirits. One system of cartomancy, however, is of a very high order and is regarded by some occultists as attracting a high-quality spirit when it is properly practised – this is the pack of symbolic cards which we now call the Tarot.

A full Tarot pack really consists of two separate packs. One of these closely resembles ordinary playing cards, in that four suites are numbered and designed in terms of numbers; the second set consist of only twenty-two cards decorated with symbolic pictures (Figure 132) and are called 'atouts' or Arcanum cards. There is a great deal of nonsense talked about the Tarot, and in the popular books on the subject it is usually said that the cards come from ancient Egypt and are very old. However, this is not true: the Tarot pack as it is now used for divination is probably not much older than the fourteenth century, though the majority of the strange images on the cards are derived from an older occult tradition. For example, the card called 'Strength' (sometimes 'Force'), which shows a woman forcing back the jaws of a lion (Figure 133), is almost certainly derived from religious art forms which are well over a thousand years old. It is interesting to compare the card in Figure 133 with the bottom image in Figure 134, which is from a thirteenth-century bronze door in the façade of San Zeno in Verona. This latter image represents one of the seven virtues. Perhaps it is in this link which the Tarot demonstrates with the religious art of the past that the occultists sense the presence of good spirits when they use the cards.

132 (above) *A set of three eighteenth-century French Tarot cards, the central one of which portrays the winged Devil between two minions. The dualism inherent in the symbolism of the two minions has been interpreted by some occultists as a link with thirteenth- and fourteenth-century European heresies which were later confused with witchcraft*

133 (left) *'Force' or 'Strength', from an eighteenth-century edition of the Marseilles set of Tarot cards*

Those who operate the Tarot cards often say that the order of the cards, and the formal pattern into which they are dealt as a preparation for fortune-telling, are determined by chance. On the other hand, many occultists claim that the method is not an application of chance at all – there is nothing random in the fall of the cards. They insist that the formal pattern is determined by spirits. Whether these spirits are good or evil seems to depend very much upon the quality of the person who deals the cards, as much as on the person who is putting the question to the Tarot.

The other method of folklore prediction by means of the hand, popularly called palmistry, has generally been frowned upon by the Church and even by the law. Under English law it was illegal to practise palmistry for a fee until well into the present century, on the grounds that palmistry was a 'pretended art', and so anyone who told fortunes from the hand was bound to be a confidence trickster. In spite of the illegality of the practice, and in spite of the fact that it was linked in earlier days with the practice of witchcraft, palmistry has always been one of the most popular of arts – if only because most people have hands and the lines upon the hand are always different. It is usual in modern times to distinguish between chiromancy, which is prediction by means of the lines on the hand, and chirognomy, which is character reading from the form of the hand as a whole.

Very many images of palmists practising their art have survived within the occult tradition, and almost all of them emphasize the drama involved in a palmist being able to read about the past and the future from lines upon the hand. Virtually all the parts of the hands, as well as many of the lines, have been linked with planetary and zodiacal symbols, though in general it is the fingers and mounts (Figure 135) which are linked with the planets, while the lines are linked with human characteristics. For example, the two lines which run across the hand, below the roots of the fingers, are called the Heart Line (magenta) and the Head Line (blue) (Figure 135) and correspond to emotional and intellectual qualities respectively. Since these two realms of human experience and expression are fundamental to the personality, the relationship between these two lines is regarded as being of great importance in palmistic character diagnosis.

The seventeenth-century painting by Piero della Vecchia in Figure 136 is another example of this sort of palmistry which incorporates astrological imagery. However, what is particularly interesting about this picture is that in the occult images employed within it there is an attempt to make the subject of palmistry acceptable. The manuscript which curls over the edge of the table (Figure 137) is not there merely for empty display; it is there to demonstrate that palmistry is linked not only with astrology, but also with the Jewish

134 (above) *A thirteenth-century image of one of the Virtues among the arcane symbols on the bronze door of San Zeno in Verona reminds us that some of the Tarot cards have an ancestry that goes back to classical times*

135 (right) *A chiromantic hand from Jean Belot's* Oeuvres *(1649). The 'Ligne Mensale' is the Heart Line (magenta) and the 'Ligne moyenne' is the Head Line (blue)*

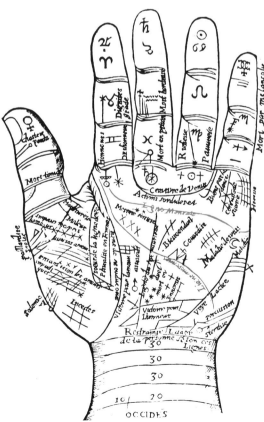

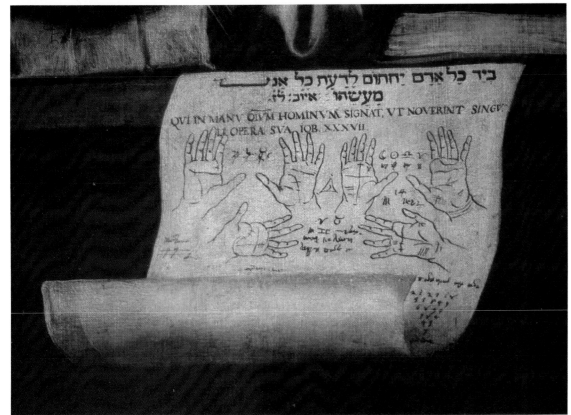

ביד כל אדם יחתום לדעת כל אנ
מעשהו איוב: לז

QVI IN MANV OIVM HOMINVM SIGNAT, VT NOVERINT SINGV
LLI OPERA SVA. IOB. XXXVII.

136 (above) The
Chiromant *by Piero
della Vecchia (1605–
78). The Pinacoteca,
Vicenza*

137 (left) *Detail of
the manuscript in
Figure 136, showing
zodiacal and
Qabbalistic symbols
used in seventeenth-
century palmistic circles*

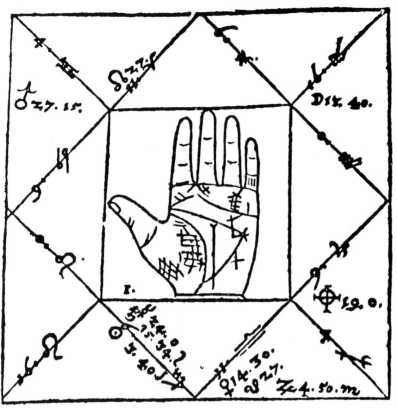

138 *Illustration from Rothmann's* Chiromantiae Theorica Practica *(1595). See text for interpretation*

Palmistry had never really been accepted by the Church in the way that astrology was by the eighteenth century; it was linked with the activity of demons and was generally viewed as being the practice of charlatans ('rogues and vagabonds', according to English law). Is there any doubt that the innocent-seeming piece of paper in Figure 137 is designed to show that palmistry, far from being one of the diabolic arts, is really a system as highly respected as the occult methods of astrology and the Qabbalistic sciences? The quotation from the Book of Job (37, 7) at the top of the manuscript appears in many early texts on palmistry (even though strictly speaking the quotation has nothing to do with hand reading at all), and so we should not be surprised to find it here. What is perhaps exceptional is that there should be a quotation in Hebrew. Since the Jews were rightly famed for their proficiency in the occult arts, is not this yet another sign that the artist was intent on showing palmistry as being among the more acceptable of the occult sciences, rather than being the concern of charlatans? Just as the developing modern science of the eighteenth century was banishing the notion of demonic influence on human life, so were those who made images of the occult.

Rothmann's view of the relationship between palmistry and astrology is worth glancing at, as it is his researches and insights which appear to have influenced several modern hypotheses about the nature of what is now called astro-palmistry. The woodcut from his *Chiromantiae Theorica Practica* of 1595 (Figure 138) attempts to relate certain line markings with the personal horoscope of the individual concerned. The hand in the centre of Figure 138 is recorded by Rothmann as a drawing of that belonging to a man born in Bratislava on 17 August 1567 (Old Style). The horoscope in the surrounding figure is cast for that date, approximately for midnight local time. Rothmann points to several confirmations in the hand of the general tenor of the horoscope. For example, he sees the rich criss-cross lines on the fleshy mound below the thumb (called in palmistry the Mount of Venus) as being linked with the significant fact that in the chart Venus is located in its own sign (Libra) and is the strongest planet in the figure. On the other hand, the three small lines on the bottom phalange of the little finger (the finger of Mercury, according to the chiromants) is said to be reflected in the fact that the planet Mercury is placed in a strong position (it is angular) in its own sign of Virgo – from which, Rothmann notes, 'we may interpret a man of excellent wit and commendable behaviour'.

Qabbala, and even that it is approved of in Holy Writ. The detail shows that the palmist has been making notes which link the lines of the hand with the planets (we can see the sigils for these alongside the hand drawings) with the signs of the zodiac (we can see the sigils for Aries, Taurus, Gemini and Libra). If that were not sufficient, we see in the bottom right a Qabbalistic system of numerology, with figures arranged in an inverted triangle.

Traditionally palmistry had always been linked with the planets, which is why the fingers had planetary names. The ring finger, for example, was linked with the Sun and called the 'finger of Apollo'; in the medieval period it was believed that there was an artery running from this finger directly to the heart, so that the gold of a ring worn on this finger found a correspondence with the heart, as gold was the metal of the Sun. However, it was not an established practice to relate other aspects of astrology to palmistry, even though one occultist called Rothmann wrote a book about the relationship between the hand and the horoscope (Figure 138). Even less directly linked with palmistry is the Jewish Qabbalistic system, so it is surprising to find that the document in the painting by Piero della Vecchia contains numerological devices linked with this system.

6 Amulets and Charms: The Invisible Power of the Evil Eye

In modern times we believe that rays of light from the world are transformed by our eyes and brain into vision. The eye is a mysterious factory where images of the world are made. This picture making is almost a magical operation, of course, reminding us that the word 'image' is linked with the word for 'magic' and 'imagination'. We believe that, in some way which is still not understood by scientists, the mind creates images from the light which penetrates the eye. In earlier days, while men realized that rays of light went into the eye, they also believed that a powerful ray was also emitted by the eye into the world. This projected visual ray had many names, but in the England of the sixteenth and seventeenth centuries it was called an 'eyebeam'. In his poem 'The Ecstasie' the seventeenth-century poet John Donne imagines two lovers looking intently at each other; they are so intense that their eyebeams intertwine and the two become prisoners to one another:

> Our eye-beames twisted, and did thred
> Our eyes, upon one double string. . . .

What were these eyebeams which were supposed to be emitted by the eye? They were rays, sent out into the world by the eye, in the opposite direction to the lightwaves which streamed in.

139 *Image of a crowned basilisk swallowing a man. Although such images are essentially derived from initiation lore (of the half-man, half-fish tradition), the basilisk is one of the most famous of amuletic images because of its supposed deadly glance. By means of its look it could kill or turn to stone. Detail from the façade of San Frediano, Lucca*

Everyone was supposed to emit such eyebeams, but it was believed that the eye forces of certain people were evil. Such people were rather like the fabled basilisk, a creature with eyes so deadly that it could kill with a glance (Figure 139). Even those who did not kill with their stare could do great damage, and were said to have the power of the evil eye. One historian, Maclagan, who quotes numerous examples of the evil eye in Scotland, records that one old woman from Mull said that the evil eye is 'just an eye with great greed and envy'. He also reports a remark made by an old man: 'It used to be said by old people that the greedy eye could split asunder the very rocks.' So evil was this rock-splitting power that, even until comparatively recently, it was widely believed in country districts that the evil eye was a gift from the Devil himself.

The idea of the evil eye was of great importance in witchcraft and black magic. Anyone with this terrible power was able to 'overlook' (or to throw evil glances) at any living thing. These people were often believed to be witches or warlocks, and it was assumed that they possessed other powers of working evil. In ancient times, whenever a child or an animal fell sick, people did not look for the cause as we might do nowadays – they took it for granted that the child or animal had been overlooked or bewitched by someone with the evil eye.

Because of this belief there were many devices used by countryfolk to drive away evil or to invite good into their lives. In the hamlet of Newchurch in Lancashire there is still a large eye built into the western side of the church tower (Figure 140). This is called by the locals the Eye of God, and it is said that it was put there when the tower was built in 1544 to drive away the evil working of witches. This eye was probably needed in that area, for just beyond Newchurch is Pendle Hill, which in the seventeenth century was infamous for its association with groups of women who were supposed to be witches. Many of the men and women who were hanged at Lancaster for witchcraft in that century came from villages in this area, and one group in particular lived in squalid homes in a forest just below Pendle Hill.

The idea of there being an evil power in the eyebeams of men and women is just about universal, and there exists in almost every language an equivalent term to 'evil eye'. In German it is the *boser Blick* (evil glance), in Italian *malocchio* – literally, 'bad eye', as in the French *mauvais oeil*. It is the Latin word *fascinum* which gives us a clue to what the evil eye really involves, however. The word *fascinum* was originally connected with the idea of binding – and indeed we have the modern word 'fascist' from the Roman *fasces*, which were the bound rods, emblems of the state. The English word 'fascinate' once meant 'to bind by magical means', and perhaps there is still a trace of this meaning in our words when we speak of a woman who is 'fascinating' because of her beauty or charm. It was believed that a witch or a warlock, or even an ordinary person with the power of the evil eye, could bind other people and things in their eyebeams, as though these beams were magical cords.

In later times this idea of binding was transferred to actual rope cords, and many pictures of witches show them carrying special thongs with which they were supposed to do their magical binding. The witches in Figure 141 are releasing winds and storms to cause a shipwreck; they had 'bound up' these winds and storms with special knots in their magical cords, so that they could release them at a time when they would do most damage.

The idea of binding is very ancient and has survived even in some innocent-seeming country rituals. There is a country custom practised even now in some parts of Britain in which an ashwood

140 *A stone eye with a pupil of blue slate, built into the tower of the parish church at Newchurch in Pendle, an area infamous for its witches. The eye, called locally the Eye of God, was actually intended as a precaution against the evil of witches*

141   *The use of witch knots* (nodi) *for wind raising, in an illustration from* Historia de Gentibus Septentrionalibus *(1555 edition). Such controlled winds could be used for sailing becalmed ships and for obtaining the right direction, as much as for destructive purposes, and there was a market in witch knots*

log is burned on the fire at Christmas Eve. This tradition comes from an ancient belief that demonic idols were made from ashwood – though some say that it was the ash which was used for the cross to crucify Christ. The custom is probably even older than Christianity, however, and some historians claim that it is linked with the burning of the sacred tree Yggdrasil (itself an enormous ash tree, with roots in Heaven and branches in Hell) at the winter solstice, which is near to Christmas time. Perhaps the origin of the custom is not so important now, however, for it is the ritual of the burning which interests us most.

It is said that the ashwood must be bound with at least three cords of subtle ash twigs (called 'binding withes'). There must be one such binding withe for each person present in the company, and each person chooses one of the binders as his own. The log is then thrown onto the fire to burn. It is said that the binding withe which bursts first indicates the person in the company who is to be most fortunate in the coming year. Bound into the withes were the wishes or expectations of those in the house.

Now this old custom is a wholesome one, yet it demonstrates quite clearly the idea that it is possible for the act of binding, or tying up, to be linked with the idea of parcelling up certain thoughts or hopes. If a witch binds up an evil thought into an object, then that object becomes unwholesome and evil.

The idea of injecting an evil power into an object by means of binding is extended into the act of hammering. Just as it was believed possible for witches to bind evil or goodness into an object, so was it possible for them to hammer evil into it. Many curious forms of what can only be called 'hammer magic' have survived in the most extraordinary ways. It was once a fairly common ritual for people to hammer nails or pins into objects, trying to think evil of a person as they were doing so. Sometimes such objects were waxen images, but at other times they were the hearts or organs of animals.

Pushing pins into waxen images or otherwise ill-treating them has always been a popular way of working evil. It is nowadays regarded as a form of what is called sympathetic magic, on the grounds that some people believe that there is a magical sympathy between things and images of those things. It is believed, for example, that if you have an image of an animal or a human being, then you have power over that animal or human. Several such waxen images, called 'poppets' (from the French *poupée* meaning 'doll'), have survived from the seventeenth and eighteenth centuries (Figure 142). You can use that power to bring evil on the living animal or person. If you do not have an image and you wish to work evil magic, then you make an image and name it after the person or animal. This last idea rests on the ancient belief that there is a magical power even in a name. There was at one time a well-developed commercial business (a black market?) in the use of waxen images for magical purposes.

A much quoted account of this is recorded in a rather dramatic pamphlet of 1613, which relates to the trial in Lancaster of a group of Pendle women suspected of being witches. One of these supposed witches, a blind lady of eighty, called Elizabeth Sowtherns, admitted that

the speediest way to take a man's life away by witchcraft is to make a picture of clay, like unto the shape of the person whom they mean to kill, and dry it thoroughly. And when you would have them be ill in any one place more than another, then take a thorn or pin and prick it in that part of the picture you would so have to be ill.

This old lady herself, tried along with others for causing the death of a man, died in jail, but some of those accused with her were hanged.

Mary the Virgin in Bottesford; it consists of three life-sized effigies, at the feet of which are two kneeling figures of children (Figure 143). Although the tomb is popularly called the Witchcraft Tomb, the inscription on the tomb does not mention witchcraft by name, only 'wicked practice and sorcerye'. The children are in fact supposed to have died of sympathetic magic practised by local witches.

This family tomb is that of the sixth Earl of Rutland, who died in 1632. The effigies of the two murdered sons are of Henry, who holds a skull in his left hand (Figure 143), and Francis, who holds a skull in his right hand, with a symbolic flower in his left. It is possible that this flower is meant as a symbol of his death, for the surname of the family of witches who are supposed to have killed him was Flower.

The Flower family consisted of a mother and two daughters, all of whom worked as servants in Belvoir Castle, where the Earl of Rutland lived. Shortly after one daughter, Margaret, was dismissed from service, the child Henry died and was buried in Bottesford in September 1613. Local gossip insisted that he had died from witchcraft or the evil eye, but it was not until 1617 that the Flower women were arrested. Margaret confessed to having cast a death spell on all the children of the earl. She had done this by stealing a glove from the little hand of Henry. This had been used to stroke their familiar (the witches' pet) and then had been cut with scissors; she insisted that this was sufficient to bring about the death of the child. Two years later they had treated another glove, this time of the younger brother, in the same way and he died young (though after the witches themselves). The mother of the witch family, Joan Flower, died prior to trial, but the two daughters were found guilty and hanged at Lincoln on 12 March 1618.

This story, preserved in the beautiful apse of Bottesford church, shows that waxen images were not always necessary to the practice of casting evil spells. If the witch could obtain something which belonged to her victim, then this would do just as well. To cut such a personal belonging with scissors or to hammer nails into it was just about the same as cutting or nailing the person to whom they belonged.

If wicked people have the power to throw evil from their eyes, to bind people and animals with magical spells, and to work evil at a distance by means of waxen images, how may any victim hope to escape? Here the answer is quite simple: anyone who suspects that evil is being thrown at him, or feels that he is being bound by a witch, may throw back the evil at the witch by means of special magical amulets. This was why the Eye of God had been built into the tower of Newchurch (Figure 140).

If the witch has cast (or thrown) a spell, then, provided it is caught before doing its evil work,

142 *A poppet or curse doll used for purposes of witchcraft. Probably early nineteenth century. Moyse's Hall Museum, Bury St Edmunds*

It is said that this idea of sympathetic power in magical images even passed into the Christian ritual of exorcism (see chapter 7, pp. 136 and 138). In certain difficult cases the priest was required to make a waxen image of the possessing devil prior to the exorcism. Having 'baptized' this image with the name of the demon, the priest would then throw it into a fire, where the flames would consume it. This ritual was designed to make the demon flee in agony.

The use of waxen or clay images was popular even in aristocratic circles, however. One famous case involved the Duchess of Gloucester, who was the ringleader of several accused in 1442 of attempting the life of Henry VI by hiring a witch to use an image 'representing the King, which by their sorcery, a little and little consumed, intending thereby . . . to waste and destroy the king's person and to bring him to death.' The duchess was found guilty and sentenced to perpetual imprisonment. It was the witch who died – not hanged for witchcraft, as was the normal procedure in England, but burned for treason.

The only tomb in an English church to be connected with witchcraft is the result of a similar sort of binding. This tomb is in the church of St

143 *Effigy of Henry, the elder son of the sixth Earl of Rutland, from the so-called Witchcraft Tomb in the church of St Mary the Virgin, Bottesford*

the same spell may be cast (or thrown) back at the witch. This word 'cast' is very interesting. We find a survival of the evil contained within it in our word 'cast' meaning a slight squint of the eye. This eye cast was once associated with the evil eye – the Latin *iacere* means 'to cast' or 'to throw away'. To this day *jettatura* (meaning 'one who throws', linked with our English word 'jettison') is one of the names given in Italy to the power of the evil eye, possessed by someone with the ability to throw or cast evil forces from his or her eyes.

What were these magical amulets which were powerful enough to throw back evil forces? Once again, as with so many occult and magical names, it is the word itself which throws light on the nature of the amulet. The word is from a Latin verb *amolior*, which means 'to do away with' or 'to baffle'. We see from this that the amulet is something which baffles the evil eyebeam of the witch. The amulet is so designed as to catch the evil and cast it back in the face of the witch. The design of amulets is one of the most intriguing fields of study in occult symbolism, for the wide variety of such designs reflects different aspects of man's belief about the nature of magic.

There are literally thousands of different amulets, all intended to baffle the evil eye. Some of them are homemade and others exquisitely wrought by craftsmen. Basically there are two different kinds of amulet – the form which is designed to protect the wearer or the building to which it is attached, and the form which is designed to repel or deflect the evil eye. An interesting Greek vase painting, made some five hundred years before Christ, illustrates very well the dual nature of amuletic symbols (Figure 144), for it shows two soldiers fighting, with a third fallen at their feet. On their shields are painted magical symbols, designed to protect the individual fighters. The bottom shield (which presumably belongs to the wounded soldier) shows a five-pointed star, while the top device is in the form of a snake. The star is a magical device, linked in ancient times with the power of the planet Venus, and is supposed to exude the protective power of this goddess on all who wear the symbol, either as a pendant amulet or as a design on clothing, on a shield or on the door of a house. It is, like the Seal of Solomon, one of the most popular of amuletic forms. No doubt the soldier had it painted on the front of his shield to protect him in battle by putting between him and his enemeies a protective aura of beneficent power. The shield above this contains a device which belongs to a different category of magical amulets: on it is painted a snake with a threatening poisonous tongue. Instead of exuding the beneficent and benign influence of a goddess, this shield is designed to exude a frightening power: it is intended to drive back the evil eye or whatever threatens the wearer. In a sense such a magical device works on the assumption that the evil projected by a witch (or, for that matter, by an enemy soldier) may be driven back by a similar evil. This vase painting therefore illustrates the two different forms of magical device which either enfolds the wearer in a protective aura or projects an evil power which will drive back evil forces.

144   *Amuletic devices on the shields of fighting Greeks and Trojans. From a sixth-century* BC *amphora in the City Museum, Rhodes*

Several of the amulets in Figure 2 are designed to protect by enfolding the wearer in a beneficient influence. For example, we have already glanced at something of the magical nature behind the form of the ankh amulet in Figure 2 – the Egyptian ankh was one of the powerful emblems of the ancient gods and as a symbol of spiritual life forces it protected the wearer from harm. Perhaps the most frequently worn of all amulets is the Christian cross, of course, but there are many beneficient magical symbols of this kind which are supposed to perform the same protective function, even if their forms are not so immediately understandable as the Christian cross, which is to some extent already contained within the Egyptian ankh, and which, as a magical protective device, is much older than Christianity. Figure 145 is an example of a similar protective symbol, for it is a Moslem amulet in the form of the name of Allah written in Arabic script; this is obviously designed to bathe the wearer in the powerful beneficence of God. As we shall see when we examine the nature of demons, occultists believe that the name for a thing is just as magical as the symbol for that thing, with the result that the most efficacious amulets are those which incorporate both the name and the symbol in a single form, as in Figure 145.

The amulets which are designed to repel the evil eye, rather than to bathe the wearer in a beneficient protective aura, are of a different order to the ankh, the cross and the Allah amulets, however. Among these are those which incorporate the image of an eye, the magical beam from which is supposed to deflect the evil eye projected by the witch. It is believed that such an amulet literally throws the eyebeam back into the eye of the evil-worker. Figure 146 is an example from Gnostic magical art, in which the eye was often surrounded by a number of power-working symbols which augmented its magical potency. The thunderbolt is a symbol for Jupiter, the lion for the Sun, the dog for Mercury, the scorpion for Mars, the stag for the Moon, and the serpent for the time god Chronos, or Saturn. Only the planet (or goddess) Venus is missing from this list of planets. This is no doubt because Venus, goddess of beauty and loveliness, was not considered a suitable image to deflect evil; she is more likely, indeed, to attract the evil eye. In place of a symbol for Venus is an owl, perched on the eye itself, to indicate that it is not of the same symbolic order as the other creatures.

The owl, with its curious staring eyes, is of course the traditional symbol of wisdom, sacred in ancient times to the goddesses Minerva and Athena. It was also a symbol of goodness and purity, and this is perhaps one reason why it is so securely perched upon the eye, to indicate quite firmly that it is a power for good, quite capable of repelling the evil beams of even the most potent witchcraft. This is one explanation, resting main-

145 *Stylized writing of the name of God used as an Islamic amulet*

146 *A woodcut of a Gnostic amulet, the symbols of which have been linked with the planets. The eye at the centre has the same magical power as the eye from Newchurch in Figure 140*

ly on the Greek and Roman view of the owl – it may, however, not be the correct one.

We must not forget that the Gnostics who designed this amulet lived in the north of Egypt, and it is likely that they made as much use of Egyptian symbolism as of Greek or Roman forms. In the Egyptian system of hieroglyphic symbols the owl stands for such things as cold, night and death. These might be more pertinent symbolic forces for an amulet designed to drive back evil. In fact, there is something about the form of the owl itself which reminds one of another form of amulet against the evil eye, one which is sometimes called the winged scarab (Figure 147). This, along with the ordinary scarab

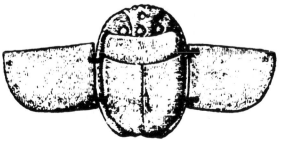

147 *A woodcut of a scarab beetle amulet, the so-called winged scarab, which was an important amulet in the death cult of the ancient Egyptians. It was believed that the scarab could resurrect from its own dung*

were also intended as word amulets, protective power sources which were to bring benefit and strength to the craft. The star Alcyone, one of the group of Pleiades in the constellation of Taurus, was regarded as a particularly important star in ancient times: it was called the Foundation Stone in Babylonian astrology, and Al Wasat, the Central One, by the Arabians. In giving such a name to a boat, the owner was calling into play all the beneficial, protective powers of this important star. The hideous dragon–fish on the front of the ship is a further reminder that the ancient figureheads on boats were large-scale protective amulets, meant either to attract benefit and safety from the sea or to frighten away the dark powers of witchcraft. This explains why some of the figureheads are often quite hideous.

A much used amulet of the hideous kind was that called the Gorgon head, which consists of an image of a woman's head with hair made from a nest of serpents (Figure 151), reminding us of the Greek serpent shield of Figure 144. The story of the Gorgon is from Greek mythology: it tells how there are three Gorgones, winged females with heads covered with serpents in place of hair, and two venomous projecting teeth. Of these three hellish monsters, only the one named Medusa was mortal, and eventually the hero Perseus was able to kill her by cutting off her head. A terrible evil force was projected from the eyes of Medusa, and anyone who looked at them was turned to stone. Perseus had managed to get near enough to this monster only by using his shield as a mirror and killed her without actually looking into her face, save as a reflection. It was inevitable that a story like this would attract the amulet makers, and thousands of Gorgon heads featuring the mortal Medusa were designed on the principle that such a demonic gaze would most effectively drive back the eyebeams of witches.

Another interesting form of amulet is not for those of a prudish cast of mind. Many thousands of tiny amulets which have been unearthed in excavations of Roman sites are actually images of human private parts. Some of these are combined with a hand, a symbol designed to ward off evil. Historians insist that such amulets were worn in ancient times even by women, and that they were designed to attract the gaze of the evil-worker, who was astonished by their form, as a result of which the evil was deflected. The image of the penis was regarded as being so powerful as an amulet that we even find examples scratched on Roman drinking cups, no doubt placed there to ward off evil influences during the course of a meal. It is interesting to see that in some amulets the forms have been combined with the head of a bull (Figure 152). This might be difficult to explain in modern times, but the fact is that in Egyptian astrological documents we find that one of the main symbols for the zodiacal sign Taurus (which is the bull of the heavens) was a crude

images, was often placed in the bandage wrappings of mummies after embalming and is said to be used to protect the soul of the departed in the postmortem realms. The winged scarab and the scarab itself are extremely interesting magical symbols and were sometimes venerated because of the T form on their backs. This shape was sometimes called the tau cross, for this was the name of the T in ancient alphabets; some insist that the tau was the form of the cross on which Christ died. Be that as it may, the scarab beetle was linked, like Christ, with the miracle of resurrection, and it was believed that this power was sufficient to drive off evil forces.

Very many amulets are designed to attract (and therefore render harmless) the attention of the witch. Some of these are actually designed in the form of hideous faces (which, of course, had eyes, or a single eye when in profile) or in the form of eyes, as, for example, in the Greek water jar which has an eye just below the rim to ensure that the liquid within is not rendered impure or poisonous by witchcraft (Figure 148). As with the eye against witchcraft in Figure 140, it is assumed that the painted eye will deflect the eyebeams and spells cast by a witch.

Sometimes the Greeks and Romans would paint such eyes on the prow of their ships to repel evil, and nowadays fishermen often carve or paint symbols of special magical power on the front of their craft for protection against harm, ranging from simple five-pointed stars (Figure 149) to complex painted carvings of dragon forms, as may be seen on a modern restoration of a traditional craft named *Alcyone* (Figure 150). This last name, which is that of a fixed star, should remind us that the names painted on the prows of boats

149 (left) *Five-pointed star on the prow of a boat in Symi, Greece. Such symbols are ultimately derived from the Egyptian hermetic tradition and are often used as amuletic devices on Mediterranean shipping*

150 (below) *Dragon-fish as a protective figure on the prow of a boat of traditional design in Rhodes harbour. It was supposed that fearsome faces would frighten away the evil eye with the same magical power as a less evil-looking eye or star*

drawing of a human penis. The life force of the bull was held in ancient times to be of great importance, and the sacrifice of bulls – whether in the Egyptian rites, in which the bull Serapis was killed after a thirty-year lifetime, or in the annual bull killing of the Mithraic religion – was thought to bring great fecundity to the earth. It is even maintained by some that the bullfights of modern Spain are really the remnants of ancient religious rites intended to ensure the fertility of the earth. If the form of the bull was so potent, then it could be used with great effect alongside a human penis against the evil eye.

As we have seen, some designers of magical pendants were concerned with making designs which were not intended to deflect the evil eye, but merely to carry a magical power for good. Similarly secret designs were often made as wall paintings or mosaics to deflect the evil eye or to attract and contain magical forces which were thought to exude beneficial influences. Very often the symbolism of these was of a hidden or specifically occult nature. The Roman mosaic in Figure 153 is an example of such an occult design, for, geometric as it may seem at first glance, it actually represents a penis and two female sexual organs. However, the penis is ejaculating semen at the pudenda to its right, and the entire figure may be seen as a magical image of creative power, of spiritual energy descending from above. One observes this in the distinctive figure of eight ∞ in which the two testicles have been arranged; this is one of the old symbols for creative force, and is said originally to symbolize the meeting of the Sun and the Moon in the heavens, which was seen as a sign of the meeting of male and female.

Not all such protective devices were so complex or so obviously sexual, though very many of the simple-seeming amuletic devices do have sexual undertones. Without doubt the most frequently used of such magical amulets is the horseshoe, which appears to have the longest history of all magic symbols. Some occultists say that its supposed power is derived from the fact that it resembles the crescent Moon ☽ , but others insist that the upright horseshoe may be imagined as a sort of container or chalice, filled with powerful magic. Whatever the reasons for this belief, literally thousands of doors in all parts of the world sport such horseshoe devices – sometimes as genuine old horseshoes, sometimes as imitations wrought into doorknobs. The practice of protecting a door by magical means is still

151 (above) *Gorgon head, representing the evil Medusa, with her hair infested with snakes. The Gorgon Medusa entered the occult tradition in the fixed star Algol*

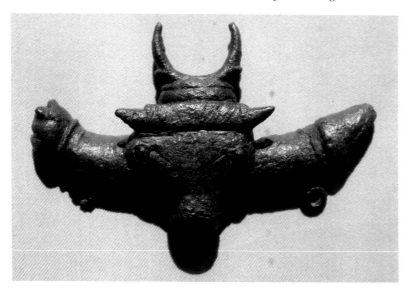

152 *An amulet made from a bull's head (note the insistence on the crescent horns) and the male sexual organ. From the Roman Museum at Augst, Switzerland*

widely popular in the Mediterranean countries, and in many Greek and Turkish cities and villages it is possible to find a wide variety of magical hand designs, intended to serve both as doorknocker and as protection against the evil eye. Presumably the idea is that, just as the eyebeam from a witch may be deflected by the power of another eye (painted or otherwise), so it may be thrown back by a hand. Figure 154 is a doorknocker from a house in the Greek city of Rhodes; it combines

two magical devices, for the hand is designed to knock against the Seal of Solomon.

Such magical symbols are regarded as protection for the house and for all who live in it. This notion has in modern times been extended from the door and house to cars. The novelist Lawrence Durrell tells an amusing story of how, when the taxi drivers of Rhodes were given new cars after the last war, they refused to drive them until they had each been provided with traditional amulets to hang in the windscreens. Little has changed since that time, for in a recent taxi drive in Rhodes I counted no fewer than three amulets on the dashboard of the vehicle, and one (a string of amuletic eyebeads) hanging from the rearview mirror. The bus journey back revealed a similar display in front of the bus driver, though he was of a more Christian frame of mind and had arranged an entire shrine with numerous amulets just above his head.

One often finds protective horseshoes fixed to the radiators of taxis and private vehicles (Figure 155), reminding us to some extent of the magical horse brasses which were fixed to the harnesses of draught horses and even to the sides of carts in former times. In fact, the magical notion behind Figure 155 is not limited merely to horseshoes, for the device proudly displayed on the front of the Mercedes is also of magical origin, as the sigil was used in late-seventeenth-century alchemical tradition as a symbol for phosphorus. One wonders if the designer of the Mercedes symbol was aware of this magical link with an element which was discovered as a byproduct of alchemical operations in Germany in 1669? Originally the word 'phosphorus' was used to denote any material which was luminescent. Such material was believed to possess magical potency, for the occultists linked it with what is now called the astral light, which is claimed to be the source of human thought. Some occultists say that the Greek myth which tells how Prometheus stole fire from Heaven is really a misunderstanding, for originally Prometheus stole phosphorus from the gods and made it available to mankind. This, of course, is a mythological way of saying that Prometheus was the one who stole the power of thinking from the gods, and thus enabled humans to think independently, because of the magical power of the astral light, or phosphorus. This explains why occultists link the demonic spirit Lucifer with the Prometheus myth, for the name Lucifer means 'light bearer', and it is claimed that, when Lucifer fell from Heaven, he brought with him the power of thinking as a gift for mankind. It is very interesting that phosphorus as a modern element is intimately bound up with the chemistry of human thought.

Certain stones, as well as powders and metals, were also credited with magical properties in earlier times. It was believed, for example, that

153 (above)   *Magical device constructed from sexual symbols. A floor mosaic on display in Sousse Museum, Tunisia*

154 (below)   *A traditional Greek doorknocker from a house in Rhodes. This example combines the hand (which wards off evil) and the Seal of Solomon on the knocking boss*

many of the jewels known to the medieval world had within them a secret power, called a virtue, which was supposed to come from Heaven. For this reason many magical stones were enclosed in gold or silver casings, to be hung around people's necks; these were worn not merely because they were beautiful to look at, but because they were powerful magic. Some magical stones were believed to have a virtue which would cure diseases or prevent certain things happening. For

155   *A Mercedes car with two horseshoes used as amulets for good luck, and a third amuletic or secret element in the Mercedes trademark symbol*

117

example, it was believed that the sapphire might be used to protect the wearer from snake bites, and the opal would protect the eyesight of anyone who wore it, and so on.

Since it was believed that a magical stone could be linked with a heavenly virtue, it was regarded as not unreasonable to group together different material things, all of which were said to contain within them the tincture of the same heavenly virtue. For example, in some medieval textbooks we find that the magical stone the crystal is linked

with the virtue of the Pleiades, and with these went the herb fennel, which contained the same magical power. Along with such associations went what have been called 'magical characters', a number of magical symbols which were also said to carry powerful protective virtues. The character for crystal (or for the Pleiades) is given in Figure 156, which is derived from a medieval textbook on the stars. Such magical symbols were often carved on stones or metal plates to act as protective devices.

The word 'charm' is often used of certain types of magical device. It is from the Latin *carmen*, which means 'song', suggesting that originally the words used in charms were intended to be chanted or sung. By the medieval period, however, when charms were used in vast numbers, they were no longer sung, but inscribed on rings, brooches or pendants. Because of the intense religious life which permeated the medieval world, most of these words or charms were linked with either the Bible or with stories from the life of Christ. It was said that the most powerful charm was the name of Jesus, or Ixtheus, one of the secret names of Christ, from the Greek word for 'fish', the initial letters of which made up in Greek a short hymn of praise to Christ. Sometimes a simple drawing of a fish was used as an equivalent for this, and at other times the symbol for the sign of the zodiac Pisces was used to represent Christ. A particularly clever combination of the idea of Pisces and of Christ may be seen in a Christian mosaic which depicts the two fishes crossed, thereby evoking both the pagan astrological symbol and the Christian notion of the cross of redemption (Figure 157).

There was much play with anagrams and magical letters in such charms. Sometimes this led to charms which are difficult to understand without explanation. We can look at one such charm in some detail to see how these things were designed. The image VV.M which is sometimes found on charms, particularly on rings, does not make much sense to those who are unacquainted with magic. One might be inclined to imagine that they merely represent the initials of the ring's owner. However, this device is one of the most powerful of all charms, and it is worth looking into its meaning.

On some rings one sometimes finds the inscription *Ave Maria gratia plena Dominus tecum*. This is the Latin version of the greeting recorded in the Bible between the Archangel Gabriel and Mary at the Annunciation. Such a ring might be given as a magical charm to a woman who was expecting a child. Sometimes the same charm would be written V.MA, which is a short form for the opening *Ave Maria* and yet at the same time stands for the initials of the Virgin Mary.

In some magical devices the curious form \\/ would be used as a charm or symbol of power.

This sigil, or letter, was no longer a reference to the Virgin, but to Christ. The reason for this is rooted in the fact that the Greek word *nike* ('victory') was used to denote Christ's victory over death in many early references to Christianity. The choice of the symbol rests upon the fact that within its form the Latin N may be found, as well as the Hebraic letter Vau (which stands for Jesus). The double V is linked with the first letter of *nike* in the Cyrillic alphabet, the lower case of which looks like a v of the Roman alphabet. Then again, the letters N and V in the sigil are regarded as being overprinted, to give the form \\/. We see, therefore, that what may be taken as a fairly simple sigil is actually replete with several levels of meaning. It is likely also that the overtones of the astrological sigil for Aries, which looks rather like a V, may have played a part in this symbolism, as in esoteric astrology Aries ♈ is the sign linked with incarnation, with the descent of spiritual energies to the earth.

When this symbol was adjusted slightly to make a Latin W, and then combined with the M, the two letters combined in a most simple form (WM) each of the notions set out above, namely: 'Christ Victorious', 'Virgin Mary' and *Ave Maria gratia plena Dominus tecum*.

We see, therefore, that the two letters (three letters, if we read the W as VV) point to Christ, to the Mother of Christ, to Christ's resurrection (that is, his victory over death), and to his incarnation. The incarnation of Christ, through a virgin birth, and his resurrection are the two main mysteries of the Christian Church, and there they are symbolized in two letters. No wonder these have been regarded as potent charms for many centuries.

Another popular amulet derived from letter forms is sometimes called the Rotas. It consisted of a magic square of letters with the outer section built up from the letters ROTAS, and its reverse SATOR:

```
R O T A S
O       A
T       T
A       O
S A T O R
```

Within this square was traced a cross, with the letters TENET:

```
R O T A S
O   E   A
T E N E T
A   E   O
S A T O R
```

The square was completed with the letters P and R:

R O T A S
O P E R A
T E N E T
A R E P O
S A T O R

The meaning of the group of words is not too clear, but within it there is a cross, and on either side of the cross are the two letters A and O, which stand for alpha and omega, the first and last letters of the Greek alphabet:

```
          T
          E
T E N E T
          E
A T O
```

These two letters were often drawn above the image of Christ or above the Cross to show that Christ has power over the beginning and end of things. Some magical amulets and magical rings often give only the form A + O.

Within the letters of the Rotas, however, it is possible to trace the letters which make up the words *Pater noster*, the opening words of the Latin prayer 'Our Father . . .'.

158 (above) *An occult symbol on the conical roof of a house (*trullo*) in Alberobello, Italy. This particular symbol contains the Christian cross surrounded by the four elements and may also be a play on the initials of the owner of the house*

159 (right) *The symbol for Venus painted on the roof of the* trullo *in Alberobello. Sometimes the symbol for Venus is used as though it were the equivalent of the Egyptian ankh. In this case it is possible that the owner is inviting the beneficent influence of the goddess Venus on his home*

```
ROTAS      ROTAS
OPERA      . PER .
TENET      . . N . .
AREPO      . . E . .
SATOR      . . T . .
```

Planetary and zodiacal symbols, initial letters
and secret devices were often combined in images
with magical jewels and used to repulse evil influences; such combinations were regarded as
highly potent magic. There is an extraordinary
town in southern Italy where many different
magical symbols derived from astrological and
occult traditions are painted on the roofs of the old
houses. The curious roofs are conical, and houses
of such design are called *trulli* in Italian. For many
years it has been the custom to paint on the *trulli*
roofs magical symbols, designed to attract good
influences on the houses, in much the same spirit
as other people will hang horseshoes on their
doors. Figures 158 and 159 show some of the
more exciting of these *trulli* symbols, but the most
frequently used are versions of the cross.

A similar use of external amuletic protection for
houses may be seen on some of the houses on the
Greek island of Mykonos, for very many of their
chimneys are marked with secret symbols (Figure
160). In this case, however, the symbols are only
rarely painted on – more usually they are built into
the brickwork or inset in pottery. Once again
there is a wide variety of different symbols, but
the majority are solar, a great number are related
to tree forms, as in Figure 160, and some (almost
inevitably in such a religious community) are
images of fish. Between them they symbolize
respectively the life force, the power of growth
and Christ. Some Mykonos chimneys combine
all three of these symbols, one on top of the other
– a sure deterrent to any threat of evil.

160 *Secret symbols on the chimney of a house on the island
of Mykonos, Greece. Such symbols include solar,
astrological and amuletic devices, magical trees and planetary
forms. Mykonos is said to be an island of a thousand
churches: it is certainly an island of a thousand magical
symbols*

7 Demons: The Unseen Workers of Evil

There is a tradition that the demons were born to Adam from his first wife, the she-devil Lilith. Perhaps there is a sly humour in this tradition, for it implies that, had man not come to earth, there would have been no devils. The blind poet Milton seems to remember this legend when he makes his great demon Sin emerge into being from the thinking of Satan at the moment that his pride leads him to consider rebelling against God. Just as the demon Sin is born of the imagination of Satan, so are devils constantly being born from the imagination of man.

The devils are reputed to be invisible by nature and inclination, and it is suggested by demonologists that all the grotesque forms with which they have been saddled (Figure 161) are really not the inventions of demons themselves, but the inventions of artists and poets. Demons are the invisible agents of evil and yet, as vast numbers of illustrations, paintings and literary descriptions make plain enough, the demons are often given forms as though they were quite visible to ordinary men. Sometimes they are made visible in men's minds as more or less shadowy pictures, as nightmares or gruesome imaginings. Most of these shadow images owe a great deal to the popular pictures of demons which are found in books and paintings – these are the demonic shapes created by artists, writers and poets. At other times, however, the demons are said to take on shapes of their own, independently of the images forced upon them by the imagination of men. It is said that when demons are conjured up by the diabolic rites of black magicians into magical circles they assume real and hideous shapes of their own making. Some of the sophisticated demonological tracts even show the demon as it first appears, and how it will appear at a second showing, after having been commanded to reappear in a more acceptable form by the magician. Figure 162 is from a nineteenth-century English book of demon lore, known as a grimoire, and shows a typical image of Cassiel, demon of the planet Saturn, in the form of a king riding a monstrous dragon, as he will appear when first conjured. When sent back by the magician, Cassiel agrees to adopt a less frightening form and usually returns in human shape.

Yet even if all the forms which have been forced upon the demons have come from the human imagination, or from the ghastly appearances which they adopt in black magic circles, this does not stop us asking where these forms came from originally. The truth is that humans are less imaginative than they like to believe; even the human imagination is rarely able to create forms out of nothing. There is usually some trace of a previous idea or image to be found in even the most outlandish or imaginative creations. We might therefore reasonably ask how the invisible demons took on their curious and frightful forms to become visible in their assumed masks of aerial matter or seeming flesh.

Almost as soon as God has formed Adam from the clay of earth, the Serpent (who is, of course, the first demon) appears to tempt Adam's wife. There is no early description of the appearance of this devil–serpent, but since the artists who illustrated Genesis knew that the Serpent could talk, they often gave it a human head. This creation of a serpent–devil did not demand a vast leap of imagination, however, for among the vast number of demons recognized in the pre-Christian world there was an Egyptian devil who was half serpent, half human. This demon was the Echidna, who had the head of a woman on the body of a serpent and was adopted into Greek mythology as the mother of several demons, of which perhaps the most famous were the many-headed dog Orthos, the mysterious Sphinx, and the monstrous Cerberus, who was guardian of the gates of Hell. The mother of such a brood was gratefully adopted by the Christian artists to symbolize the sweet-tongued Serpent of the Garden of Eden, and a thousand medieval images of the temptation give the Serpent the head of a woman and coil her snake-like body around the tree on which the fruit of the Fall of man hangs (Figure 163); sometimes the demon is shown trampled beneath the foot of Mary, whose Son redeemed the work of the Serpent. Most of the artists who drew this serpentine form did not realize that they were portraying an ancient Egyptian monster.

This story of the origin of the image used for the earliest named demon is the story of almost every demon in the world. Since the demons are

161   *The mouth of Hell and demonic temptations. From a fourteenth-century manuscript in the British Library*

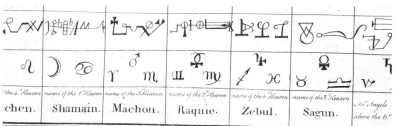

162 *The Saturnian demon Cassiel astride his dragon. From a hand-coloured plate in Francis Barrett's* The Magus *(1801)*

strange images of her as a goggle-eyed bird, even though for the Babylonians she was merely invisible and (with the normal power of demons) capable of adopting almost any form she chose in the material world.

Another early night monster was the incubus, a demon who appeared to women in their dreams and made passionate love to them. Sometimes the incubus would appear in the form of a monster and sometimes as a beautiful lover. The name 'incubus' carries no mysteries, however, for it is from the Latin *incubare*, meaning 'to sleep', and in Greek and Roman times it was often used in connection with sleeping in temples for healing purposes. The female form of the demonic lover (who took men as her victims) was called a succubus – again, sometimes beautiful or sensual, at other times frightful in appearance. Some churchmen argued that such demons as succubi and incubi were not real, but figments of the dreaming mind. Others, however, insisted that they were so real (that is to say, so material) that they were able to collect the semen of those whom they excited in dreams and to use this for demonic procreation.

Both Lilith and the incubus were described in literature, and a vast gallery of portraits of both demons have existed from ancient right up to modern times. It is instructive, for example, to compare the rather hideous image of Lilith in her Babylonian form (Figure 164) with the modern painting of her attending a dying man in Figure 58. In this interesting picture the ideas of Lilith and of the incubus begin to merge, for the demonic Lilith has become a sort of demon–lover. It is said that Lilith comes to all sinning men on their deathbeds and induces them to make love to her. Although she is a demon, she disguises this from the dying man by presenting towards him the body of a beautiful woman. Her back, which is hidden from the man, is a hideous semi-matter rather like rotting vegetation. When the man reaches out to take this woman, only then does he discover that he has grasped a demon in his hands, and that he has made that final move towards death.

This interesting image of Lilith points to one of the keys to the traditional notion of how demons make themselves visible to men. Most textbooks on demons say that they do not have real bodies, but 'aerial forms', made of a 'subtle air'. Some insist that the body of a demon is made of a specially thickened air. At the same time demons are supposed to have the power to make this aerial form even thicker, so that it becomes visible to those on earth. Since demons are not restricted to any particular physical body, they can mould their thought body to any shape they wish before thickening it. A demon can therefore appear on earth in any shape it likes, and it is a reflection of the demonic love for evil that it chooses so often to appear in monstrous form. Lilith comes in two

invisible to ordinary man, the artist tends to rely for his imaginative creations on old images which he finds in the pictures of demons or outlandish monsters of earlier times.

According to some, the serpent–demon was not the first devil. It is said that the nightmare demon Lilith preceded even the Serpent in the story of man's Fall. She was named as the first wife of Adam, before Eve came on the scene; as a result of their union the brood of Lilin – the first demons – came into the world. In Babylonian literature her name is especially feared, and a special class of priests was concerned with warding off the terrible witchcraft and evil which she spread in the world. Images of Lilith have been found by archaeologists (Figure 164), and she was also described in ancient texts, yet she really came into her own in Hebraic literature, in which she insinuated herself into a dominant position over childbirth. To this day spells and magical symbols are constructed to drive away Lilith during pregnancy and birth in certain households. In the Bible, where she is named in Isaiah, Lilith is linked with the night owl and is said to be a night monster. Such clues as these have led to many forms in Figure 58 – as a dying vegetative body because she is a demon who rules over death, and as a feminine mask so that she might be found sensually attractive by the man and therefore all the more easily tempt him to sin with her.

In their real habitat the demons were invisible, and even when they came to earth they generally remained so. The idea in ancient times was that demons lived in the astral plane, the spiritual realm which is part of the material world, a sort of life power for that world, yet invisible to it (see chapter 2). Human beings and all things which have material bodies live immersed in this astral world, usually unaware of its existence, much as fish swim in the waters of the sea, probably without being aware of the water itself. On the whole demons prefer to do their evil work in a hidden way – they prefer to remain invisible to men. Yet sometimes a situation arises in which they might become visible. For example, it was taught in the ancient mystery schools that, by means of assiduous disciplines and study, any man might so cleanse his inner being that he would be able to see on every plane of existence. As a result of such cleansing he would be able to see all the levels of being normally hidden to man, including the astral plane. He would be like a fish, suddenly becoming aware of the water itself, even of the existence of the land and its strange inhabitants beyond the surface of its own world. Such a man might at will have conversations with the angels or see the demons.

One of the demonic themes which was popular with artists in former times was the temptation of those men who set out to challenge the power of the dark forces in the astral world. Monks were depicted as being tempted by monstrous, foul creatures (Figure 165), which were really nothing more than demonifications of the inner passions. These demons were the symbolic forms of man's own inner hell, which every person who wishes to achieve higher states of initiation must inevitably encounter and learn to control. Once a person had learned to control the lower part of his or her being, to keep the demons and passions in their place, then he or she was regarded as being pure enough to learn how to live within the higher realms of the astral plane. Such people were often symbolized as half fish or half dragon, to show that they had integrated their lower nature and were in control of the darker part of their being. This is one reason why such men who had attained inner vision and were now initiates were so often pictured as half man, half fish (Figure 167), and why accounts of such initiations are often clothed in the story of the candidate being swallowed by a fish or a snake (Figure 139). Such initiates were, so to speak, at home in two worlds, and we should not be surprised to find them called 'fish–men', 'snake–men' or even 'dragon–men'. Such names, when misunderstood, gave rise to demonic forms, as may be seen in the demons

163 (above) *The tempting demon of the Fall in the form of a human-headed serpent. This image is derived ultimately from that used for an Egyptian demon, the Echidna. Medieval stained glass from St Etienne, Mulhouse, Alsace*

164 (right) *The demon Lilith, from an Assyrian bas-relief in the British Museum*

165 Sixteenth-
century engraving based
on a painting by
Brueghel the Elder,
showing St James in an
alchemist's den
inhabited by demons.
The picture is
sometimes wrongly said
to represent a Sabbat

166 Demonic fish-
man whispering into the
ear of a human. Such
images are derived
ultimately from
initiation symbolism.
From the façade of San
Michele in Pavia

portrayed on the façade of San Michele in Pavia (Figure 166).

According to this occult theory, therefore, under certain conditions man might penetrate into the higher world, where the invisible angels and demons had their existence. Equally, the demons might wish to descend into the material plane in a visible form. Although they preferred to remain invisible, sometimes it was necessary for them to take on a physical form so that they could do their evil work more effectively. What were these appearances which a devil might take on when interpenetrating the time and space of the world natural to man?

The use of demon images in mockery of the initiate wisdom of occultism is nowhere more obvious than in the pictures of demons with long or grotesque tongues. The tongue is often used in post-Christian symbolism as a sign of the spoken word, and by extension it is also a symbol of the Word itself – that is, of Christ as the Logos. It does not take much power of imagination to see that the demons with grotesque tongues, such as may be seen in Figure 168 from the façade of Lincoln cathedral, may represent a demonic mockery of the power of Christ. As is so often the case with the medieval demons which infest the façades and towers of the great cathedrals, however, there is always an element of humorous mockery in such images: they are there merely to remind man that the world of demons is ever present in ordinary life. In medieval times the images of demons were used much more freely as part of decorative

167 *Vishnu as a celestial fish–man in an oriental initiation image*

motives, for theologians and sculptors were well aware of the important role such creatures had in the divine plan. The tendency in medieval times was to treat demons, as well as the images of demons, with respect and with a trace of humour, for it was felt instinctively that, had there been no demons, there would have been no Fall of man, and, had there been no Fall, it is unlikely that there would have been the great redemptive act of Christ upon which Christianity itself rests.

One humorous account we have of a demon visiting the material world is in a tale called *The Search of Belphegor*. The story tells how it has been rumoured in Hell that there is such a thing on earth as married bliss. Now, the demons know quite well that human beings are not designed to live together in harmony, and the very idea of domestic bliss puzzles them. Eventually they send one of their number, the demon Belphegor, to find out if there is any truth in the rumour. His adventures on earth are very wittily described in the several surviving legends, but what is

interesting is that, because Belphegor does not wish to draw attention to himself, he adopts a form as near to the human as possible. Being a demon, he cannot appear entirely as a human, as he wishes: for example, he cannot disguise his horns or his animal-like feet, and therefore he has to go out in the world in these impediments (Figure 169). This semi-human form is the most respectable appearance that the demon can adopt in the material world.

Where did the 'respectable demon' get his horns, and where did the majority of demons get their cloven hooves? If the demons were really invisible, where did this widespread notion of horns and hooves arise? The answer to both these questions is not easy to come by, but it is likely that the horns were a symbol of the crescent Moon. Once upon a time people believed that the Moon was itself the home of the demons. They did not believe that the demons lived on the Moon, but that they swarmed in the space between the Moon and the earth – in what the ancients called the sphere of the Moon. The lunar sphere, sometimes called the starry region of the demons, was that vast aerial space between the earth and the physical body of the Moon: the earth 'swam' in this spiritual sphere, which was the natural habitation of the demons. It was, in effect, the astral sphere, or the lowest and darkest level of the astral sphere, the word 'astral' meaning 'star-like'. The horns of the Devil were really the outer symbol which linked the Devil, and the thinking of the Devil, with the Moon. As we have seen, there are many images of the Virgin Mary standing on the crescent of the Moon to show that she has overcome evil; so, by a reversal of the symbolism, the demons wear crowns of the lunar crescent to show that they are dominated by evil.

Sometimes the crescents are disguised, for at times the horns are nothing more than short stumps (Figure 168), while other times they are long and undulating, as in the demon that is dragging away a boy who has been sold to him by

170 *A hairy red demon dragging away a boy sold to it by the child's parents. Hand-coloured woodcut of the late fifteenth century. The 'hairy' demon was not uncommon in medieval art; it may have been derived from Asmodeus of Babylonian demonology*

his parents (Figure 170). This particular demon is very hairy, reminding us somewhat of the original Asmodeus (see below), but his feet are not hooves, as is often the case with medieval demons.

The emphasis on horns may also be a result of how the Bible chose to describe one of the most awful of demons in the Book of Revelation. This demon was the Beast with seven heads and ten horns, the Beast 'which was, and is not', and which came from the bottomless pit. The imagery of seven heads and ten horns is fairly definitive, and many medieval artists tried visualizing this demon with pencil and brush.

The cloven hooves of demons are perhaps a little easier to trace. Some demonologists insist that the goat-like hooves are merely a throwback to Roman times, when the nature spirit Pan was pictured as half man, half goat, with hairy legs and cloven feet. Some medieval images of the Devil

suggest a direct line between the demons and this ancient Pan (Figure 171). However, other demon-ologists reject the Pan theory of demonic hooves, and claim that the image of the devil goes back to the *Seirizziim* of the ancient Hebrews, a word which was used for the Devil but which also meant 'goat'.

It is surprising just how many of the medieval demons are relics of the ancient pre-Christian gods. For example, the terrible Astaroth was a demon who would appear in conjuration rites riding a hideous dragon, with a snake in his right hand. Originally Astaroth was a female fertility god of the Semitic races, called Ashtart. She was turned into a demon is a most curious way: in ancient times certain rabbis decided to insert in the names of a number of foreign gods the vowels from the word *boshet* (*bOshEt*), which means 'abomination'. By means of this change the fertil-ity goddess Ashtart became 'AshtOrEth' and by a

171 *The Devil blowing a horn to summon witches to the Sabbat. After the* Lectionum Antiquarum *of Ludovicus Ricchierus (1571 edition)*

been the beautiful angel Lucifer (the name in Latin means 'light bearer'), but after the fall he became an enemy of God, Satan. And the name Satan, where did that come from? Almost certainly it is from the Hebraic *saitan*, which is one of the general names for demons, used to denote those invisible devilish beings who work against the creative power of God.

Asmodeus is a curious name, for it may be traced back to a Babylonian word *ashema-deva*, meaning 'hairy demon'. The last part of this name, *deva*, appears to have come from an ancient Indian (Sanskrit) term for a god. In other words, just as many of the Christian demons were really ancient gods, so some of the Persian demons appear to have been gods in far distant times.

Now the interesting thing about Asmodeus is that he is one of the demons mentioned in Holy Writ. He is the demon who possessed Sarah, the woman whom Tobias had fallen in love with and wished to marry. This demon had killed off seven of her previous suitors, however, and Sarah was no longer high on the list of those seeking a wife. With the help of an archangel, Tobias manages to exorcise this demon and all ends happily. When in later times artists sought to illustrate the apocryphal Book of Tobit in which the story of this exorcism is found, they had to visualize the demon in some form or another. The tradition of the demon of wrath as a furry demon had been lost by this time. At the same time, the magical tradition (found mainly in the black books of demons, demonology, pact, and so on, which we now call the grimoires) presented Asmodeus as a terrible monster in a form which was just not appropriate for a biblical illustration. So what could an enterprising illustrator do? He ignores tradition and makes of his Asmodeus an ordinary demon with horns and hooves, adding for good measure a rather hideous face and tail. This conventional demon may be seen to the right in Figure 172, being driven off by the Archangel Raphael.

Because of the widely held notion that demons were fallen angels, many pictures of demons show them with wings. However, it is only rarely that such wings are like those of exotic birds, or made from peacock feathers, like those of angels; it is more usual for the wings of demons to look like those of bats or other creatures of the night. In his great poems on Purgatory and Hell the Italian poet Dante often mentions that the demons have wings, and so most of the illustrations to his *Divina Commedia* show demons with bat wings in the fallen angel tradition (Figure 174).

The fact that many of the terrible demons of the late-medieval period were really debased pagan gods is revealed in the triple-headed demon Haborym (Figure 173). His cat head is derived from the Egyptian pagan goddess Bastet, who was cat-headed and sometimes called Mau, meaning 'little cat'. Besides being feline, she is also linked with fire, for she and her cat goddess sister

few strokes of the pen was transformed into an abominable demon.

Lucifer is another demon with a history of decline from godhead to demonhood. His name was used to denote the lovely star Venus, when she was visible as the Morning Star, preceding the Sun in the dawn sky. The poet Milton was merely following an old idea when he gave the name Satan (meaning 'enemy') to Lucifer after his fall from Heaven. In the morning of the world he had

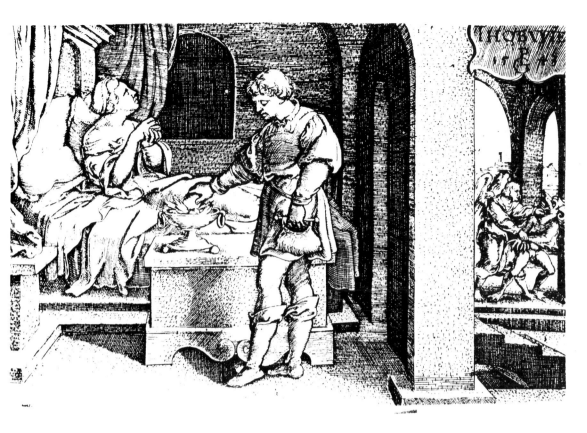

172 (above) *Engraving by Georg Pencz (1540) showing Tobias burning the innards of his magical fish, enabling the Archangel (right) to drive away the devil Asmodeus, who has killed seven men*

173 (right) *The demon Haborym as visualized by Collin de Plancy in 1863, from material supplied by traditional grimoires. It is possible that the three heads hark back to a half-digested Egyptian demonology*

Bubastis killed the serpent Apep by burning him in flames. The snake god was cold and evil, like our own Devil (Figure 117), so we may see in the two blue heads of Figure 173 a reference to the underlying duality of heat and cold derived from Egyptian symbolism. In medieval grimoires Haborym was recognized as the demon of incendiarism, yet his triple heads point to an occult tradition that the realm of man (the demonic human head at the centre) is bordered by dualities, here expressed as a feline symbol of warmth and a viperish symbol of cold.

Each new religion seems to make demons from the gods of earlier religions. It is interesting to observe that a little earlier we looked at the fish–man of Figure 167 and saw that it related to the idea of a wise initiate who had gained insight into the two worlds. A similar image of a fish–man from ancient Babylonia is linked with the same notion – it depicts the hero–king Gilgamesh in the symbolic gear of an initiate (Figure 176). This curious fish-like headgear is said by some to be the origin of the papal headdress, which does

174 *The winged Erynes, as visualized by Gustave Doré in his illustrations to Dante's* Inferno *(canto ix)*

175 *Detail from Albrecht Dürer's engraving of* Knight, Death and the Devil, *1513*

indeed have all the appearance of being a huge fish mouth gaping at the skies – the symbolism pointing to the idea that the Pope is a high initiate. What is of real interest to demonologists is that the fish–man, who in Babylonian times represented the highest level of initiation and was known by the name Dagon, was in later times misunderstood and demoted in the same way as many of the ancient gods. In some of the medieval demon lists and grimoires we find mention of the devil Dagon who is part man, part fish.

For all their many names, and for all they were very often revisualizations in demonic form of god-like beings, there was nothing in the lists of demons compiled in pre-Christian times that might compete with those which developed in medieval Europe. The true medieval demon is really a product of the demented imagination of the witchcraft delusions and trials, their faces and forms resembling animals rather than humans (see Figures 172 and 178). Such demons were probably never seen either by witches or by their trial judge save in their imaginations, yet a million woodcuts which illustrate the witchcraft stories portray the Devil himself as a horned and cloven-hoofed human with a hideous face (Figure 175). It was believed that the Devil, who worked his evil on earth through his thousands of witch and warlock slaves, must himself adopt a semi-human form. Since the slaves and minions of the Devil were human, it was felt reasonable to portray even the archfiend himself in a form which resembled the human. It was only after the full terror of the witchcraft persecutions was over that the popular books began to turn the Devil back into a monster with a non-human form. Once again artists felt free to portray the Devil as a goat-like monster, set within a framework of occult symbols.

The image of the Devil in Figure 177 was drawn by a well-known occultist in the nineteenth century, and he knew very well that the star on the head of his Satanic Majesty was itself very ancient. This five-pointed star had indeed been used in Egyptian hieroglyphics as a symbol of God and spiritual power, and in later times became one of the most important symbols of purity and spirituality in occult lore. One might therefore consider it surprising (if not shocking) to find this image of purity and goodness in a diabolic image. However, if you look carefully at the figure, you will be able to trace a reversal of this star in the shape of the Devil's face. The two horns are the upper points of the star, the two ears are the horizontal points, and the sharp, bearded chin forms the lower point. Now the interesting thing is that this second star can be considered as the forehead star reversed. The forehead star has one point directed towards the heavens, whereas this larger star has its point directed towards the earth, or, indeed, towards Hell at the centre of the earth. In fact, the whole image deals with reversals: there are two crescent moons – one white, one black; the two snakes arising from the sexual parts of the devil are black and white, and so on. This notion of reversal is linked with the important Satanic concept that the Devil is God inverted. Demonologists never tire of claiming that the reversed five-pointed star looks like a primitive drawing of the Devil's head, with horns and a goat-like beard. The symbol is deeper than this, of course, for it really represents the upturning or reversal of the ancient power and goodness of the gods, and the placing of this power in the hands, or claws, of the devils.

In its darker days the Christian religion created myriads of demons, more numerous than can be counted. When St Macarius prayed to God to be allowed to see the hosts of invisible demons, he was astounded to find that indeed their name was legion; 'they are as numerous as bees,' he wrote later, still shaking. In the sixteenth century the French physician John Weyer confounded popular and legal opinion by maintaining that the accounts of devil worship at Sabbats were merely 'imaginary'; he insisted that the goat–devil of the witches was nothing other than the product of sick minds. And yet even a man of such insight still calculated that there were seventy-two

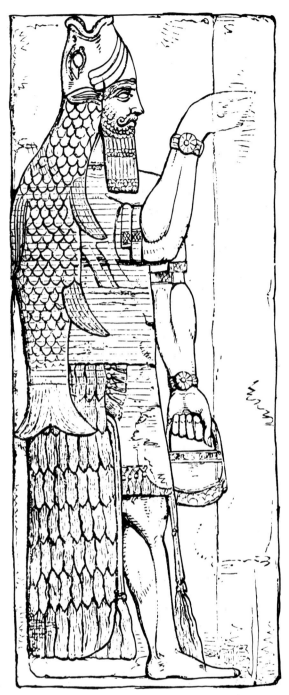

176 *Representation of the Babylonian sun-god hero Gilgamesh. Note the headdress of a fish body, which originally pointed to the idea of Gilgamesh being an initiate into the ancient mysteries. In later times such images were misinterpreted as being demonic – see, for example, Figure 166*

demon princes of Hell, in command of nearly seven and a half million devils.

This number seventy-two was not really haphazard, for Weyer (who had been a student of the notorious sixteenth-century occultist Cornelius Agrippa) had taken the number from a special book of black magic called the *Lemegeton*. The *Lemegeton* is a strange text on black magical rites, listing seventy-two demons by name and rank as though they were so many soldiers on the side of evil. More important, this same text gives instructions on how these demons might be conjured from within the safety of the special protective magic circle which keeps the demon from doing any evil to the conjuring magician.

177 *An extravagantly symbolic representation of the Devil as visualized by the journalist and occultist Eliphas Levi in his influential* Dogme et Rituel de la Haute Magie *(1856)*

The *Lemegeton* takes it for granted that all the demons are normally invisible. However, the text also insists that if someone who has learned the dangerous art of conjuration follows the correct rites, and commands by name one of the demons to appear, then these demons do so in a personalized and recognizable form. The *Lemegeton* actually describes the demonic forms in which these devils will show themselves: few of them are pleasant, as might be expected. Baal, one of the most powerful of demons, would appear with the head of a toad or a cat, in an image which is once again a throwback to the Egyptian gods, and in this form he would teach 'knowledge of all kinds, and tell the magician of the secrets of invisibility'. Naberius appears with three heads, is 'bird-like', and suffers from a sort of demonic St Vitus's dance, as the grimoires insist that he is 'unable to

stand still'. In fact, the notion of a demon with a bird-like head seems to have survived from ancient Egyptian images of gods, among which the heads of the ibis, the heron and the falcon were depicted on human bodies to denote certain gods. The double-headed demon Maymon in Figure 178 is probably linked with this old tradition.

In other cases the outer form of the demon appears to symbolize its inner nature. Behemoth, for example, was a demon particularly linked with gluttony and the delights of the belly, and so in the illustrations which show his form he is portrayed as a fat, elephantine monster (Figure 179). When the great artist William Blake decided to illustrate this demon as part of his book on Job, he preferred to ignore the tradition of the *Lemegeton* and went back to the biblical descriptions of Behemoth (in Job, 60), which suggest that Behemoth was a sort of armour-plated hippopotamus (Figure 181). For all the inventiveness of such artists as Blake, however, the traditional notion of demons as horned, animal-like creatures seems to have persisted more strongly than any other idea, and very often there are traces of humour in even the most ghastly image. The remarkable demons from the medieval stained-glass window in Fairford church (Figure 180) show several traditional demons torturing those souls consigned to Hell. However, at the bottom right is a more imaginative demon, with a grotesque face in his belly, and the mouth of his head open as though waiting to receive the soul of the sinner being wheeled towards him in a wheelbarrow by a blue, horned demon.

Although he is not mentioned in the *Lemegeton*, the leader of the ghastly crew of seventy-two demons of Solomon is Beelzebub, about whose name specialists have argued for centuries. Some insist that the word is from the old *beel-ze-bul*, meaning 'god of the dunghill'. In the certain knowledge that some ancient Greeks would make an annual sacrifice to flies (which swarmed around dunghills), Beelzebub was later called Lord of the Flies. This in turn meant that when he was portrayed in popular grimoire literature he was visualized as a huge fly (Figure 182). The piratic skull and crossbones on the wings in this image are merely an imaginative addition of the nineteenth-century artist, for they are not mentioned in any of the descriptions of Beelzebub. By the nineteenth century the demons were no longer the living reality they had been during the witchcraft delusions. The skull and crossbones were more likely to strike terror into the heart of someone than was an image of a monstrous fly. This is another example of how the images of unseen things, such as demons, are drawn or painted according to ideas current in the mind of the artist.

One of the reasons why the grimoire literature insisted upon providing the names of the seventy-

178 *The demon king Maymon from a fifteenth-century grimoire. The image of a double-headed bird is derived from alchemical illustrations. Private collection*

two demons was because it was widely believed that knowledge of the secret name of a demon gave a magician power over that demon in a magic circle. The name was a secret power or password, but it was not the only secret by which a demon might be conjured and bossed around. There was another way in which a demon might be controlled: this was by means of a secret personal symbol, sometimes called a 'seal', a 'character' or a 'sigil'. A number of these sigils, for the demons Belial, Morax, Naberius, Shax and Vepar, all from a sixteenth-century grimoire manuscript, are reproduced in Figure 183.

By the sixteenth century there was scarcely anything secret about these magical graphics, for they were copied in thousands of grimoires; yet even so large numbers of magicians insisted that it was still possible to conjure up the demons by means of these curious figures. While they are very interesting, they do not tell us anything about the demons themselves. The sigil for the demonic Shax would not suggest that he is conjured because of his ability to strike people deaf, dumb and blind, or to reveal to the magician the site of hidden treasure. Nor would we guess that his favourite appearance was in the form of a bird. Nor does the sigil for Morax hint at his minotaur-like appearance (he is said to appear as a bull-headed man), or that he will teach the magician such things as occult knowledge, astrology and the magical use of stones and herbs. The boat-like sigil for the demon Vepar, on the other hand, might hint that he is a sea demon who appears in the guise of a mermaid, and who will, on the command of the conjuring magician, cause shipwrecks, storms and death by drowning.

135

As we have seen, many of the early Babylonian demons were named and described, which would suggest that at least someone had seen them, or at least pretended to have seen them. It was claimed even in those days that the initiates trained in the secret schools had power to see both angels and demons, and perhaps such descriptions as were set down in writing came from these initiates. Certainly the story of one Babylonian plague demon appears to have come from one of the schools in which initiates were trained. The devil Namtar of Babylonian mythology was a plague demon: he is the one who smites the lovely Ishtar with a ghastly disease when she goes to Aralu (the Babylonian equivalent of Hell) in search of Tammuz. Later, on the orders of the demon queen Allatu, Namtar sprinkles Ishtar with the Waters of Life to remove the disease and bring her back to perfect health. This ritual is paralleled even today in the Church process of exorcism, for the person possessed by a demon is sprinkled with holy water at the very beginning of the rite designed to drive out the devil.

179 (above)   *The demon Behemoth visualized by Collin de Plancy in 1863. The biblical tradition is continued only in the demonic head*

181 (right)   *The demons Behemoth and Leviathan as visualized by William Blake in his illustration to the Book of Job (1825). Blake's demonology is intensely personal and often reverses the established concepts*

180 (right)   *Sections of stained glass showing Purgatory and Hell in the west window of the church of St Mary at Fairford. Satan (to the bottom right) has a gaping fish's head as a crown, recalling such 'demonic' images as Figure 176*

Can any understand the spreadings of the Clouds
the noise of his Tabernacle

Also by watering he wearieth the thick cloud
He scattereth the bright cloud also it is turned about by his counsels

Of Behemoth he saith, He is the chief of the ways of God
Of Leviathan he saith, He is King over all the Children of Pride

Behold now Behemoth which I made with thee

WBlake invenit & sculpt

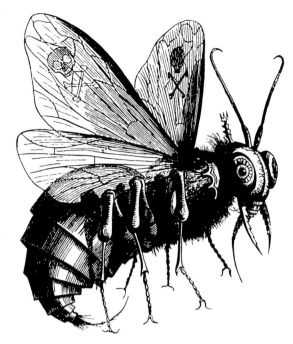

182 (right) *The demon Beelzebub as Lord of the Flies, after Collin de Plancy, 1863*

183 (below) *A medieval grimoire with marginal glosses including some of the sigils for the demons. Private collection*

In ancient images of exorcism, as in medieval Christian images, we see demons being driven away by specially trained priests, and always they leave the body of the possessed by way of the mouth (Figure 184). This notion might be linked with the idea that demons lived in the invisible aether, or spiritual air, and humans may 'breathe in' demons through their noses or mouths. There may also be a link with the idea of the demonic names; some demonologists believe that it is possible to control demons only if we know their names. If a person possessed by a demon can pronounce its real name, then he may in a sense breathe it out from his body, along with his breath. This is almost certainly the reason why so much attention was placed by demonologists on the name (sometimes on the secret name) of the individual demon.

Just as knowledge of a demonic name or sigil is essential in conjuration, so is such knowledge important in exorcism. Unwanted demons often obsessed or possessed unfortunate humans and even animals, so that one of the many duties of the medieval priests was concerned with keeping back demons, or in getting rid of demons who had succeeded in taking control over an unfortunate human being. Part of this ritual of exorcism required that the priest (having made certain that the person was indeed possessed by a devil) should attempt to learn the name of the demon. It was recognized that some illnesses had similar symptoms to possession, and that some people would pretend to be possessed for their own personal gain. One nun who found herself pregnant pretended to be possessed by three demons, and the officiating priest 'exorcised' two of them before her real condition became evident. Fortunately the priest had an excellent set of rules by which he could determine whether or not a person was possessed, and these included fainting fits, paroxysms, the vomiting of strange objects (pins, needles, stones, clots of blood, even eels, insects and mice). Additionally the one possessed would speak with a different voice, and his or her appearance might change, becoming more and more demonic as the possession persisted. In such cases the demon was, as it were, making himself visible through the body of a living human being.

Having made sure that the person to be exorcised was not shamming in any way, the priest would then command the demon to give his name and rank. The knowledge of the demon's name was essential to genuine exorcism, for the name (or the seal of the demon) was the only way by which a demon might be identified and then controlled. A typical response can be found in a famous exorcism of a lady of high birth in Auch in 1618: in answer to the questions put to it by the numerous priests charged with the exorcism, the devil named himself as Mahonin and said that he was a fallen archangel who normally dwelled in water.

In fact, one of the most interesting lists of demon names and demonic secrets was provided during such an exorcism. One Father Sebastien Michaelis, who had been made responsible for a convent of nuns in Aix-en-Provence, had to rid one of the nuns, Sister Madeleine, of a demon which was causing her a great deal of trouble. He left an account of this exorcism, in 1612, and tells us that he started it in the normal way, sprinkling the nun with holy water and then demanding that the demon should reveal its name and rank. He was, however, surprised to find that this devil, after admitting that he was the infamous Balberith, who specialized in hatred, murder and blasphemy, proved also to be hypertalkative. Balberith provided the astonished Michaelis with a blueprint of the complete hierarchy of Hell, which was a dark mirror image of the angelic hierarchy of Heaven. Sixteen of the demons he listed were the most famous in demonology – Beelzebub, the Lord of the Flies, was there as leader, while Leviathan, Asmodeus and Astaroth were a little lower down the scale.

Although Balberith gave the names of sixteen demons, he freely admitted that there were nine ranks of demons, stretching from the fallen Seraphim to the fallen Angels. This list of nine ranks is upside down, like the five-pointed star we traced in Figure 177, for it was supposed in medieval times that there were nine ranks of angels, stretching from the Seraphim to the Angels. The ranks of Hell were a parody of the ranks of Heaven: instead of God being at the top of the angelical ranks, the Devil was placed at the bottom of the demonic ranks and located at the centre of the earth. The number nine is a magical number, being three times three, the Trinity tripled, but it was also a magical number before the Christians emphasized the Trinity in their symbols. There used to be a Roman ceremony during the festival of the Lemuria (held on 9, 11 and 13 May each year) designed to propitiate the demons or shades called the *lemurae*. The Roman writer Ovid tells us that it was the practice of those haunted by such shades to throw nine black beans over their heads, and shout at the spectres nine times to leave the house. It was a well-established practice to wear an amulet designed to ward of demonic evil for exactly nine days, and lovers of Shakespeare will remember that the three witches in Macbeth prepare their magical

184   *San Zeno exorcising a woman by driving the demon from her mouth. From a twelfth-century bronze panel on the doors of San Zeno, Verona*

stew with a chant evoking three times three to make up nine, which they clearly regarded as a diabolic number. Perhaps such symbolism is the reason why Milton insists that, when the rebel angels fell from Heaven to become the first demons, they plummeted down for nine full days?

8 Alchemy: The Secrets of Inner Rebirth

The popular notion of the alchemist is that of an old man working at a hot furnace in a laboratory filled with curiously shaped bottles (Figure 185), perhaps even with a stuffed alligator or monstrous fish hanging from the ceiling. It is believed that such a man was intent on trying to make gold or silver from ordinary metals, such as lead or iron.

Without doubt there were people who thought that it was possible so to refine metals and stones as to obtain from them a secret gold. No doubt some of them really believed that they might find in nature a magical stone or powder which would make them rich beyond their wildest dreams. However, the genuine alchemist was not working towards these ends. The gold he sought was really not a metal at all. Rather than taking the path to worldly riches, the alchemist was seeking an inner secret, looking for the way to develop his own inner world of vision and understanding. The gold of the alchemists was sometimes called Mercury or the Inner Sun. In choosing the name Mercury to denote the thing for which they

searched, the alchemists had in mind that the god Mercury was in ancient times the one responsible for communication with the gods; they too were seeking for a way of communicating directly with the spiritual realm of the gods. The secret path they sought was really the pathway to Heaven, and their riches were not the riches of this earth.

The genuine alchemists was concerned with spiritual things. They did not look into dross metals, such as lead or iron, to seek out their magical gold. Instead they looked into the dross of man, that ordinary, untransformed inner life of man, which they visualized as a sort of dead weight, containing more riches of miraculous powers than anyone could ever imagine. They believed that, if they worked at this lower part of man, they might so refine it as to change it into the higher life. A perfectly natural event which alchemists liked to compare with their art is the way in which a dark, ugly chrysalis turns into a beautiful butterfly. This transformation of ugliness into beauty is one reason why from very

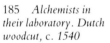

185 *Alchemists in their laboratory. Dutch woodcut, c. 1540*

ancient times the butterfly was linked with the human soul. The serious alchemist sought to discover a secret whereby the wonderful powers he could feel in his own soul, or which he could sense within his own inner being, might be released into the world in their full glory.

In the Tarot cards the first image is that of 'The Fool', who walks along a road with a sack on his back, a curious animal clawing his legs (Figure 186). It was said that this fool carried in his sack an unbelievable wealth of treasure, but that he was too foolish to bother looking inside the sack in order to find what was weighing him down. This image was said by occultists to be a parable of human life, in that few people are concerned with looking into their inner life to discover its hidden riches of the soul. It is only such a view of alchemy that explains why some occult pictures show an alchemist using a bellows to heat up a huge cauldron in which stands a man who is presumably being boiled alive (Figure 187).

There was almost something religious in the attitude of the real alchemist, and one should not be surprised to find a statue of a man wearing an alchemist's hat (Figure 188) in a cathedral. This figure, hidden away among the gargoyles of the towers of Notre Dame in Paris, is even to this day called 'The Alchemist'. One modern writer, Walter Lang, having admitted that alchemy is a sort of religion, points out that there are many alchemical symbols in the stone carvings of Notre Dame. 'It has long been believed that the Gothic cathedrals were secret textbooks of some hidden knowledge: that behind the gargoyles and the glyphs, the rose windows and the flying buttresses, a mighty secret lay, all but openly displayed.'

Alchemists called their search for the inner gold the 'Great Work' or the 'Hermetic Secret'. The word 'hermetic', which is often nowadays used in the idea of hermetically sealing a bottle or some such container, was actually derived from the name of the Greek equivalent of Mercury, the god Hermes, who is supposed to have taught the secrets of alchemy to men. A large number of the processes of the alchemists are shown in strange pictures which depict changes and transformations taking place in hermetically sealed bottles (Figure 189). The bottle is usually nothing more than a symbol of the human soul or body, and the secret changes taking place inside the bottle are symbols for the soul's growth. The work of the alchemists remained a hermetic or hidden art, sealed off from those who were in one way or another unfit to have the secret knowledge, restricted only to those few who were prepared to pass their lives in meditative discipline and quiet research, or who had been fortunate enough to find a successful alchemist who could teach them the art. To ensure that the secrets of alchemy were preserved, almost every stage in the process of the Great Work was hidden behind a complex sym-

186   'The Fool' card of the Tarot pack, from an eighteenth-century edition of the Marseilles design. For all its title, the card is usually taken by occultists as representative of the seeker after knowledge, as the initiate who has higher knowledge and therefore often appears foolish to those around him

bolism, so that nowadays it is often difficult to understand what such stages were.

One of the popular notions about alchemy is quite reasonable, however. This is the idea that the alchemist had huge furnaces on which he heated his chemicals. These furnaces certainly did exist in a number of houses and secret laboratories, at least of those alchemists who followed the more practical side of the secret art. In most alchemical textbooks, however, these furnaces are once again usually symbols – this time of heat. The huge bath furnace of Figure 187 was designed by the occultist to resemble a font. In the early days of Christianity (even in those times when alchemy was practised), the rite of baptism was conducted in huge fonts and involved total immersion, usually three times, once for each member of the Trinity. The symbolism of Figure 187 therefore shows that the text to which this is an illustration is more concerned with the spiritual background to alchemy than with anything strictly materialistic.

In fact, the various furnaces and heating apparatuses (Figure 190) used by alchemists play an important part in occult symbolism, and the reason why may be seen in Figure 187. It was

141

187 *The alchemist as a spiritual worker nourishing the growth of the inner man, within a framework of Christian symbolism. From the manuscript called 'Splendour Solis' in the British Library*

188 *Gargoyle on the parapet to the east of the west front of Notre Dame in Paris. The figure is that of an alchemist, the most obvious sign being his hat, which is similar to those used in initiation imagery, particularly in images associated with the Mithraic cult. Presumably the figure is presiding over the alchemical symbolism on the cathedral façade below*

believed that the first stage which the alchemist had to follow in the difficult work of transforming the inner man was to burn away (or boil away) all the darkness and dross of what was sometimes called the 'lower man'. The inner or higher man was eternal, linked with the eternal stars, and the alchemists believed that this could be reached and developed if everything lower was purged away by flame. Naturally, this does not mean that the aspiring alchemist therefore leaped into the fire of his furnace, for this heat or burning was of a symbolic kind, just as were the ashes and carbon which were left from the consuming flames. The true alchemist wished to burn away for ever the lower part of his being and have access to the stars. One direct result of this concern (real or symbolic) with furnaces was that the alchemists were often called 'fire philosophers'.

The alchemists themselves called their fire by many names, but one of the most frequently used terms for fire was 'the Sun', by which they meant the Inner Sun. Figure 191 must appear most strange to someone who is not aware of the symbols which alchemists used to disguise their inner search. Why is the lion green, and why is it eating the Sun? The name 'Green Lion' was used by alchemists to denote one of the stages of their inner work. In the sequence of the work there are the 'Old Lion', the 'Ordinary Lion' and the 'Red

Lion'. We might understand this idea to some extent by seeing the lion as the dark, lower part of man – the beast – which needs to be refined by the open warmth and light of the Sun. If this animal nature is tamed, then the whole man is perfected and he will attain great inner strength. Certainly the alchemical texts say that when the Green Lion has been prepared – which is to say, when it has taken the Sun into its being – then the inner process of transmutation is completed. The leading Arabic alchemist Avicenna writes: 'when the Green Lion is complete, then it has the power to change a thousand times its own weight into pure gold.' There is a level on which one may take this digestion of the Sun as being yet another heating or refining symbol which is so popular in alchemy.

The symbolism of the lion is derived mainly from astrology, for Leo the Lion is itself ruled by the Sun, which in turn rules the human heart. This should illustrate that alchemy, more than any other occult science, has called to its service the symbols of all other magical systems, from astrology and demonology to amuletic magic and initiation symbolism. In particular it made use of the symbols designed by an occult brotherhood known as the Rosicrucians, who employed alchemy as a convenient system of symbols to hide behind its complex forms their own spiritual

189 *The symbol of spiritual growth within a hermetically sealed bottle. Around the central image are the children of Mercury (Hermes), those who fall under his rule and participate in mercurial enterprises. The secret or spagyric art is sometimes called the hermetic art. From the 'Splendour Solis' manuscript in the British Library*

teachings. Many of the remarkable images which have survived from the heyday of alchemy are filled with occult symbols (Figure 192), with snippets of lore from talismanic magic and from herbalism or the use of precious stones, with images derived from the religious life, and with secrets derived from the traditions concerned with zodiacal, planetary and elemental beings. But it is astrology which played the most important role in alchemy. It was said that no successful Great Work could be done unless the alchemist had calculated a beneficial time, or a good horoscope, to begin his work.

The seven metals favoured by the alchemists were gold, silver, mercury, copper, iron, tin and lead. Each of these was linked with a particular planet, the idea being that the nature of each planet was reflected on the earth through its distinctive metal. The relationship was: gold – Sun; silver – Moon; mercury – Mercury; copper – Venus; iron – Mars; tin – Jupiter; lead – Saturn.

The Sun and Moon were sometimes called by their Latin names *Sol* and *Luna*, as may be seen in the names at the top of Figure 193. The seven planets and the seven metals were linked with a very large number of occult correspondences. For example, the seven days of the week were also associated with planets and metals: this explains why, in Figure 193, Saturday is portrayed as an old man leaning on a stick. Saturday is Saturnday, and the old image of Saturn was derived from the Greek god Chronos, the time god. The curious curved knife in the hand of Saturn really goes back to the idea of Old Father Time's scythe. Saturn is sometimes portrayed as a crippled old man, which explains why this image for Saturday is using a crutch. The goat in the black roundel is a reference to the zodiacal sign Capricorn, which is ruled by the planet Saturn. The roundel behind the figure is meant to depict the waterbearer Aquarius (the upturned water jug is all that one can make out), which is also ruled by Saturn. Each of these seven images of the days of the week are linked with the seven planets, the zodiacal signs and a whole host of other symbols.

The names for planets and metals were regarded as being interchangeable, and it was believed that the planets and metals existed inside every human being. It was the balance between these that made up the human temperament, personality and even the physical appearance. As a result the alchemical and occult traditions insist that there are seven different types of person, linked with the seven planets or metals. The Saturn type, for example, is one who is of a morose and melancholic disposition (an emotional cripple). Such a man was said to be suffering from an excess of Saturn, or from lead poisoning. The opposite cosmic force to the heavy Saturn was the Moon, which appears to move so quickly in the sky (Saturn appears to be the slowest planet). For this reason a man

190 (left) *Alchemist separating the impure (at the bottom of his vase) from the pure. To his left is the Bath of Mary, a method of gentle heating often interpreted by occultists as a reference to a special spiritual exercise*
191 (below) *'Green Lion', a standard alchemical term, marks the consummation of the preparation of 'Red Stone' from* Prima materia *or dross. The relationship between this image and Figure 133 is obvious. From* Rosarium Philosophorum *(1550)*

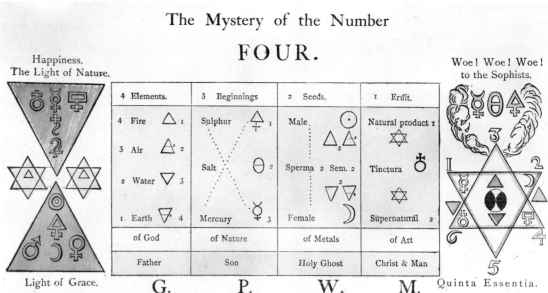

The Mystery of the Number
FOUR.

Happiness.
The Light of Nature.

Woe! Woe! Woe!
to the Sophists.

4 Elements.	3 Beginnings	2 Seeds.	1 Fruit.
4 Fire △ 1	Sulphur ⚴ 1	Male ☉	Natural product 1 ✡
3 Air △ 2	Salt ⊖ 2	Sperma 2 Sem. 2 △ △ 2	Tinctura ☿
2 Water ▽ 3			
1 Earth ▽ 4	Mercury ☿ 3	Female ☾	Supernatural 2 ✡
of God	of Nature	of Metals	of Art
Father	Son	Holy Ghost	Christ & Man
G.	**P.**	**W.**	**M.**

Light of Grace.

He who understands this figure, will see how one thing originates from
another one. Everything exists fundamentally of four elements. They produce
three Beginnings, and from these originate two sexes, Sun and Moon, but
the latter two produce the Son, the mortal and the divine Man.

Quinta Essentia.

Smoke will arise above
your heads from eternity
to eternity, and be a torture to you.

192 *A hermetic
commentary on the
magic of four, from a
hand-coloured edition of
the 1785 translation of*
Geheime Figuren der
Rosencreuzer

suffering from the moodiness of Saturn might be cured by taking into himself a little of the Moon – which is, of course, silver. Very many of the old alchemical texts are really nothing more than medical treatises, indicating how the human being may be healed by means of the proper administering of earths, powders, stones and plants.

One result of this way of thinking is that many alchemical documents and figures are often filled with astrological symbols and ideas. A fairly typical example of this is seen in Figure 194, in which the astrologer is pointing to the image of the zodiacal sign Scorpio, which we must presume is beneficial for the operation he intends for his great furnace and jars. A more complicated example is seen in Figure 195, which is a pair of horoscope charts relating to alchemical operations. Each of the animals, birds and flowers around these figures has a symbolic importance – the five-petalled flower at the top has a different significance to the four-petalled flower at the bottom, for example.

Besides making use of such astrological and occult symbols from other secret arts, the alchem-

193 *The seven
planets, with the
zodiacal signs over
which they have rule,
apportioned to the seven
days of the week. From
an early sixteenth-
century English
'Shepherd's Calendar'*

ists invented their own symbols from things found in their laboratories and among their chemical preparations. As we have seen, curiously shaped bottles in which the hermetic process of transmutation were said to take place were often meant to be symbols of the human body, within which the 'secret Sun' was hidden. Within these precious bottles – sometimes called alembics – the inner innocent soul was prepared to fly into the world. Some symbols were therefore special to the alchemists. For example, in the process of transmutation there were several clearly marked stages, the first of which was that of heat. This was called 'calcination', which involved reducing the crude matter to a sort of ash, sometimes called 'carbon'. This probably explains why the huge furnace so often dominates pictures of the alchemist's laboratory. In the process of refining the dross materials and other preparations to obtain from them their hidden virtues, there were four methods of heating, each one linked with one of the four elements – Earth, Air, Fire and Water. The most gentle of these was called the *Bain Maria* (Bath of Mary), which was a method of obtaining a slow, general heat, with the pan itself contained within a second protective pan of water: this was 'heat by Water'.

It is in such strange names and images that one begins to see the level upon which the true alchemist worked. To one who was not aware of the inner content of his work, the alchemist might appear to be concerned with warming things in water baths and so on. However, the very term *Bain Maria* points to the Virgin Mary and the idea of washing oneself clean in an image of the power of the ideal woman. This idea of the healing force of the name or image of the Virgin (who was, among other things, a symbol of the perfect soul within each human being) was much more widespread in medieval days than it is in the present time. The picture in Figure 7 demonstrates this, for its shows ordinary people carrying wax models of their sick limbs, or waxen models of sick people, to an image of the Virgin Mary. This is a picture of the pure magic with which medieval Christianity was interwoven, and which was also merged into the practice of alchemy.

Many of the secret processes which took place in the glass jars of the alchemists were symbolized by means of Christian images which had once been pagan. In view of the fact that alchemy was what might be termed a science of the soul, and in view of its connection with the refining of the soul life of man, we should not be surprised that images of the sea, of sea creatures and of fish (Figure 196) frequently appear. In occult symbolism the sea has always been an image of the soul or spirit. The two fish in Figure 197 are from a seventeenth-century textbook on alchemy. These fish are swimming in opposite directions, which, of course, reminds us of the ancient image for the zodiacal sign Pisces (Figure 45). The Latin text

194 (above)   *Alchemists disputing the correct astrological conditions under which to conduct an alchemical operation. Sixteenth-century woodcut*

195 (below)   *Horoscopes cast to determine the times for starting alchemical operations. From Thomas Norton's* Ordinall of Alchemy *(1652 edition)*

Figura II.

Mare est Corpus, duo Pisces sunt?
Spiritus & Anima.

196 (above) *The winged queen as a mermaid. The left-hand pond is a 'cutout' of the burning stick, a reference to the inversion of space which takes place during an alchemical operation. From the 'Sapientia Veterum Philosophorum' manuscript in the Bibliothèque de l'Arsenal, Paris*

197 (right) *The two fishes of Pisces (spirit and soul) submerged in the sea of the unconscious. From Lambsprinck's* De Lapide Philosophico *(1677)*

below Figure 197 explains why they swim in opposite directions – it is because one represents spirit and the other soul, which pull against each other, the spirit longing to return to its proper home in Heaven and the soul, which has fallen in love with the delights of the flesh, pulling to the earth. Such an image is very important in alchemy, for the theory of the fire philosophy was based on the teaching that man consists of body, soul and spirit, and the alchemists used very many symbols to denote these three.

As we saw in the section on demons (chapter 7, p. 125), the fishtail in occult images is usually a sign of the initiate – of one who has earned insight into two worlds, symbolized in the image as the inner (watery) world and the normal outer world. The alchemical image of the siren (Figure 196) is of the same order, and is usually intended to indicate a state in which the alchemist has reached the point of breaking through into the other world, piercing through the veil which hangs between the material realm and the spiritual beyond. The source of the initiate fish–man may be seen in images as widely separated as Hindu images of the initiate–god Vishnu (Figure 167) and the Christian image of Jonah and the whale (Figure 198). It is possible to see the story of Jonah being swallowed by a large fish as an occult symbol for a man who gives up his own lower personality (dies, as it were, to the world) and is then reborn into the world as a new man, with his higher faculties awakened. This rebirth of soul was the aim of the alchemists, of course, and we should therefore not be surprised to find that fishtailed men and women, or siren figures, appear very frequently in alchemical symbols. The water in which these fish–men swim is not the ordinary water of the physical sea or lakes – it is a symbol of a higher level of consciousness, of what the alchemists themselves often called the Quintessence.

The miraculous power of the Quintessence (which we glanced at in our study of earth magic – p. 82) plays as important a part in alchemy as it does in occult symbolism. This is mainly because one of the aims of the alchemist was to attempt to release from ordinary matter (that is, from the fourfold elements) the powerful and magical force of the Quintessence. In the fifteenth century a monk who had occupied himself a great deal with alchemical research wrote that 'alchemy is the science of the elements – it is nothing other than the conversion of these elements into one another.' If it is really possible to derive from the four elements the higher fifth element, which is really the element of life itself, the great healing power, then the true art of transformation would have been discovered.

Some of the strange images used to symbolize the four elements, and the magical Quintessence occur again and again in alchemical documents. It is no accident that the five-petalled flower is at the top of the horoscope charts in Figure 195. This is the transformed four-petalled flower, indicating that by means of the secret art the four elements are harmoniously combined with the magical fifth element – four become five. The symbolism of this is deepened by the fact that the five-petalled flower, symbol of the successful work, is placed over the Sun!

Alchemists often used special symbols for each of the four elements. In some cases the element of Air is symbolized as a chameleon (Figure 199). This may seem strange to us in the modern age, but in the medieval period it was seriously believed that the chameleon ate nothing but air. In other images a more conventional Air symbol was used, as, for example, the form of a bird. The symbol for Fire was more often than not the salamander, sometimes with six legs, sometimes with only four (Figure 200), which likes to live in the flames of fire. Water was symbolized sometimes as a fish, sometimes as water flowing in a stream or from a water jug. Earth had many symbols: sometimes a squirrel, on the ground that the squirrel buried the nuts and seeds which would root in the earth and grow into plants or trees.

Spirit and soul were often visualized as being linked with Water, while the body was associated with Earth. It is the body which is turned to the dark ash of carbon in the alembic, after the first operation. This ash is sometimes called the *Caput mortum* or 'Death's Head', a symbolic skull intended to show that there was nothing still alive in such an ash. It is possible that the pirates' skull and crossbones were derived from the alchemist imagery – their message was that, when the pirates caught another ship, everything would be reduced to useless ashes. The crossed bones were a cynical reference to the cross of Christ, through which symbol he brought healing to the world.

198 (above) *Jonah and the whale – a scarcely disguised reference to initiation imagery (see, for example, Figure 167). Medieval stained glass from St Etienne at Mulhouse, Alsace*

199 (left) *Detail of the title page of* Septem Planetae *(see Figure 88) showing the chameleon as a symbol for the element of Air. The clouds in the picture are also a standard Air symbol (see, for example, Figure 196)*

200   *The salamander or fire newt bathing in the flames. Detail from a plate in Lambsprinck's* De Lapide Philosophico *(1695 edition)*

If we look at the title page from one of the most famous of all books on alchemy, the *Musaeum Hermeticum* (Figure 201), we will find examples of each of the alchemical symbols already mentioned. At the top right the pelican is tearing at its breast to feed its young ones. Below is a man carrying a torch and a bowl of fire – to his left is a four-legged newt which is really a salamander. Below this image is a symbol of Water in the form of a man pouring water on the earth – behind him is a whale and a ship. Opposite, on the left side of the page, a man carries a spade, a fairly ordinary symbol of the earth. In his right hand he carries a squirrel. Above this Earth symbol is the Air symbol, a man walking through wind-blown clouds with a bird perched on his left hand. In the large oval at the bottom of the picture, flanked by images of the Sun (with the lion of Leo) and Moon (with the crayfish, symbol of zodiacal Cancer), is a most curious image. This shows two hermits, old men with sticks, carrying simple lanterns, following a woman who holds in her right hand a Seal of Solomon from which streams a bright light. This Seal of Solomon, as we have already noted (chapter 1), is a symbol of the four elements united by the Quintessence, or fifth element. There is hardly a single part of this curious page which does not contain some occult symbol.

There is one important alchemical symbol which we have not yet looked at, however. In the top left of the page we find an image of the phoenix bird, burning to death in a pyre. The phoenix is one of the most important of all alchemical images, and it is therefore worth look-

ing a little more closely at the occult tradition in order to grasp the meaning behind its symbolism.

The phoenix, which is sometimes called the 'Arabian bird', reminding us that the alchemy which was used in medieval Europe had come mainly from the Arabs, appears in several different myths. The most widely circulated tells how the bird will live for a period of five hundred years, at the end of which it builds itself a nest of precious spices. The nest completed, the phoenix sings a doleful song and then flaps its wings rapidly to set the nest on fire. The bird is soon burned to ashes, and from this mass of carbon there miraculously springs to life a new phoenix. Most occultists link this myth with the idea of human reincarnation, but however the alchemists regarded its esoteric content, we may see in it certain ideas which must have appealed to them: for example, that from the ashes of burned material forms there could spring forth new life. It was with this aim – so to consume themselves in flame that they might find eternal inner life – that the true alchemists worked.

Sometimes the phoenix, which is linked with the Sun, is also presented by the occultists in the form of a peacock (Figure 189). This symbolism is probably connected with a medieval story which tells how the peacock is filled with pride at the beauty of its own tail. Sometimes, however, as it struts around, it glances down at the earth, and there it sees a black cross. The peacock is seeing its own claws, and because it cannot believe that such beauty is carried by such a fragile thing as a cross it screams like a child. The medieval scribes who recorded the story pointed out that it is a parable, for the peacock represents human pride, and that the whole of human life (so deeply enmeshed in pride) is supported by the sacrifice of Christ, which is the cross. The alchemists turned the symbol inside out and presented the beautiful peacock as an image of what man might become when the darkness is removed from his being (Figure 189). This is one reason why the phoenix–peacock was an important symbol for the fire philosophers. Indeed, it became so popular that the bird was eventually adopted by chemists as a symbol of their trade. However, for many centuries before the medieval period it had been used as a symbol of resurrection in Christian circles.

In an important alchemical text called *Treasure of the Alchemists* the sixteenth-century doctor–magician Paracelsus describes a complex operation to make what he calls 'Iliaster', the union of Sulphur, Salt and Mercury. He says that this Iliaster is also called the 'alchemical phoenix'. With such a name as this, the Iliaster must be a very important product, and we must therefore ask ourselves what the union of Sulphur, Salt and Mercury might be.

201 (opposite)   *Title page of* Musaeum Hermeticum, *a famous collection of alchemical texts (1677 edition)*

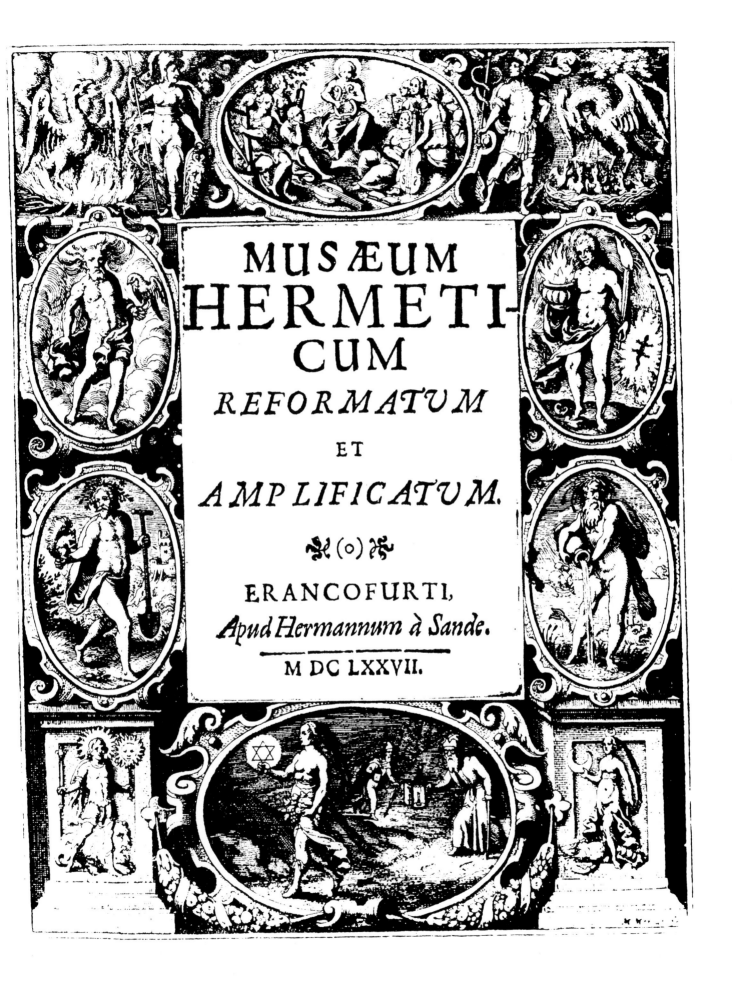

MUSÆUM HERMETI-CUM

REFORMATUM

ET

AMPLIFICATUM.

⚜(o)⚜

ERANCOFURTI,

Apud Hermannum à Sande.

MDC LXXVII.

202 *The third table from Law's edition of Boehme, with a door opened to reveal Hell (or Purgatory) at the feet of the burning man. For the preceding stage, see Figure 82*

From what we have already seen about these three 'substances', we can safely assume that alchemical Sulphur, Salt and Mercury have little or nothing to do with those things which pass under the same names in modern times. The very symbols used to denote them (Figure 84) are confirmation of a deep inner meaning. In fact, the alchemists wrote at great length (in a secret script very difficult to decipher) about these three things, and we may be certain that within the human being Sulphur represents the will forces, Salt the thinking forces, and Mercury the heart forces or the emotional life of man. A union of the three (which is the Iliaster of Paracelsus) is actually a well-balanced, moral man.

It is worthwhile looking a little more closely into this symbolism of what alchemists called the Three Principles. Sulphur, representing the will of man, is located in the stomach and in the sexual parts. In some alchemical images (Figure 82) this is shown as a burning area, as though Hell itself were situated in this part of the body. This picture is one of a series in which certain parts of the picture can be folded back to reveal the inside of the man. The inside is spiritual, rather than material, as one might expect from an alchemical text. It is interesting to compare Figure 82 with Figure 202, which shows a development of the inner man, revealing that, in terms of the alchemical view of man's nature, his lower part is bathed in the flames of fire. The idea behind this symbolism is that the will forces in man are (like flames)

constantly striving upwards and, were they not controlled, they would explode outwards rather like the flames from an active volcano. This is probably one reason why in occultism Hell itself is linked with fire and will with sulphur, and why in popular lore the Devil is reputed to leave behind the smell of sulphur. The alchemists used the symbol ♀ to represent Sulphur. It is made from the symbol which represents Fire (see p. 62).

Salt represents the thought process in man. Occultists link this process with death. Thought itself is said to be a living substance, made of living images, but once it has entered into the human being, it dies and turns to Salt. Thinking takes place in the head, and it is therefore no accident that the alchemists wrote of Salt as being contained in human tears, which stream down towards the Fire within the lower part of the body. As we have seen (pp. 62–3), one alchemical text, *A Discourse of Fire and Salt*, uses a symbol which is essentially that of two triangles interlinked – the one with its apex pointing upwards represents Fire (Sulphur), and that with its apex pointing downwards represents Salt (Water) (Figure 83).

Fire rises and Water sinks. If the two were always meeting, then the human being would be in a state of constant agitation, as they exploded together in steam. For this reason the alchemists insisted that there was a miraculous barrier between them, something which was capable of uniting with both Sulphur and Salt, yet at the same time maintaining its own nature. This mira-

152

HERMES BIRD.

culous substance was Mercury; within the context of the human being, this Mercury is symbol of the human emotional system. It is the emotional realm of man which keeps the intellect of Salt away from the life forces of Sulphur. If one examines the ancient sigil for Mercury ☿ one sees that its design expresses something of its power of mediation between Salt and Sulphur: it is as though it is designed to catch the tears of Salt in its upper crescent, and to keep down the fires of Sulphur with its fourfold cross. In some alchemical images of Mercury we find a small dot within the sigil ☿ to link it with the sacred Quintessence.

This power of Mercury to keep apart the two polarities of man explains to some extent why Mercury is called the Great Healer. The fact that

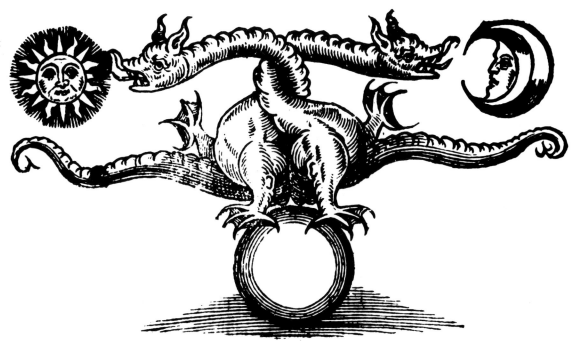

FLEGMAT   SANGVIN

MELANC   COLERIC

205 *Alchemical woodcut of the seventeenth century showing the androgyne composite of man–woman, surrounded by the sigils for the zodiac and set within a quadrature representing the four temperaments*

the Greek name for Mercury is Hermes should also lend a clue as to why the phoenix is often called the Hermes bird (Figure 203): we have noted already that the phoenix was adopted by chemists as a symbol of their trade (p. 150), and now we see why – for the Hermes bird–phoenix is itself involved with healing, and the chemists were originally those people who provided all the mineral and vegetative specifics designed to help heal the sick.

Yet we must recall that the phoenix burns itself periodically to be reborn. Is this merely a reference to the healing process in man or does it have some other significance? In his writings Paracelsus leaves us in no doubt that the alchemical phoenix or Iliaster is nothing more than a symbol of the completely healed, or perfected, human being, who has burned away all the dross of his lower demonic being and is free to fly. The perfected human being is one, with the three parts of his being in their proper place and in harmony: the Mercury of his emotions balances the Salt of his intellect with the Fire of his will. This perfected human being is the true Hermes bird, the aim of the secret practices of the alchemists.

Three is an important number to the alchemists, mainly because of the place which the Three Principles play in their work and literature. Sometimes the three are symbolized in planetary terms, at other times in strange images. The double dragon of Figure 204 is an example of this, for the male planet of the Sun is on one side and the female planet of the Moon is on the other. The two-headed, two-tailed dragon balances on a globe, which might be the earth itself. Where have we already come across the idea of something balancing two other forces? It is the idea of Mercury balancing Sulphur and Salt. Here the dragon, which is the dragon in every human being, is balancing the cosmic male and female, and is balanced on the earth. It is one of the most remarkable ideas of the alchemists that every human being is a hermaphrodite – which is to say that within every man there is a spiritual woman, and that within every woman there is a spiritual man. Certain modern schools of psychoanalysis have been deeply influenced by this alchemical notion, especially that arising from the alchemical insights of C. G. Jung, or, in modern times, psychosynthesis. In addition to there being a woman in every man, and vice versa, there is also a dragon. Every ordinary man leads a dragon, and every ordinary man is also a sort of St George who must eventually slay or tame that dragon.

This dragon is not altogether a wholesome being, therefore, and there is a stage in the alchemical operation in which the alchemist must symbolically fight or control the dragon, to free himself of its influence – an operation which is far from easy. However, when the dragon is tamed or killed, then it is possible for the hermaphrodite to live in harmony. In alchemy the Sun–male is often called the King, and the Moon–female is often called the Queen. There are very many pictures of the King and the Queen together, sometimes as lovers, sometimes as a hermaphrodite (Figure 205). In such images we have again a symbol of harmony, of the whole man/whole woman – for all the image looks as though it consists of two parts (male and female), it really consists of three, for somewhere is the dragon which used to dominate them. One of the secrets of alchemical imagery is that, when you see only two elements, then you should look for the missing third. It is more often than not the missing element which is a clue to the meaning of an alchemical picture. There is often something missing, some secret element, within important alchemical images, and it is this that places them among the most interesting examples of occult art.

There is no picture which illustrates more fully the religious or inner nature of alchemy than the one in Figure 203, a title-page design for a work called 'Hermes Bird'. In this we see the familiar double dragon, with its two heads snarling at the Sun and Moon, much as in Figure 204, but in this

154

206 *Greek alchemical manuscript showing the self-devouring dragon Ouroboros*

207 *The winged dragon Ouroboros, the sixth secret figure in* De Lapide Philosophico *of Lambsprinck (1677)*

case descending from the clouds is a bird, the Hermes bird. It is drawn in exactly the same form as the dove, the ancient Christian symbol of the Holy Spirit!

The most recurrent of all alchemical symbols, then, is the dragon, and from among the many forms which the dragon takes the most frequently used is the Ouroboros or dragon–snake which bites its own tail (Figure 207). Such an image is found in the earliest manuscripts, as, for example, in Figure 206 from a Greek text on astrology, through to a popular collection of occult texts printed in the nineteenth century (Figure 95). The occult significance of this image is very profound and may be studied on many levels. Perhaps the most obvious level is that which takes the dragon as a symbol of time. The dragon is eating its own tail, devouring itself in much the same way that time seems to swallow up itself and the world. The past disappears and time itself is lost – or so it would appear to those who live submerged in time. In devouring its own tail the dragon forms a circle, and it is therefore a convenient image of space, of the inner space, which is itself linked with the passage of time. The alchemists made use of deep symbolism to reflect upon the way this space within the Ouroboros might be used. In

Figure 207, for example, one sees at the centre of the circle of dragon coils the four-clawed foot of the dragon. This image reminds us of the story of the black cross which carries the proud beauty of the peacock, and we might indeed see one level of the occult symbolism of Figure 207 as representing the secret form $\oplus$. This symbol is used in a variety of different occult contexts. In astrology, for example, it is the basis of the horoscope chart, which (as we have seen in chapter 1) represents the emergence of soul into the cross of space and time. In alchemy, however, this symbol is a secret symbol for a magical virtue which is called Azoth. This word carries us into the very heart of alchemy, for Azoth is, in the words of the great alchemist Paracelsus, 'that medicine which cures all diseases in the three kingdoms of Nature'. The three kingdoms are those of Salt, Sulphur and Mercury, which is to say man himself. The curious winged dragon of Figure 207 is therefore nothing more than a symbol of that extraordinary curative power which can make man whole and baptize him into a new world of being. The whole man is just another alchemical symbol for the initiated man, for one on whom has been bestowed knowledge of the inner and outer worlds.

At times occultists have made serious attempts to represent in a single diagram the whole of the complex symbolism behind their chosen arcane realm. The etching by Merian, dated 1698 (Figure 208), represents a most interesting example of such an attempt. Almost every line in this etching contains a symbolic element, and it may interest the general reader to examine it with a view to determining what he or she has learned about the nature of secret symbolism. Note how the four symbols for the elements are near the bottom of the picture, the 'rising' elements of Fire and Air guarded by the phoenix, the 'sinking' elements of Water and Earth guarded by the eagle. These birds (symbolic of processes in alchemical transmutation) are then surmounted by a beast and a human. The warm side is symbolized by a lion and a man, who support between them the Sun. The other side is lunar, for the stag (associated with the lunar Diana) and the cosmic female hold between them a symbol of the Moon. Between these elemental and cosmic symbols is a man standing on a single-headed lion (perhaps the Red and Green Lions of the alchemists, merged by the secret art into a single union). The man combines

the lunar and the solar, for half of him is light, the other half dark, reminding us of the two heads of the demon Haborym (Figure 173). Around him are growing plants, symbol of the etheric world, marked with the sigils of the planets and with alchemical symbols. Above there are also dualities, for the lower register is swathed in clouds, while the upper register is cloudless and penetrated by the clear rays of the sun or of the spiritual hierarchies. In the cloudy area we see half a circle which combines the five most important symbols of the alchemical process, from the black crow of Saturn, to the fire-born phoenix linked with Mercury, and between them the pelican of Venus, the cockatrice of Mars and the Jupiterian bird which the modern occultists call the Hansa bird. Above, in the cloudless area, are the Christian symbols of lamb and dove, along with the name of God, three symbols together marking the Trinity. Thus the celestial Trinity at the top is the fruition of the two (separated) male and female trinities on earth (Fire–phoenix–Air and Water–eagle–Earth). This is the human ternary in seed, each a symbol of what man might become if he follows the strict rule of occultism.

208 *An etching of 1698 by Merian entitled* Tabula Smaragdina *(The Emerald Tablet), a reference to a document which was supposed to contain all the secrets of the alchemists in a brief symbolic form*

Index

Page numbers in *italic* refer to the illustrations and captions

abstract art, 49–50
Acheron, river, 76
Adam, 122, 124
Adam Kadmon, 24, *24*
Adams, Michael, 50, *50*
Addingham Moor, *89*
Aegean Sea, 38
Africa, 83
Agrippa, Henry
 Cornelius, *62*, 74, 133
Air, 24, 28, 29, 56, 67, *68*,
 70, 71, 80–2, *80*, 147–50,
 149, 157
Aix-en-Provence, 139
Alberobello, *120*
Albigensians, 100
Albumasar, *33*, 37
alchemy, 7, 18, 22, 62–5,
 64, *65*, 90–1, 116–17,
 140–57, *140–57*
Alcyone, 114
Algol, *116*
Allah, 113
Allatu, 136
alphabet, 7
Alt-Oetting, *11*
Amiens Cathedral, *14*, 29
amulets, *8*, 18, 22, 38, 66,
 110–21, *112–21*, 139
anagrams, 119
Andromeda, 38–40, *39*
angels, 43, 55–6, 130, 139
Anima mundi, *60*, 61, 62, 72
animals, 42–3, 56
ankh, 8, *8*, 12, 113
Anubis, 66, *66*
Apep, 131
Apollo, 70, 75–6, 106
Apsu, 40
Aquarius, 27, 29, 37, *37*,
 40, 68, 145
Ara, 40, *40*
Arabs, 16, 100, 114, 150
Ariadne, 78–9
Aries, 29, 30, 50, 59, 61,
 62, 68, 70, *70*, 72, 106,
 119
Aristotle, 28
Ascendant, 28
ashwood, 108–9
Asmodeus, 128, *129*, 130,
 131, 139
Astaroth, 129–30
Astral body, 18, 43, 44, 46,
 47, 50–1, 56–7
astral light, 117
astral travel, 84
astral world, 42–57,
 42–57, 66, 90, 91, 125
astro-palmistry, 106

astrology, 7, 16, 26–40,
 100–2, 104, 106, 143–6
astronomy, 23
Astroth, 139
Athena, 113
Atlantis, 82–3, 84
Atlas, 41
Auch, 138
Avicenna, 143
Azoth, 18, 156

Baal, 134
Babylonians, 33, 40, 114,
 124, 130, 131–2, *133*, 136
Bain Maria (Bath of Mary),
 145, 147
Balberith, 139
Barrett, Francis, *124*
basilisk, 18, *107*, 108
Bastet, 130–1
Beast, 38, *38*
Beelzebub, 134, *138*, 139
Behemoth, 134, *136*
Belial, 135
bellman, 11, *12*
Belot, Jean, *104*
Belphegor, 127–8, *128*
Belvoir Castle, 110
Bern, 31, *32*
Berri, Duc de, *59*
Besant, Annie, *48*
Betelgeuse, 23
Bethlehem, 16
Bible, 119, 124, 128–9
binding, 108–10
birth, 26–8
black magic, 22, 51,
 90–100, 108, 122, 133
Black Virgin, 82
Blake, William, 19, 61, *61*,
 134, *136*
Blavatsky, Madame, 47
boats, 114, *115*
Bodin, 98
Boehme, Jacob, 21–2, *21*,
 29, *63*, *152*
Boethius, *41*
Boguet, Henri, 92, 94, 95,
 98
Boroughbridge, 84, *84*
Bottesford, 8, *12*, 110, *111*
Botticelli, Sandro, *Mars
 and Venus*, 18–20, *20*, 21
Bracken House, London, *29*
brain, 24, 34, 61, 64
breathing, 64, 66
Brocken, *96*
Brueghel, Pieter the
 Elder, *126*
Bruges, 37
Bry, Johann de, *60*
Bubastis, 131
bulls, 10–11, 68, 114–15,
 116

Butleigh, 86, *87*
butterflies, 140–1

calendar, 31
Cancer, *8*, *16*, 21, 24, 26,
 26, *30*, 68, 70–2, *72*, 75,
 150
Capricorn, 27, 28, 59, 68,
 145
cars, 116, *117*
cartomancy, 102–4
Cassiel, 122, *124*
Cassiopeia, 38
Castelwitch, *54*
Castor and Pollux, 32, 70
cathedrals, *16*, 74, 76–80,
 100, 126–7, 141
cats, 130–1
Centaurus, 38, *38*
Central America, 83
Cepheus, 38
Cerberus, 122
Cetus, 38, 40
chalk figures, 84, *85*
chameleons, 149, *149*
charms, 119
Chartres Cathedral, *16*, *16*,
 76, 78–80, *79*, 82, *82*
Chelmsford, *94*, 95
Cherubim, 55–6, *56*
China, 102
I Ching, 102, *102*
chirognomy, 104
chiromancy, 104
Choleric temperament, 29,
 67, 68, *68*
Christ, 24, 40, 43, *43*, 46,
 82, 109, 114, *118*, 119–20,
 126–7, 149, 150
Christianity: angels, 43,
 55–6, 130, 139; and the
 astral world, 46;
 astrological symbols, 16;
 baptism, 141; Cross, 113,
 114, *120*, 149, 150;
 demons, 133; exorcism,
 110; fish symbol, 40, 119;
 gargoyles, 8, 11, *12*, 16,
 16, 141, *143*; Trinity, 10,
 11, 139, 141, 157; and
 witchcraft, 100
Christmas, 109
Chronos, 27, 113, 145
churches, 11, 16
CND, 11, 15
colours, astral world, 42,
 46–51, 56–7
Compostella, 76
constellations, 30–8, *31–5*
cosmology, 23–6, 28, 59
Crete, 79, 82
crosses, 28, 113, 114, *120*,
 149
crows, *19*

Crystalline Heavens, 24
Cunningham, J. Wade, 53
curse dolls, 109, *110*

Daedalus, 79
Dagon, 132
Dante, 79–80, 102, 130,
 132
Davis, A. J., *44*
'De Sphaera', *72*
dead spirits, 76, 91
death, 44–6, 47, *48*, 64, 66
Delphi, 75–6, 77
demons, 7, 22, 51, 55, 56,
 74, 75, 91–4, 96–8,
 100–2, 110, 122–39,
 123–39
'Desire body', 43
Devil, 66, 79–80, *80*, 84,
 91–8, *98*, 100–2, *101*,
 103, 108, 128–9, *130*,
 132–3, *134*, 152
Devil's Arrows, 84, *84*, 89
Diana, 33, 157
divination, 74–6, 100–6,
 102
dogs, 42, 113
Donne, John, 107
doorknockers, 115–16,
 117
Doré, Gustave, *132*
Doubler Stones, 89, *89*
dragons, 18, 84, *85*, 114,
 115, *153*, 154–6, *155*, *156*
Druid Stone, 89
Druids, 82
Dürer, Albrecht, *31*, *34*,
 35, *35*, 55, 91, *93*, *132*
Durrell, Lawrence, 116
dwarfs, 66–7

Eagle of the Moon, 64
Eagle of the Sun, 64
Earth, 24, 28, 29, 56, 67,
 68, 71, 80–2, *80*, 147–50,
 157
earth magic, 74–89, 102
earth powers, 76–8, *86*,
 89
Echidna, 122, *125*
ectoplasm, 54–5, *54*
Eglington, William, 54–5,
 54
Ego, 43, 57
Egypt, 8, 10, *10*, 33, 66,
 83, 103, 113, 114–15, 122,
 130–1, 134
emotions, 42–3, 44–7, 64
Ephyra, 76, 77
Erynes, *132*
Etheric body, 18–20, 21,
 43, 56
etheric plane, 41, 42, *51*
Ethiopia, 38

evil eye, 107–8, *107*, 110–15
exorcism, 110, 136–9, *139*
eyebeams, 107–8, 113, 116
eyes, *8*, 107–8, *107*, 110–15, *113*, *114*

Fairford, 134, *136*
fairy stories, 66–7
Fall of Man, 122, 124, *125*, 127
familiars, 94–5
fascism, 11
Fates, 41–2, *41*, 44
figureheads, 114, *115*
fire, 10, 12–15, *14*, 43, 46, 143
Fire (element), 24, 28, 29, 56–7, 62, 63, 64, *64*, 67, *68*, 71, 80–2, *80*, 147–50, 152, 157
Firmament, 24, *24*, 29, 36
fish, 40, *118*, 119, 121, 125, *126*, 127, 131–2, 147–8, *148*
flames *see* fire
Flower family, 110
flowers, 148–9
Fludd, Robert, *23*, 60
fortune-telling, 74–6, 100–6, *102*
four elements, 18–19, 24, 28, 29, 56–7, 67, 68, 80–2, 147–50
four humours, 67–8, *68*
four temperaments, 29, 67–8, *68*
fourfold model, 67
France, 108
Francis, St, 46, *46*
Freher, Dionysius, 20–2, *21*
Fulcanelli, 18, 79
furnaces, alchemy, 141–3, 147

Gabriel, Archangel, 24, 119
gargoyles, *8*, 11, *12*, 16, *16*, 141, *143*
Geheimer Figuren der Rosencreuzer, *146*
Gemini, *8*, 21, 32, *33*, 36, 37, 40, 59, 68, 70–1, *71*, 72, 106
Geneva, Palace of the Nations, 32, *32*
geomancy, 7, 74–5, *74*, *75*, 76, 100, 102
Germany, 11, 108, 117
ghosts, 51–5, *53*, *54*
giants, 66–7, 83, 84, 88
Gichtel, Georg, *9*
Gilgamesh, 131, *133*
Glastonbury, 86–8, *86*, *87*
Gloucester, Duchess of, 110
Gnostics, 100, 113, *113*
Godhead, 21
Goethe, Johann Wilhelm von, *27*, 28, *96*
Gog-Magog Hills, 84
gold, 66, 106, 140
gondolas, 8
Gorgon, 114, *116*

Gounod, Charles François, 49, *49*
Grail legend, 59
Greece, 83, 113, 134; amulets, *8*, *9*, 10, 112, *112*, 114, *114*, *115*, 116, *117*, 121, *121*; astrology, 16, 27, 64, 100; calendar, 31; mythology, 33, 38, 79, 114, 117, 122; prediction, 75–6
Green Lion, 143, *145*
grimoires, 122, 130, 132, 134–5, *135*, *138*
Guazzo, 98

Haborym, 130–1, *131*, 157
Hades, 76
halos, 10
hammer magic, 109, 110
Hansa bird, 157
hares, 96
Harz Mountains, *96*
Heaven, 43, 117, 139, 140
Heinfogel, *31*, *35*
Hell, 62, 75, 79–80, *80*, 82, 102, 122, *123*, 127, 130, 133, *136*, 139, 152, *152*
Henry VI, King, 110
Hercules, 70
Hermes, 141, *144*, 154
'Hermetic Secret', 141
Hildegarde of Bingen, 56, *57*
Hinduism, 148
Historia de Gentibus Septentrionalibus, 109
Hollidge, Alfred, *53*
Homer, *Odyssey*, 76
hooves, cloven, 129
Hopkins, Matthew, 95, *96*
horoscopes, 27–8, *27*, 29, 100, 106, 146, *147*, 156
horse brasses, 116
horseshoes, 115, 116, *117*, 121
Hyginus, *30*, *70*, *71*, *72*

Iliaster, 150–2, 154
Ilkley, 89
imps, 95
incubus, 92, 124
initiation, 16, 27, 29
Inquisition, 96, 98, 100
Intelligencies, 24
Ireland, 83
Ishtar, 136
Isis, 82
Islam, 113, *113*
Italy, 8, 10–11, 24, 108, 112, *120*, 121

James, St, *126*
Jasper, 99
jewels, 117–19, 121
Jews, 104–6
Joan of Arc, 100
Job, Book of, 106
Jonah, 148, *149*
Jung, C. G., 154
Jupiter, *27*, 70, 113, 145, 157

Kandinsky, Wassily, 49–50
Keighley, 88, 89

Kelly, Edward, *52*
Kingsweston, 86, *87*

'labours of the month', 35, *36*
labyrinths, 78–80, *79*, *80*, 82
Lambsprinck, *148*, *150*, *156*
Lancaster, 91, 108, 109
Lang, Walter, 141
Law, William, 63, *152*
Law of Two, 22
Leadbeater, C. W., 47–50, *47–9*, 56
Leda, 70
Legmeton, 133–4
Lemuria, 139
Leo, 21, 26, *26*, 35, *36*, 37, 43, 68, 87, 143, 150
Lethbridge, T. C., 84, *85*
letters, amulets, 119–21
Levi, Eliphas, 73, *134*
Leviathan, *136*, 139
ley lines, *86*
Libra, *9*, 26, *37*, 38, *39*, 68, 106
Lichtenberger, Johannes, 27
life force, 29, 41, 42, 64
Lilith, 44–6, *44*, 122, 124–5
Limbourg brothers, 59, *59*
Lincoln, 110, 126, *128*
lions, 42–3, 44, 86, 87, 113, 143, *145*, 157
Lisbon, 55
Lord of the Flies, 134, *138*, 139
Lucca, 79, *80*, 107
Lucifer, *44*, 117, 130
Lully, Raymond, *44*
lunar zodiac, 36, *36*
Lupercalia, 98–100

Macarius, St, 133
Maclagan, 108
Madeleine, Sister, 139
Magi, 16, 20, 29
magic, 7; black magic, 90–100, 108, 122, 133; earth magic, 74–89
magical characters, 119
magicians, 51
Mahonin, 138
Malleus Maleficarum, 96
man, zodiacal, 59–61, *59*, 68–73
Mars, 18, *20*, 28, 113, 145, 157
Mau, 130–1
Maymon, 134, *135*
mazes, 74, 78–80, *79*, *80*, 82
Medusa, 38, 114, *116*
Mehren, *42*, *43*, 46
Melancholic temperament, 29, 67, 68, *68*
melothesic man, 59–61, *59*, 68–73
Mercedes cars, 11, 15, 116–17, *117*
Mercury, 18, *19*, 64, 65–7, 66, 70, *71*, 106, 113, 140, 141, *144*, 145, 150–4, 156
Merian, 157, *157*

mermaids, 18, *18*, *148*
metals, alchemy, 145–6
Michael, Archangel, 24
Michaelis, Father Sebastien, 139
Milton, John, 122, 130, 139
Minerva, 113
Minos, King, 79
Minotaur, 78–9, *79*
Mithraic cult, 115, *143*
Molitor, Ulrich, 92, 94, *95*
monkeys, 61–2, 66
Moon, 24–6, 35–6, *36*, 42, 43, 55–6, *55*, 75, *75*, *80*, 82, 113, 115, 128, 145–6, 150, *153*, 154, 157
Morax, 79, 135
Mother Goose, *92*
Mulhouse, St Etienne, *125*, 149
Musaeum Hermeticum, 150
music, 11, 49, *49*
Mykonos, *8*, *9*, 10, 121, *121*

Naberius, 134, 135
names, power of, 109, 113, 114, 119, 134–5, 138–9
Namtar, 136
natural magic, 74
Nazcas culture, 84, *86*
Nazism, 11
necromancy, 76, 91
Neptune, 38
Nereids, 38
Newchurch, Lancashire, 108, *108*, 110
nike, 11, 119
Norton, Thomas, *147*, *153*
Nothius, 40, *40*
numerology, 20, 106

Odysseus, 76
Old Man of the Sea, 66
Oracle of the Dead, 76
Orion, 33–4, *34*, 36, 38
Orthos, 122
Osiris, *10*, 33
ouija boards, 102
Ouroboros, 27, 73, *155*, 156, *156*
Ovid, 139
owls, 113

Padua, Palazzo della Ragione, 37, *37*
paintings, 18–20, 46–50
palingenesis, 90–1, *90*
palmistry, 104–6, *105*, *106*
Pan, 64, 96, 99, 129
Pancake Stone, 89
Pandora, *6*
Paracelsus, 150–2, 154, 156
Paris, Notre Dame, 16, *16*, 18, *19*, 141, *143*
Parma, 24, *26*
Pavia, San Michele, 18, *126*, 129
peacock, 150, 156
Pegasus, 38
Pemmo Altar, *15*
Pencz, Georg, *131*

Pendle Hill, 88, *88*, 91, 108, *108*, 109
penis, amulets, 114–15, *116*
Perseus, 38, 114
personality, 67–8, *68*, 145
Peru, 84, *86*
Philosophic Mercury, *19*
Phlegmatic temperament, 29, 67–8, *68*
phoenix, 150, 154, 157
phosphorus, 11, 15, 116–17
photography, spirit, 51–5, *53*, *54*
pilgrimages, 76–8, 82, 89
Pisces, 29, *30*, 37, *37*, 59, 68, *118*, 119, 147, *148*
Plancy, Collin de, *128*, *131*, *136*, *138*
planets, 24, 28, 29, 104, 106, 145–6, *146*
plants, 41, 42, 43, 90–1, 148–9
Pleiades, 114, *118*, 119
Pomerance, Fay, *44*
Popes, 131–2
'poppets', 109, *110*
prayer stars, 15
prediction, 74–6, 100–6, *102*
Primum mobile, 24, *24*, 29
Prometheus, 117
Ptolemaic universe, *24*, 80
Purgatory, 75, 79, 130, *136*, *152*

Qabbala, 23, *23*, 24, *24*, *105*, 106
Quintessence, 19, 28–9, 37, 39, 40, 41, 46, 55, 56, 63, 73, 74, 82, 148–9, 150

Rackham, Arthur, *6*, 91, *92*
Raleigh, Sir Walter, 12, *13*, 21
rams, 68
Raphael, Archangel, 130, *131*
Regulators, 24
reincarnation, 150
Remus, 99
'The Resuscitated Rose', 90, *90*
Rhodes, *115*, 116, *117*
Ricchierus, Ludovicus, *130*
rock carvings, 88–9, *88*, *89*
Romans, 16, 66, *66*, 75, 76, 98–9, 100, 113, 114, 115, 139
Rome, 99
Romulus, 99
roofs, *trulli*, *120*, 121
Rosenroth, 24
Rosicrucians, *9*, 64, 143–5

Rotas, 119–21
Rothmann, 106, *106*
Rumbolds Moor, *88*
Rutland, 6th Earl of, 110, *111*

Sabbat, 92, 94, 95–8, *96*, 100, *130*, 133
Sacra di San Michele, *40*, 100–2, *101*
Sagittarius, 26, *26*, 38, *38*, *39*, 68, 88, *101*
saints, 55
salamanders, 14–15, *14*, 149, 150, *150*
Salisbury plain, 82–3, *83*
Salt, 62, 63, 64, *64*, *65*, 73, 150–4, 156
Sanguine temperament, 29, 67, 68, *68*
'Sapientia Veterum Philosophorum', *148*
Sarah, 130
Satan, 130, *136*
Saturn, 24, 27, *27*, 113, 122, *124*, 145–6, 157
satyrs, 18–19
Scale of Being, 43, *44*
scarabs, 113–14, *113*
Schultz, *30*
science, 61–2
Scorpio, *16*, 26, *26*, 27, 28, 68, 146
Scorpius, 33, 38, *39*, *101*
Scot, Michael, 75, *75*
Scotland, 83, 108
sea, 40
Seal of Solomon, 8–9, *8*, 21, 29, 42, 56, 63, 64, 73, *73*, 80–2, *82*, 112, 116, 117, 150
seances, 7, 53–5, *54*, 91
The Search of Belphegor, 127–8
Sephirah, 23
Septem Planetae, *68*, 149
Seraphim, 55–6, 139
Serapis, 115
serpents, *19*, 27, 43, 55, 70, 113, 114, *116*, 122–4, *125*
sexual symbols, 114–15, *117*
sexuality, 92, 95, 96
Shakespeare, William, 139
Shax, 135
sheep, 46, *46*
'Shepherd's Calendar', *10*, *68*, *146*
Sindbad, 66
sirens, 148, *148*
skull and crossbones, 149
snakes *see* serpents
soul, 27–8, *39*, *44*
Soul of the World, *60*, 61
Southern Fish, 40, *40*
Sowtherns, Elizabeth, 109

Spain, 76, 115
Sphinx, 122
Spica, *37*
spirit photography, 51–5, *53*, *54*
'Splendour Solis', *142*, *144*
Stabius, *31*, *35*
stags, 113, 157
standing stones, 74, 88–9
stars: amulets, 112, 114, *115*; astral world, 42; constellations, 30–8, *31–5*, 87; cosmology, 28–9; Firmament, 24, *24*, 36; lunar zodiac, 36; star symbols, 8–10, *9*, 15–16, *15*, 20, 21, 29, 39, 46
Stead, W. J., 53
Stellatum, 24, 30, 36
stone circles, 74, 82–4, *83*, 88–9
Stonehenge, 82–3, *83*
stones, magical, 117–19
succubus, 92, 124
Sulphur, 62, 63, 64, *65*, 73, 150–4, 156
Sun, 9, 10, 24, 29–31, 35, 36, 70–1, 82, 106, 113, 115, 145, 150, *153*, 154, 157
swastikas, 11
Swinburne, Algernon Charles, 7
Switzerland, 31
Symi, *115*
sympathetic magic, 109–10

talismans, 22
Tammuz, 136
Tarot cards, 39–40, *39*, 70, 103–4, *103*, 141, *141*
Taurus, 9, 21, *27*, 29, 36, 59, 68, 70, *70*, 72, 106, 114–15
temperaments, 29, 67–8, *68*
Theosophical Society, 46–7
Theseus, 78–9, *79*, 80
thought, 42, 47, *48*, 61, 63–4, 66, 70, 117, 152
Three Principles, 64–6, 67, 152, 154
threefold model, 61–7
Thrones, 27
Thwaites and Reed, *29*
Tiamat, 40
Tiresias, 76
Tobias, 130, *131*
tongues, 126, *128*
trees, 23–4, *23*, 121
triangles, 62–3, 80–2
Trinity, 10, 11, 40, 139, 141, 157
Troy, 76, *112*

trulli symbols, *120*, 121
Turin, 8, 10–11, *11*
Turkey, 116
Twelve Apostles (stone circle), 89

Uffington, 84, *85*
Underworld, 76

Vallemont, 90, *90*
Vecchia, Piero della, 104–6, *105*
Venice, 8, *8*
Venus, 8, 9, *10*, 18, 20, *20*, 28, 106, 112, 113, *120*, 130, 145, 157
Vepar, 135
Verona, San Zeno, 42, 103, *104*, *139*
Vezelay, St Madeleine, 78, *78*
Vicenza, Chiericati Palace, 38, *39*, 40
Virgin Mary, 10, *11*, 24, 55, *55*, 79–80, 82, 119, 122, 128, 147
Virgo, *16*, 21, 26, 28, 30, 37, *37*, 68, 88, 106
Vishnu, *127*, 148
Vital body, 18–20
Vreede, *30*
Vril, 83

Walton-le-Dale, *52*
Wandlebury Hill, 84, *85*
Waring, *52*
warlocks, 91–2, 95, *96*, 108
Water, 24, 26, 28, 29, 56, 67, *68*, 71, 80–2, *80*, 147–50, 152, 157
Waters of Life, 37
waxen images, 109, 110, 147
Weyer, John, 133
White Horse of Uffington, 84, *85*
wind raising, *109*
witch knots, *109*
witchcraft, 7, 11, 91–100, *91–9*, 108, 109–12, *110*, 114, 132–3
wolves, 42, *42*, 46, 99
Wyllie, 53, *53*

Yggdrasil, 109
Yorkshire, 89

Zeno, San, *139*
zodiac, *16*, 24, 26–8, *26*, 29–38, *29*, *30*, *32*, *37*, 87, 100, 106; earth zodiac, 86–8, *87*, *88*
zodiacal man, 59–61, *59*, 68–73